国内外经典教材辅导系列·英语类

胡壮麟《语言学教程》（第5版）笔记和考研真题详解

主编：圣才考研网
www.100xuexi.com

中国石化出版社

内 容 提 要

本书是语言学经典教材《语言学教程》(第5版)(胡壮麟主编)的学习辅导书。全书完全遵循该教材的章目编排，共分12章，每章由两部分组成：第一部分为复习笔记(中英文对照)，总结本章的重点难点；第二部分是考研真题与典型题详解，精选名校经典考研真题及相关习题，并提供了详细的参考答案。

圣才考研网(www.100xuexi.com)提供胡壮麟《语言学教程》辅导方案【视频课程、电子书、题库】。购书即可享受大礼包增值服务【本书电子书(电脑版、手机版)+全国名校真题详解电子书】。手机扫码(本书封面右上角)领取本书大礼包。

图书在版编目(CIP)数据

胡壮麟《语言学教程》(第5版)笔记和考研真题详解/圣才考研网主编．—北京：中国石化出版社，2018.2(2021.6重印)
(国内外经典教材辅导系列)
ISBN 978-7-5114-3697-9

Ⅰ．①胡…　Ⅱ．①圣…　Ⅲ．①语言学-研究生-入学考试-自学参考资料　Ⅳ．①H0

中国版本图书馆CIP数据核字(2018)第022982号

中国石化出版社出版发行
地址：北京市东城区安定门外大街58号
邮编：100011　电话：(010)57512500
发行部电话：(010)57512575
http://www.sinopec-press.com
E-mail：press@sinopec.com
武汉市盛宏源印务有限公司印刷
全国各地新华书店经销
*
787×1092毫米16开本14.25印张357千字
2018年3月第1版　2021年6月第2次印刷
定价：58.00元

序 言

我国各大院校一般都把国内外通用的权威教科书作为本科生和研究生学习专业课程的参考教材，这些教材甚至被很多考试(特别是硕士和博士入学考试)和培训项目作为指定参考书。为了帮助读者更好地学习专业课，我们有针对性地编著了一套与国内外教材配套的复习资料，并提供配套的名师讲堂和题库。

《语言学教程》(第5版)(胡壮麟主编)一直被用作高等院校英语专业语言学教材，被绝大多数院校指定为英语专业考研必读书和学术研究参考书。作为该教材的学习辅导书，本书具有以下几个方面的特点：

1. 梳理章节脉络，浓缩内容精华。每章的复习笔记以该教材为主并结合其他教材对本章的重难点知识进行了整理，并参考了国内名校名师讲授该教材的课堂笔记，因此，本书的内容几乎浓缩了经典教材的知识精华。

2. 中英双语对照，突显难点要点。本书章节笔记采用了中英文对照的形式，强化对重要难点知识的理解和运用。

3. 精选考研真题，补充难点习题。本书精选名校近年考研真题及相关习题，并提供答案和详解。所选真题和习题基本体现了各个章节的考点和难点，但又不完全局限于教材内容，是对教材内容极好的补充。

另外，在笔记部分，对于在《语言学教程》第三版或第四版提到而第五版删减的知识点我们也予以保留，并用“*”标明，部分院校考研真题依旧会涉及这些知识点的考查。相对于第三版或第四版，对于在第五版新增加的知识点用“▼”标明，以便于使用不同版本教材的读者使用。

购书即可享受大礼包增值服务【本书电子书(电脑版、手机版)+全国名校真题详解电子书】。手机扫码(本书封面右上角)领取本书大礼包。

圣才考研网(www.100xuexi.com)是圣才学习网旗下的考研考博专业网站，提供考研公共课和全国500所院校考研考博专业课辅导【一对一辅导、网授精讲班等】、电子书、题库、全套资料(历年真题及答案、笔记讲义等)、国内外经典教材名师讲堂、考研教辅图书等。

考研辅导：kaoyan.100xuexi.com(圣才考研网)
资格考试：www.100xuexi.com(圣才学习网)

圣才考研网编辑部

目　录

第1章　语言学导论

1.1　复习笔记

本章要点：

1. The definition and the design features of language
   语言的定义与特征
2. The origin and the function of language
   语言的起源和功能
3. Main branches of linguistics study
   语言学研究的范围和内容
4. Important distinctions in Linguistics
   语言学的一些重要区分

本章考点：

1. 有关语言的常考考点

语言的定义；语言的基本特征(任意性、二重性、多产性、移位性、文化传递和互换性)；
语言的功能(提供信息、人际交往、施为、表达情感、寒暄、娱乐、元语言)；
语言的起源[神授说，人造说(“汪汪”，“噗噗”，“哟－嘿－吼”理论)，进化说]等。

2. 有关语言学的常考考点

(1) 语言学的定义，现代语言学与传统语法学研究的三个显著区别。
(2) 语言学研究的四个原则及其简要说明。语言学中几组重要区别，每组两个概念的含义、区分及其意义。
(3) 普通语言学的主要分支学科及各自的研究范畴。
(4) 宏观语言学及应用语言学的主要分支及各自的研究范畴。

本章内容索引：

Ⅰ. Definition of language

Ⅱ. Design features of language

1. Arbitrariness
2. Duality
3. Creativity
4. Displacement
5. Cultural Transmission
6. Interchangeability

Ⅲ. Origin of language

1. The Biblical account
2. The bow-wow theory
3. The pooh-pooh theory

4. The yo-he-ho theory
5. The evolution theory

Ⅳ. Functions of language

1. Informative function
2. Interpersonal function
3. Performative function
4. Emotive function
5. Phatic function
6. Recreational function
7. Metalingual function

Ⅴ. Definition of linguistics

Ⅵ. Branches of linguistics

1. Microlinguistics
2. Macrolinguistics

Ⅶ. Important concepts and their distinctions

1. Descriptive vs. Prescriptive
2. Synchronic vs. Diachronic
3. Langue vs. Parole
4. Competence vs. Performance
5. Traditional Grammar vs. Modern Grammar
6. Linguistic Potential vs. Actual Linguistic Behavior

Ⅰ. The definition of language Language is a system of arbitrary vocal symbols used for human communication. This definition has revealed five essential factors of language: systematic, arbitrary, vocal, symbolic and most importantly human-specific.	**Ⅰ. 语言的定义** 语言是用于人类交流的任意的有声符号系统。该定义揭示了语言的五个要素：系统，任意，口头，符号，人类特有。
Ⅱ. The design features of language 【考点：名词解释 & 填空】 The features that define our human languages can be called design features which can distinguish human language from any animal system of communication.	**Ⅱ. 语言的定义特征** 语言的定义特征是人类语言区别于其他动物交流系统的特点。
1. Arbitrariness It is the core feature of language, which refers to the fact that there is no intrinsic connection between the forms of linguistic signs and their meaning. Arbitrariness exists in the relationship between a particular sound and the meaning it is associated with. But it is not entirely arbitrary at all levels. Some words, such as the ones created in the imitation of sounds by sounds are motivated in a certain degree.	**1. 任意性** 任意性是语言的核心特征，是指语言符号的形式与所表示的意义没有天然的联系。符号的声音与意义之间存在任意性。虽然语言从本质上讲是任意的，但也不是完全任意的。一些词语，例如一些拟声词的发音与其意义还是有一定联系的。

2. Duality

Duality refers to "the property of having two levels of structures, such that units of the primary level are composed of elements of the secondary level and each of two levels has its own principles of organization." (Lyons, 1981: 20) The property of duality only exists in the system with both elements (e. g. sounds, letters) and units (e. g. words). Primary units 'words' (meaningful) consist of secondary units 'sounds' (meaningless).

3. Creativity

Creativity means language is resourceful due to its duality and recursiveness, which enables human beings to produce and understand an infinitely large number of sentences in our native language, including the sentences which were never heard before.

4. Displacement

Displacement refers to the fact that human language allows users to employ language symbols to represent objects, events and concepts that are not accessible in time and space at the moment of communication. The generalization and imagination given by displacement benefit human beings immensely.

5. Cultural Transmission

Language is culturally transmitted. It cannot be transmitted through heredity.

6. Interchangeability

Interchangeability refers to the fact that man can both produce and receive messages, and his roles as a speaker and a hearer can be exchanged at ease.

Ⅲ. Origin of language

1. The Biblical account

Language was God's gift to human beings.

2. The bow-wow theory

Language was an imitation of natural sounds, such as the cries of animals, like quack, cuckoo.

3. The pooh-pooh theory

Language arose from instinctive emotional sounds, such as the expression of pain, anger or joy.

4. The yo-he-ho theory

Language arose from some rhythmic grunts made by a group of people engaged in joint labour or effort—lifting a huge hunted game, moving a rock, etc.

2. 二重性

二重性是指拥有两层结构的这种属性，底层结构是上层结构的组成成分，每层都有自身的组合规则。二重性只存在于这样的系统之中，既有元素又有它们组合成的单位。上层单位"词"(有意义的)由底层单位"语音"(无意义的)组成。

3. 创造性

创造性指语言的能产性，它能够使人造出和理解无穷的长句，其中很多句子是以前从未听过的。

4. 移位性

移位性是指人类语言可以让使用者在交际时用语言符号代表时间上和空间上并不可及的物体、事件和观点。移位性赋予人们的概括和想象力使人类受益无穷。

5. 文化传递性

语言不是靠遗传，而是通过文化传递的。

6. 互换性

互换性是指人可以是信息的发出者，也可以是信息的接受者，即人作为说话者和听话者的角色是可以随意更换的。

Ⅲ. 语言的起源

1. 圣经的记载

语言是上帝的恩赐。

2. "汪汪"理论

语言是模仿自然的声音，例如动物的叫声，如(鸭子)的刮刮声，嘎嘎声，布谷鸟的叫声。

3. "噗噗"理论

语言来源于人本能的情感声音，表达疼痛、愤怒或喜悦。

4. "哟-嘿-吼"理论

语言起源于原始人共同劳动或者努力举起猎物、搬动石头等时发出的有节奏的哼哟声。

5. The evolution theory Language originated in the process of labour and answered the call of social need.	**5. 进化理论** 语言起源于劳动的过程，满足了社会的需求。
Ⅳ. Functions of language 【考点：判断所描述的是语言的何种功能 & 名词解释】	**Ⅳ. 语言的功能**
1. Informative function Language is used to tell something, to give information, or to reason things out. The informative function is regarded as the most important function. Declarative sentences serve this function.	**1. 信息功能** 语言用来陈述某件事情，提供信息或用作推理。信息功能是语言最重要的功能，一般出现在陈述句中。
2. Interpersonal function The interpersonal function means people can use language to establish and maintain their status in a society. It can be regarded as the most important sociological use of language.	**2. 人际功能** 人际功能是语言最重要的社会功能。人们由此建立和维持他们的身份和社会地位。
3. Performative function The performative function of language is mainly used to change people's social status, such as in wedding ceremony, the blessing of infants and the naming of ships at a voyage ceremony. In these speech acts, language is usually very formal, even ritualized.	**3. 施为功能** 语言的施为功能主要是用来改变人的社会地位，例如在婚礼，为孩子祈福和在首航仪式上为船命名。在这些言语行为中，语言通常是非常正式的，甚至是仪式化的。
4. Emotive function The emotional function of language plays a key role in changing the audience's attitude towards or against someone or something. Therefore, it can be regarded as one of the most useful functions of language.	**4. 感情功能** 语言的感情功能在改变听者赞成或反对某人、某物的态度上作用非常关键因此，它是语言最有用的功能之一。
5. Phatic function The phatic communication means people always use some small, seemingly meaningless expressions or expression like slangs, jokes and jargons to help define and maintain interpersonal relations.	**5. 寒暄功能** 寒暄功能是指通过一些短小、看似无意义的表述，或者俚语、玩笑、行话等来帮助确立和维持人际关系。
6. Recreational function The recreational function refers to the use of language for the sheer joy of it, such as a baby's babbling or a chanter's chanting.	**6. 娱乐功能** 语言的娱乐功能是指纯粹为了娱乐而使用语言，例如婴儿的牙牙学语，歌者的吟唱。
7. Metalingual function The metalingual function refers to the fact that our language can be used to talk about itself.	**7. 元语言功能** 语言的元语言功能是指语言可以用来讨论语言本身。

V. Definition of linguistics	**V. 语言学的定义**
Linguistics is usually defined as the science of language or, the scientific study of language. It not only focuses on a particular language, but is based on the systematic investigation of linguistic data, conducted with reference to some general theory of language structure. The four principles which make linguistics a science are exhaustiveness, consistency, economy and objectivity.	语言学通常被定义为研究语言的科学，或对语言的科学研究。它不仅仅关注某种特定的语言，而是基于一些语言结构的综合理论，对语料进行的系统研究。语言学研究的科学性可以归纳为：穷尽性、一致性、简洁性以及客观性。
VI. Branches of linguistics	**VI. 语言学的分支**
1. Microlinguistics—Intra-disciplinary divisions	**1. 微观语言学**
Phonetics	语音学
Phonology	音系学
Morphology	形态学
Syntax	句法学
Semantics	语义学
Pragmatics	语用学
2. Macrolinguistics—Interdisciplinary divisions	**2. 宏观语言学**
Psycholinguistics	心理语言学
Sociolinguistics	社会语言学
Applied linguistics	应用语言学
Computational linguistics	计算语言学
Neurolinguistics	神经语言学
VII. Important concepts and their distinctions	**VII. 重要概念及其区分**
1. Descriptive vs. Prescriptive	**1. 描写式与规定式**
Linguistics takes a descriptive approach to language: it tries to explain things as they actually are, not as we impose upon them other rules. Prescriptive linguistics aims to lay down rules about how a language should be used instead of how it is actually used. The distinction lies in describing how things are and prescribing how things ought to be.	语言学对语言采取描述性的方法：它试图解释事物的真实状态，而不是强加给他们其他的规则。规定式语言学旨在制定有关如何正确使用语言而不是实际使用语言的规则。它们最主要的区别就在于前者描述事情怎样而后者规定事情应该如何。
2. Synchronic vs. Diachronic	**2. 共时与历时**
Language can be studied at a given point in time or over time. When we study language at a particular time, it is called synchronic linguistics. When we study language developments through time, it is called diachronic or historical linguistics. Synchronic linguistics focuses on the state of language at any points in history while diachronic linguistics focuses on the differences in two or more than two states of language over decades or centuries.	语言研究可以是在一个给定的时间也可以是一段时间。当我们集中在某一点时间来研究语言时就叫做共时语言学。当我们研究随着时间发展的语言时就叫做历时语言学。共时语言学集中研究历史任何时期点的语言现状，而历时语言学集中研究几十年或几百年的时期内两个或比两个更多的语言状况的差异。

3. Langue vs. Parole According to Saussure, langue and parole can be used to distinguish the speaker's linguistic competence from the actual phenomena. Langue refers to the abstract linguistic system shared by all the members of a speech community. Parole refers to particular realizations of langue.	**3. 语言与言语** 索绪尔用语言和言语来区分说话者的语言能力和言语上的实际表现。语言是指一个语言群体的所有成员所共有的抽象的语言系统。言语是指语言的具体实现和运用。
4. Competence vs. Performance 【考点：解释 Saussure 和 Chomsky 的两对概念的异同】 (1) Chomsky made the fundamental difference between competence and performance. (2) Linguistic competence refers to the underlying knowledge about the system of rules which a language user has mastered. (3) Performance refers to the real-world linguistic production in concrete situations.	**4. 语言能力和语言应用** (1)乔姆斯基提出了语言能力和语言应用的根本区别。 (2)语言能力是指语言使用者对于语言规则系统的潜在认识。 (3)语言运用指在具体场景中语言的实际运用。
5. Traditional Grammar vs. Modern Grammar Traditional grammar can be considered as prescriptive; it is based on "high" (religious, literary) written language. It sets models for language users to follow. But Modern linguistics is descriptive; its investigations are based on authentic and mainly spoken language data. It is supposed to be scientific and objective and the task of linguists is supposed to describe the language people actually use, whether it is "correct" or not.	**5. 传统语法与现代语法** 传统语法是规定式的，是基于"高度的"书面语。它为语言使用者提供可供遵循的模式。但是现代语法是描写式的，对语法的研究是基于真实的并且主要是口语化的语言数据。它应该是比较科学和客观的，而语言学家的任务也应该是描述人们如何在实际中使用语言，无论其是否"正确"。
6. Linguistic Potential vs. Actual Linguistic Behavior Halliday thinks that with language, there is a wide range of things that a speaker can do in the culture he is in. The set of possibility for "doing" is termed linguistic potential from a functional language's view. What a speaker actually says on a particular occasion to a particular individual is what he has selected from the many possible things he could have said. This actual selection of things from what one could have is termed actual linguistic behavior.	**6. 语言潜势与实际语言行为** 韩礼德认为，通过语言说话者可以在其生活的文化环境里做一系列广泛的事情。从语言功能的角度来看，"做"的可能性就被定义为语言潜势。说话者在某一特定的场所对某个特定的个体来说，是从其所能说的多种可能的内容中挑选而来的。这种说话者从言语中所做的实际选择就叫做实际言语行为。

1.2 考研真题与典型题详解

I. Fill in the blanks.

1. Arbitrariness of language makes it potentially creative, and __________ of language makes learning a language laborious. For learners of a foreign language, it is this feature of language that is more worth noticing than its arbitrariness. (大连外国语学院 2008 研)
2. In Saussure's view, the relationship between signifier (sound image) and signified (concept) is __________ (北二外 2005 研)

3. Human language is arbitrary. This refers to the fact that there is no logical or intrinsic connection between a particular sound and the __________ it is associated with. (人大 2007 研)
4. The features that define our human languages can be called __________ features. (北二外 2006 研)
5. Human languages enable their users to symbolize objects, events and concepts which are not present (in time and space) at the moment of communication. This quality is labeled as __________. (北二外 2007 研)
6. By __________ is meant the property of having two levels of structures, such that units of the primary level are composed of elements of the secondary level and each of the two levels has its own principles of organization. (北二外 2005 研)
7. Halliday proposes a theory of metafunctions of language, that is, language has __________, interpersonal and textual functions. (中山大学 2008 研)
8. Our language can be used to talk about itself. This is the __________ function of language. (中山大学 2005 研)
9. __________ function is realized by mood and modality. (中山大学 2006 研)
10. __________ refers to the role language plays in communication(e. g. to express ideas, attitudes) or in particular social situations(e. g. Religious, legal). (北二外 2016 研)
11. Some sentences do not describe things. They cannot be said to be true or false. The utterance of these sentences is or is a part of the doing of an action. They are called __________. (大连外国语学院 2008 研)
12. When language is used for establishing an atmosphere or maintaining social contact rather than exchanging information or ideas, its function is __________ function. (北二外 2005 研)
13. Linguistics is usually defined as the __________ study of language. (北二外 2003 研)
14. The branch of linguistics which studies the sound patterns of a language is called __________. (北二外 2003 研)
15. The branch of grammar which studies the internal structure of words is called __________. (北二外 2004 研)
16. __________ mainly studies the characteristics of speech sounds and provides methods for their description, classification and transcription. (北二外 2005 研)
17. Semantics and __________ investigate different aspects of linguistic meaning. (北二外 2007 研)
18. In linguistics, __________ refers to the study of the rules governing the way words are combined to form sentences in a language, or simply, the study of the formation as sentence. (中山大学 2008 研)
19. __________ can be defined as the study of language in use. Sociolinguistics, on the other hand, attempts to show the relationship between language and society.
20. The branch of grammar which studies the internal structure of sentence is called __________. (北二外 2008 研)
21. Psycholinguistics is concerned primarily with investigating the psychological __________ of linguistic structures. (中山大学 2006 研)
22. Saussure distinguished the linguistic competence of the speaker and the actual phenomena or da-

ta of linguistics (utterances) as __________ and __________. The former refers to the abstract linguistic system shared by all the members of a speech community, and the latter is the concrete manifestation of language either through speech or through writing. (人大 2006 研)

23. __________ grammars attempt to tell what is in the language, while __________ grammars tell people what should be in the language. Most contemporary linguists believe that whatever occurs naturally in the language should be described. (人大 2006 研)

24. One of the important distinctions in linguistics is __________ and performance. (人大 2006 研)

25. An approach in linguistic study which attempts to lay down rules of correctness as to how language should be used is __________. (北二外 2008 研)

26. Chomsky initiated the distinction between __________ and performance. (北二外 2007 研)

27. By __________, we mean language is resourceful because of its duality and its recursiveness. (北二外 2013 研)

28. The idea of __________ was first developed by Roman Jacobson (1896 – 1982) in the 1940s as a means of working out a set of phonological contrasts or oppositions to capture particular aspects of language sounds. (中山大学 2011 研)

29. Theory that primitive man made involuntary vocal noises while performing heavy work has been called the __________ theory.

30. Modern linguistic is __________ in the sense that the linguist tries to discover what language is rather than lay down some rules for people to observe.

31. The description of a language as it changes through time is a __________ study.

32. Linguistic potential is similar to Saussure's langue and Chomsky's __________.

33. One of the important distinctions in linguistics is __________ and parole. The former is the French word for "language", which is the abstract knowledge necessary for speaking, listening, writing and reading. The latter is concerned about the actual use of language by people in speech or writing. Parole is more variable and may change according to contextual factors.

Ⅱ. Multiple Choice

1. Which of the following is NOT a frequently discussed design feature? (大连外国语学院 2008 研)

   A. Arbitrariness B. Convention C. Duality

2. Which of the following words is entirely arbitrary? (西安交通大学 2008 研)

   A. tree B. crash C. typewriter D. bang

3. By __________ we mean language is resourceful because of its duality and recursiveness. (西安外国语学院 2006 研)

   A. arbitrariness B. duality C. creativity D. displacement

4. When language is used to get information from others, it serves an __________ function. (北二外 2003 研)

   A. informative B. directive C. interrogative

5. The functions of language do NOT include __________. (大连外国语学院 2008 研)

   A. informative function B. interpersonal function

   C. metacognitive function

6. The study of physical properties of the sounds produced in speech is closely connected with

__________. (大连外国语学院 2008 研)

A. articulatory phonetics B. acoustic phonetics

C. auditory phonetics

7. Which of the following is a main branch of linguistics? (大连外国语学院 2008 研)

A. Macrolinguistics B. Psycholinguistics

C. Sociolinguistics

8. Saussure is closely connected with __________. (大连外国语学院 2008 研)

A. Langue B. Competence C. Etic

9. Saussure took a(n) __________ view of language, while Chomsky looks at language from a __________ point of view. (西安交通大学 2008 研)

A. sociological... psychological B. psychological... sociological

C. applied... pragmatic D. semantic... linguistic

10. According to F. de Saussure, __________ refers to the abstract linguistic system shared by all the members of a speech community. (西安交通大学 2008 研)

A. parole B. performance C. langue D. Language

11. __________ refers to the system of a language, i. e. the arrangement of sounds and words which speakers of a language have a shared knowledge of. (西安外国语学院 2006 研)

A. Langue B. Competence

C. Communicative competence D. Linguistic potential

12. The actual production and comprehension of the speech by speakers of a language is called __________. (北二外 2010 研)

A. grammar rules B. competence

C. performance D. language device

13. The study of language at one point in time is a __________ study. (北二外 2010 研)

A. historical B. synchronic C. descriptive D. diachronic

14. Which of the following statements is true of Jacobson's framework of language functions?

A. The referential function is to indulge in language for its own sake.

B. The emotive function is to convey message and information.

C. The conative function is to clear up intentions, words and meanings.

D. The phatic function is to establish communion with others.

15. "An refer to Confucius even though he was dead 2,000 years ago." This shows that language has the design feature of __________.

A. arbitrariness B. creativity C. duality D. displacement

16. The function of the sentence "Water boils at 100 degree Centigrade" is __________.

A. interrogative B. directive C. informative D. performative

Ⅲ. True or False

1. It is conclusive that Chinese is regarded as the primeval language. (清华 2000 研)
2. Wherever humans exist, language exists. (对外经贸 2006 研)
3. According to Saussure, the relation between the signified and the signifier is arbitrary. (大连外国语学院 2008 研)

4. The features that define our human languages can be called DESIGN FEATURES.（大连外国语学院 2008 研）
5. Onomatopoeic words can show the arbitrary nature of language.（清华 2000 研）
6. The bow-wow theory is a theory on the origin of language.（大连外国语学院 2008 研）
7. When language is used to get information from others, it serves an informative function.（清华 2001 研）
8. Historical linguistics equals to the study of synchronic study.
9. Duality is one of the characteristics of human language. It refers to the fact that language has two levels of structures: the system of sounds and the system of meanings.
10. Prescriptive linguistics is more popular than descriptive linguistics, because it can tell us how to speak correct language.

Ⅳ. Explain the following terms.

1. Displacement（南开大学 2010 研；清华 2001 研）
2. Duality（北二外 2010 研；南开大学 2010 研；西安交通大学 2008 研）
3. Arbitrariness（四川大学 2006 研）
4. Phatic function(communion)（武汉大学 2005 研）

Ⅴ. Short answer questions

1. What is the directive function?（西安交大 2008 研）
2. How well, in your opinion, does the word "communication" represent the function of human language?（北二外 2008 研）
3. Briefly explain what phonetics and phonology are concerned with and what kind of relationships hold between the two.（北外 2002 研）
4. What makes language unique to human beings?（北航 2010 研）
5. What are the major differences between phonology and phonetics?（西安交通大学 2008 研）
6. Why do people take duality as one of the important design features of human language? Can you tell us what language will be if it has no such design feature?（南开大学 2004 研）
7. Why do we say linguistics is a science?（北外 2011 研）
8. One of the design features of human language is creativity. What is it? And what makes it possible?
9. Explain the characteristic of arbitrariness. What are the relationships between arbitrariness & onomatopoeic words and arbitrariness convention?

Ⅵ. Essay questions

1. What are the seven functions of human language?（人大 2006 研）
2. Is it possible to separate semantics and pragmatics? Why or why not? What are the implications of your answer for second language teaching?（北外 2005 研）
3. Examine the following two statements about language, and discuss the similarities and differences between them. Do you agree with the two statements? Explain your answer.
   (1) Sapir (1921: Language): "Language is a purely human and non-instinctive method of communicating ideas, emotions and desires by means of voluntarily produced symbols." (p. 8).

(2) Bloch and Trager (1942: Outline of Linguistic Analysis): "A language is a system of arbitrary vocal symbols by means of which a social group co-operates." (p. 5). (北外 2005 研)

4. Shakespeare has Juliet say:

   What's in a name? That which we call a rose.

   By any other name would smell as sweet.

   What do the above lines say to you about the relationship between the form (sounds) and meaning (concept) of a word in spoken language? Explain with positive evidence as well as exceptions from the English language. (北外 2004 研)
5. Make comments upon the relationship between arbitrariness, convention, and motivation. (四川大学 2006 研)
6. Illustrate the significance of studying speech Sounds in linguistics. (大连外国语学院 2008 研)
7. Saussure puts forward the concept of langue and parole, and Chomsky puts forward the concept of competence and performance. Please dwell upon the differences and similarities, if any, of the two pairs: langue and parole vs. competence and performance. (北京交通大学 2007 研)
8. What are the three metafunctions of Systemic Functional Grammar? Illustrate each of them with specific examples. (武汉大学 2011 研)
9. How do you compare the traffic light system with a human linguistic system?

参考答案及解析

I. Fill in the blanks.

1. conventionality

   (语言学习过程中学习者必须识记一些固定搭配或约定俗成的习语谚语等，因此使得语言学习比较费力。)
2. arbitrary

   (索绪尔认为符号的形式或声音与其意义之间没有逻辑联系，所以两者之间的关系是任意的。)
3. meaning

   (参见第 2 题解析。)
4. design

   (人类语言区别于其他动物交流系统的特点是语言的区别特征，是人类语言特有的特征。)
5. displacement

   (移位性是指人类语言可以让使用者在交际时用语言符号代表时间和空间上不可及的物体、事件和观点。)
6. duality

   (双重性是指拥有两层结构的这种属性，底层结构是上层结构的组成成分，每层都有自身的组合规则。)
7. ideational

   (韩理德将儿童的语言功能范围逐渐缩小，简化成为一套高度符号化和抽象化的功能：概念、人际、语篇功能。)
8. metalingual

（语言的元语言功能是指语言可以用来讨论语言本身。）

9. Interpersonal

（人际功能通过语气情态实现。）

10. Function

（本题考查语言学中对“语言的功能”的定义。功能指的是语言在沟通中(例如表达观点、态度)或在特定社交场合(如宗教、法律)中所起的作用。）

11. Performative

（施为句是用来做事的，既不陈述事实，也不描述情况，且不能验证其真假。）

12. phatic

（寒暄功能是指那些有助于确立和维持人际关系的表达，例如俚语、玩笑、行话、礼节性的问候、社会方言或地域方言的转用等。）

13. scientific

（语言学通常被定义为研究科学的语言，或对语言的科学研究。）

14. phonology

（音系学研究支配语音分布和排列的规则以及音节的形式。）

15. morphology

（形态学研究词语的内部结构组织。）

16. Phonetics

（语音学研究语音，以及语音的描写和分类。）

17. pragmatics

（语义学研究词作为词的意义，语用学是在语境中研究意义。）

18. syntax

（句法学研究形成正确句子的规则。）

19. Pragmatics

（语用学是在语境中研究意义。）

20. syntax

（句法学研究语言中组合成句子的支配规则，或简单地说，研究句子的构造。）

21. reality

（心理语言学研究语言与意识之间的联系，实质就是心理活动与语言结构之间的关系。）

22. langue；parole

（语言指一个语言集团的所有成员共享的抽象语言系统，言语是指语言在实际使用中的实现。）

23. Descriptive；prescriptive

（描述性语言记录语言共同体的成员所遵循的规则，规定式的语言学目的在于为正确使用语言定下各种规则。）

24. competence

（语言能力指理想的语言使用者关于语言规则的语言知识，语言应用指语言交际中关于语言规则知识的实际使用。）

25. prescriptive

（规定式的语言学目的在于为正确使用语言定下各种规则。）

26. competence

（乔姆斯基提出了语言能力和语言应用的根本区别。）

27. creativity

（本题考查语言的定义特征中的创造性。创造性指语言的能产性，它能够使人造出和理解无穷的长句，其中很多句子是以前从未听过的。）

28. distinctive features

（区别性特征第一次由 Roman Jacobson 提出。）

29. yo-he-ho

（语言的起源有“汪汪”理论，“噗噗”理论和“哟嘿吼”理论。“哟嘿吼”理论语言起源于原始人共同劳动时发出的有节奏的哼哟声。）

30. descriptive

（把语言说成描述性的科学是说语言学家试图发现和记录一语言共同体的成员所遵循的规则，并不是强加给他们其他规则或正确的标准。）

31. diachronic linguistic

（历时语言学集中研究几十年或几百年的时期内两个或比两个更多的语言状况的差异。）

32. competence

（索绪尔的语言与乔姆斯基的语言能力相似，因为二者都指抽象的语言知识，不是实际使用中的语言。）

33. langue

（索绪尔用语言和言语来区分说话者的语言能力和言语上（表达的）的实际表现或语料。）

Ⅱ. Multiple Choice

1. B （语言的区别性特征主要是指任意性，双重性，创造性和移位性。）
2. A （crash 是一个缩略语，typewriter 是复合词，bang 是拟声词，所以只有 tree 的形成比较任意。）
3. C （创造性指语言的能产性，它能够使人造出和理解无穷的长句，其中很多句子是以前从未听过的。）
4. C （疑问功能是指以语言为媒介探求信息，一般用于疑问句中。信息功能是指语言用来陈述某件事情，提供信息或用作推理。信息功能是语言最重要的功能，一般出现在陈述句中。）
5. C （语言的主要功能包括信息功能，人际功能，施为功能，感情功能，寒暄功能，元语言功能和娱乐功能。）
6. B （声学语音学研究语音的物质特征。）
7. A （语言学主要分为宏观语言学和微观语言学，宏观语言学又包括社会语言学，心理语言学和人类语言学。）
8. A （索绪尔提出了言语与语言，乔姆斯基提出了语言能力与语言应用。）
9. A （索绪尔的语言指语言社团中的语言，所以是从社会的角度研究语言。乔姆斯基是从使用者本身掌握的语言知识研究语言，是从心理角度研究语言。）
10. C （参见第 9 题解析。）
11. A （语言指一个言语社团所有成员共享的抽象语言系统。）
12. C （语言应用指在语言交际中关于语言规则知识的实际使用。）

13. B （在某一时间点上对语言的描写是一种共时研究。）
14. D （所指功能是指用语言来传达信息，情感功能是表达一种态度，感受；意动功能是通过命令和恳求说服影响他人。）
15. D （移位性是指人类语言可以让使用者在交际时用语言符号代表时间和空间上不可及的物体、事件和观点。）
16. C （语言的信息功能是指语言用来陈述某件事情，提供信息或用作推理。）

Ⅲ. True or False

1. F （汉语是经过长期发展而来的高级语言而不是一种原始语言。）
2. F （语言是在人类出现相当一段时间之后才出现的。）
3. T （索绪尔认为语言符号的形式与意义没有天然联系，两者之间的联系是任意的。）
4. T （能定义人类语言的特点就是语言的基本特征。）
5. F （拟声词表明语言并不是完全任意的，一些拟声词的发音与其意义还是有一定联系的。）
6. T （语言的起源包括“汪汪”、“噗噗”等理论。）
7. F （语言是用来陈述某件事情，提供信息或用作推理，信息功能是语言最重要的功能，一般出现在陈述句中。）
8. F （历史语言学相当于历时研究。）
9. T （二重性是人类语言的一个基本特征，因为语言有两层结构：声音系统和意义系统。）
10. F （描写式和规定式的语言学是分析语言的两种不同的方法，不能简单的说谁好谁坏之说。）

Ⅳ. Explain the following terms.

1. Displacement: Language can be used to refer to what is present, what is absent, what happens at present, what happened in the past, what will happen in the future or what happens in a far-away place. This property of language enables language users to overcome the barriers caused by time and place. For example, we can talk about Sapir, who is already dead; we can even talk about next week, which is in the future.
2. Duality refers to the fact that in all languages so far investigated there are two levels of structure or patterning. At the first, higher level, language is analyzed in terms of combinations of meaningful units (such as morphemes, words etc.); at the second, lower level, it is seen as a sequence of segments which lack any meaning in themselves, but which combine to form units of meaning. For example, a syllable is the smallest unit that is normally spoken by itself, and scores of syllables become the carriers of hundreds of meaningful segments of words that are called morphemes.
3. Arbitrariness: Arbitrariness refers to the fact that the forms of linguistic signs have no natural relationship to their meaning. Arbitrariness of language makes it potentially creative, a conventionality of language makes a language be passed from generation to generation. For example, it is unable to explain why a book is called a /buk/ and a pen a /pen/.
4. Phatic function: The phatic function of language refers to the use of the language which often consists of small, seemingly meaningless expression for setting up a certain atmosphere or maintaining social contacts rather than for exchanging information or ideas. For example, greetings,

farewells, and comments on the weather in English could serve this function.

V. Short answer questions

1. Directive function is one of functions of language. Language is used to get the hearer to do something. Most imperative sentences are of this function. For example, the sentence "Close your book and listen to me carefully!" performs a directive function. Other syntactic structures or sentences of other sorts can, according to J. Austin and J. Searle's "Indirect speech act theory" at least, serve the purpose of direction too, e. g., "If I were you, I would have blushed to the bottom of my ears!"
2. We use language for an almost infinite number of purposes, from writing letters to gossiping with our friends, making speeches and talking to ourselves in the mirror. But the primary function of language is to transmit information and to convey commands, feelings and emotions. That is, language is a tool of communication. The term "communication" can be used to cover much of the function of language. This function can be further divided into more specific functions, such as phatic function/communion, directive function, informative function, interrogative function, expressive function, evocative function, performative function etc.
3. By definition, phonetics is the study of speech sounds, including the production of speech, while phonology is the study of the rules governing the structure, distribution, and sequencing of speech sounds and the shape of syllables. Both phonetics and phonology are concerned with speech. Phonetics is the study of the production, perception, and physical properties of speech sounds; phonology attempts to account for how they are combined, organized, and convey meaning in particular languages. Phonetics is the study of actual sounds, that is, the analysis and modeling of the speech signal; phonology is concerned with a more abstract description of speech sounds and tries to describe the regularities of sound patterns in different languages or within a language. In this sense, phonetics is concrete, while phonology is abstract. What phonetics studies is the speech sound, namely phone, what phonology studies is phoneme.
4. The design features of language which refer to the defining properties of human language tell the difference between human language and any system of animal communication.

   Arbitrariness is a core feature of language, which means that there is no logical connection between meanings and sounds. Duality, which means the property of having two levels of structures, such that units of the primary level are composed of elements of the secondary level and each of the two levels has its own principles of organization. Creativity means language is resourceful because of its duality and its recursiveness. Because of duality the speaker is able to combine the basic linguistic unites to form an infinite set of sentences, most of which are never heard before. Displacement means that language can be used to refer to things which are present or not present, real or imagined matters, in the past, present, or future, or in far-away places. So all these features make language unique to human beings.
5. Phonetics studies speech sounds, including the production of speech, that is how speech sounds are actually made, transmitted and received, the sounds of speech, the description and classification of speech sounds, words and connected speech, etc. Phonology studies the rules governing the structure, distribution, and sequencing of speech sounds and the shape of syllables. Put it

simply, phonetics simply describes the articulatory and acoustic properties of phones (speech sounds) while phonology studies how sounds interact as a system in a particular language.

6. Duality makes our language productive. A large number of different units can be formed out of a small number of elements—for instance, tens of thousands of words out of a small set of sounds. And out of the huge number of words, there can be astronomical number of possible sentences and phrases, which in turn can combine to form unlimited number of texts. Most animal communication systems do not have this design feature of human language.

   If language had no such design feature, then it would be like animal communicational system which consists of only a number of basic sounds and this would be highly limited. Then we would not be able to produce a very large number of sound combinations (e. g. words), which are distinct in meaning. In other words, the number of messages one can send would be restricted to the number of basic sounds.

7. Linguistics is generally defined as the scientific study of language. It tries to answer the basic questions "What is language?" and "How does language work?" Linguistics studies not any particular language, e. g. English, Chinese, Arabic, and Latin, but it studies languages in general.

   It is a scientific study because it is based on the systematic investigation of linguistic data, conducted with reference to some general theory of language structure. In order to discover the nature and rules of the underlying language system, what the linguist has to do first is to collect and observe language facts, which arc found to display some similarities, and generalizations are made about them; then he formulates some hypotheses about the language structure. But the hypotheses thus formed have to be checked repeatedly against the observed facts to fully prove their validity. In linguistics, as in any other discipline, data and theory stand in a dialectical complementation; that is, a theory without the support of data can hardly claim validity, and data without being explained by some theory remain a muddled mass of things.

   (此题考查语言学作为一门学科其科学性，为开放性试题，从其研究内容及方法角度作答即可。)

8. The creativity of language means that users can understand and produce sentences they have never heard before. Creativity is a property unique to human language. It is one of design features that only human language has.

   Human language is resourceful because of its duality and its recursiveness. The speaker is able to combine the basic linguistic units to form all infinite sets of sentences, most of which are never before produced or heard. The fact that human language is recursive could be shown in that words can be used in new ways to mean new things, and can be instantly understood by people who have never come across that word before. For example, I could make a sentence like *The old lady who is waiting for the girl who is talking to the boy who is playing with a basketball is my grandma.*

   Recursiveness also includes coordination and subordination, conjoining and embedding, hypotactic and paratactic. recursiveness, together with openness, is generally regarded as the core of creativity of language.

9. Arbitrariness refers to the fact that the forms of linguistic signs bear no natural relationship to their

meaning. Onomatopoeic words are the words that sound like the sounds they describe. Only when people know the meaning can they infer that the linguistic sign is appropriate for the exact sound. Arbitrariness of language makes it potentially creative, and conventionality of language makes a language be passed from generation to generation.

VI. Essay questions

1. According to Hu Zhuanglin, language has at least seven functions, and they are illustrated as follows:

(1) Informative function. It means that language is the instrument of thought and language serves an informational function when used to tell something. It is also called ideational function in the framework of functional grammar. The declarative sentences such as "This is a book." are the typical illustration of this function.

(2) Interpersonal function. The interpersonal function means people can use language to establish and maintain their status in a society. It is the most important sociological use of language. In the framework of functional grammar, this function is concerned with interaction between the addresser and addressee in the discourse situation and the addresser's attitude toward what he speaks or writes about. For example, the ways in which people address others and refer to themselves (such as Dear Sir, Dear Professor, Johnny, yours, your obedient servant) indicate the various grades of interpersonal relations.

(3) Performative function. The performative function of language is primarily to change the social status of persons, as in marriage ceremonies, the sentencing of criminals, the blessing of children, the naming of a ship at a launching ceremony, and the cursing of enemies. The kind of language employed in performative verbal acts is usually quite formal and even ritualized. The performative function can extend to the control of reality as on some magical or religious occasions. For example, in Chinese when someone breaks a bowl or a plate, the host or the people present are likely to say *sui sui ping an* (every year be safe and happy) as a means of controlling the forces which the believers feel might affect their lives.

(4) Emotive function. The emotive function is one of the most powerful uses of language because it is so crucial in changing the emotional status of an audience for or against someone or something. It is a means of getting rid of the nervous energy when people are under stress, for example, swear words, obscenities, involuntary verbal reactions to beautiful art or scenery; conventional words/phrases, for example, *God*, *My*, *Damn it*, *Wow*, *Ugh*, *Ow*, etc.

(5) Phatic communion. The phatic communion refers to the social interaction of language. People always use some small, seemingly meaningless expressions such as *Good morning*, *God bless you*, *Nice day*, etc., to maintain a comfortable relationship between people without any factual content.

(6) Recreational function. The recreational function means people use language for the sheer joy of using it, such as a baby's babbling or a chanter's chanting.

(7) Metalingual function. The metalingual function refers to the fact that people can use language to talk about itself. For example, I can use the word "book" to talk about a book, and I can also use the expression "the word book" to talk about the sign "b-o-o-k" itself.

2. Though both semantics and pragmatics have to do with the meaning of language, and link language to the world, we think it is possible to separate semantics and pragmatics in linguistic study. Semantics is the study of literal meaning of linguistic expressions, particularly meaning of words, phrases and sentences. In using the term sense rather than reference, the focus of semantics is on the way people relate words to each other within the framework of their language. Pragmatics starts from the observation that people use language to accomplish many kinds of acts, broadly known as speech acts thus it is the study of how to do things with words or of the meaning of language in context. This kind of meaning in pragmatics usually refers to as speaker's meaning, utterance meaning, or contextual meaning. Its interpretation depends more on who the speaker of the sentence is, who the hearer is, when and where it is used. Thus the distinction between semantics and pragmatics is clear: the former is more closely related to the words used, the more constant, inherent side of meanings; the latter is more closely related to the context, the more indeterminate side, or something extra.

The first implication for second language study involves the appropriate use of the target language. The teaching of a foreign language in a classroom involves two types of instruction: one is informational and analytical and can be diagrammed on the axis of general semantic information about the language. But language learning also has a crucially important skill component, which involves the development of the ability to use the language, actively through speaking and writing and passively through listening and reading. This is the pragmatic turn in second language teaching. The language use should be analyzed in relation to the context of communication, and that language teaching and learning should focus on the appropriate use of the target language, oral and written, according to situational and wider social context.

The second implication is concerned with vocabulary learning and translation. The learning of second language's vocabularies involves the understanding and memory of their meanings. Since the differences between the first and second language's culture, there may be no corresponding meaning underlying the same sayings. Teachers should explain the different usage or implication of the target language's items. This is of much importance for cross-cultural translation practices.

3. Similarities:

(1) Both definitions stick to the fact that language is primarily a matter of speech because the primary medium of language is sound. Sapir illustrates this idea by implying that the produced symbols are auditory and Bloch and Trager by explicitly using the word "vocal".

(2) Both definitions allude to the fact that the association between the words and the things that they denoted is rarely inherent, Sapir by using the word "symbols" and Bloch and Trager by placing emphasis on "arbitrary" and "symbols".

Differences:

(1) Sapir's definition emphasizes that language relates to communication between human beings. It is very different from the communication systems of other creatures, such as bird songs and bee dances. Bloch and Trager do not clearly indicate this property, only saying that it is possessed by a social group.

(2) Sapir also considers that language is "non-instinctive" and "voluntarily produced". Thus for him language does not include such instinctive forms of communication as smiling and cries of pain, etc. However, Bloch and Trager's definition do not include this feature.

(3) The element "system" in Bloch and Trager's definition reflects the fact that language provides us with the framework for generating appropriate utterances rather than providing us with an infinite store of ready-made utterances. Still elements of lacunae are combined according to rules.

(4) The function of language is indicated differently in two definitions. Sapir sees language as for communicating ideas, emotions and desires, while Bloch and Trager considers it for a social group's co-operation. Sapir's definition proposes "communication" as the principal function of language and specifies what is communicated; Bloch and Trager only vaguely point out that language can be used for co-operation.

Each of the two definitions has its own special emphasis, and it is not totally free from limitations. We think the two definitions grasp some defining properties of language that distinguish it from any animal system of communication, for example, "vocal", "arbitrary", "symbol", "purely human", "a system". But either has some limitation. As for Sapir's definition, whether one considers language to be instinctive or not is an issue. Language is instinctive in so far as we are all born with a predisposition to speak, we all acquire a language without tuition and when we speak we do not consciously convert our thoughts into speech. Language is, however, non-instinctive in that we can choose what to say or whether to say anything at all. Both the definition's description of language's function is not precise. Sapir's definition confines language only to communicating ideas, emotions and desires, and Bloch and Trager's definition does not point it out at all.

4. The lines said above show that the relationship between the form (sounds) and meaning (concept) of a word in spoken language is arbitrary in nature. That means there is no logical connection between forms (sounds) and meaning (concept). Different sounds are used to refer to the same object in different languages.

   Sounds are just symbols; they are associated with objects, actions, ideas, etc. by convention. In this example, the rose can be called by many names in different languages but its smell never changes. Another example, different languages have different forms for referring to dog in English, such as Chinese "狗(gou)", French "chien (n. m.)". While language is arbitrary by nature, there are some exceptions as well. The best examples in English are the onomatopoetic words and compound words. For example, some onomatopoetic words "rumble", "crash", "crackle" "bang" are uttered like the sounds they describe, thus seem to have a natural basis. Besides, some compound words are also not entirely arbitrary. For example while "photo" and "copy" are both arbitrary, the compound word "photocopy" is not entirely arbitrary, thus seem to be motivated. Anyhow, non-arbitrary words make up only a small percentage of the vocabulary of a language.

5. Arbitrariness of language makes it potentially creative; a conventionality of language makes a language be passed from generation to generation, and makes learning a language laborious. The link between a linguistic sign and its meaning is a matter of convention.

The terms motivation and constraint describe the extent to which the signified determines the signifier. The form of the signifier of a generalized car or a traffic sign is determined by the convention that is accepted by the users of the code.

Motivated signs are iconic signs; they are characterized by a natural relation between signifier and signified. A portrait or a photograph is iconic, in that the signifier represents the appearance of the signified. The faithfulness or the accuracy of the representation—the degree to which the signified is re-presented in the signifier—is an inverse measure of how conventionalized it is. It is important to recognize that (i) in signs of high motivation, the signified is the determining influence, and (ii) in signs of low motivation, convention determines the form of the signifier. Therefore, convention plays a key role in our understanding of any sign. Convention serves as the social dimension of signs. We may not understand the unmotivated verbal sign for car the French use, but we understand the road signs in France in so far as they are iconic.

6. Language is first and foremost a "system of vocal symbols". Human beings are capable of making all kinds of sounds, but only some of these sounds have become units in the language system, as we have seen in the discussion of language Speech sounds had existed long before writing was invented, and even today, in some parts of the world, there are still languages that have no writing systems. Therefore, the study of speech sounds is a major part of linguistics.

   Analysis of speech sounds can be approached on two levels: phonetics and phonology. The former deals with speech organs and their functions, speech sounds, waves carrying speech sounds, analysis and processing of the sounds by the listener. The latter is concerned with the organization of speech within specific languages, or with the systems and patterns of sounds that occur in particular languages. Both phonetics and phonology are main branches of linguistics.

   To study speech sounds, linguistics need to analyze the minute processes and activities of the speaker and explain the way speech organs move to convey meaning. The theory and methods thus developed can be applied to numerous other fields. For example, people who work in recording, language description and language teaching all have some interest in phonetic knowledge while those who work in audiology, speech therapy and speech pathology must have a solid foundation in phonetics and phonology.

7. According to F. de Saussure, langue refers to the abstract linguistic system shared by all members of a speech community; while parole refers to the realization of langue in actual use.

   For Chomsky, a fundamental distinction between linguistic competence and performance should be made. A language user's underlying knowledge about the system of rules is called linguistic competence. And performance refers to the actual use of language in concrete situations. In light with this, competence enables a speaker to produce and understand an indefinite number of sentences and to recognize grammatical mistakes and ambiguities. A speaker's competence is stable but his performance is often influenced by psychological and social factors, and thus would involve imperfections such as slips of tongue, false starts, unnecessary pauses, and so on. Thus, the point is that a speaker's performance does not always match his competence.

   Saussure's distinction is somewhat similar with Chomsky's in the sense that they both refer to the constant factor which underlies the utterances that constitute parole/ performance. However, their difference is quite obvious. Saussure's language is a social product, a set of conventions for a speech community. Chomsky regards competence as a property of the mind of each individual. Saussure looks at language more from a sociological point of view while Chomsky looks at it more from a psychological point of view.

8. According to Halliday, the adult's language becomes much more complex and it has to serve many more functions, and the original functional is gradually reduced to a set of highly coded and abstract functions, which are three metafunctions: the ideational, the interpersonal, and the textual functions.

First, the ideational function ("experiential" and "logical") is to convey new information, to communicate a content that is unknown to the hearer. Present in all language uses, the ideational function is a meaning potential, because whatever specific use one is making of language he has to refer to categories of his experience of the world.

The ideational function mainly consists of "transitivity" and "voice". This function not only specifies the available options in meaning but also determines the nature of their structural realisations. For example, John built a new house can be analysed as a configuration of the function roles:

Actor: John

Process: Material: creation: built

Goal: affected: a new house

Second, the interpersonal function embodies all uses of language to express social and personal relations. This includes the various ways the speaker enters a speech situation and performs a speech act. Because the clause is not confined to the expression of transitivity, there are non-ideational elements in the adult language system.

Interpersonal function is realised by mood and modality. Mood shows what role the speaker selects in the speech situation and what role he assigns to the addressee. If the speaker selects the imperative mood, he assumes the role of one giving commands and puts the addressee in the role of one expected to obey orders. Modality specifies if the speaker is expressing his judgement or making a prediction. For example, "Give me that teapot!"

Mood is made up of two parts: the "Subject" and the "Finite" element. The subject can be a noun, a noun phrase, or a clause.

Third, the textual function refers to the fact that language has mechanisms to make any stretch of spoken or written discourse into a coherent and unified text and make a living passage different from a random list of sentences. Although two sentences may have exactly the same ideational and interpersonal functions, they may be different in terms of textual coherence.

The textual function fulfils the requirement that language should be operationally relevant, having texture in a real context of situation that distinguishes a living passage from a mere entry in a grammar or a dictionary. It provides the remaining strands of meaning potential to be woven into the fabric of linguistic structure.

For example, analyze the sentence "John likes linguistics." on three levels of metafunctions.

Ideational Mental Process Reaction	John	likes	linguistics
	Senser	Mental reaction	Mental reaction
Interpersonal Declarative	Mood		Residue
	Subject	Predicator	Adjunct
Textual Unmarked Theme	Theme	Rheme	
	Given		New

（考查韩礼德功能语法中三项元功能，并举例说明。）

9. Both the traffic light system and human linguistic system can symbolize some information in communication whereas the linguistic system is more complicated. However, the linguistic system has several distinctive features that no other systems have, including the traffic light system.

(1) Language is arbitrary which means that there is no logical connection between meanings and sounds. But in traffic light system, there are direct logical connections between the light signals and their meanings.

(2) Language is hierarchical, that's to say linguistic system has two levels of structures, such that units of the primary level are composed of elements of the secondary level and each of the two levels has its own principles of organization. However, the traffic light system has no hierarchical system and the structure is composed by a single level.

(3) Language is creative. By creativity we mean language is resourceful because of its duality and its recursiveness. Because of duality, speaker is able to combine the basic linguistic units to form an infinite set of sentences, most of which are never before produced or heard. But there is no recursive nature in traffic light system which means that it can not produce new meaning.

第2章　语音

2.1　复习笔记

本章要点：

1. Speech Organs 发音器官
2. Distinction, Classification and the Criteria of Description between Consonants and Vowels
   辅音和元音的区别、分类及描写规则
3. Coarticulation and Phonetic Transcriptions
   协同发音和语音转写
4. Phonemes and Allophones
   音位和音位变体
5. Phonological Processes, Phonological Rules and Distinctive Features
   音系过程、音系规则和区别特征
6. Syllable Structure, Stress and Intonation
   音节结构、重音和语调

常考考点：

1. 语音学

语音学的定义；音姿的定义；发音器官的英文名称；英语辅音的定义、发音部位、发音方法和分类；英语元音的定义和分类、基本元音；发音语音学；听觉语音学；声学语音学；语音标记，国际音标；严式与宽式标音法。

2. 音系学

音系学的定义；音系学与语音学的联系和区别；音素、音位、音位变体、最小对立体、自由变体的定义；音位理论；自由变异；音位的对立分布与互补分布；语音的相似性；区别性特征；超语段音位学；音节；重音(词重音、句子重音)；音高和语调。

本章内容索引：

Ⅰ. The Definition of Phonetics and Phonology

1. Phonetics
2. Three Major Research Fields of Phonetics
3. Phonology

Ⅱ. Speech Organs

▼1. Gestures
2. Speech organs
3. Voiceless sounds
4. Voiced sounds
5. IPA

Ⅲ. Consonants and Vowels

1. Definition
2. Consonants
   (1) Manner of Articulation and Place of Articulation
   (2) Classification of Consonants
3. Vowel
   (1) Cardinal vowels
   (2) Criteria of vowel description
   (3) Monophthongs, Diphthongs and Triphthongs

Ⅳ. Coarticulation and Phonetic Transcriptions

*1. Coarticulation

*2. Phonetic Transcription

Ⅴ. Phonemes and Allophones

1. Phoneme
2. Allophones

Ⅵ. Phonological Processes and Distinctive Features

1. Phonological processes
2. Assimilation

*3. Distinctive features

Ⅶ. Suprasegmentals

1. Suprasegmental features
2. The Syllable Structure

▼3. Sonority Scale

▼4. Stress
   (1) Change of the stresses due to suffixes
   (2) Stresses in compounds and phrases

5. Intonation and Tone

Ⅰ. The Definition of Phonetics and Phonology

1. Phonetics

Phonetics is the study of speech sounds and their production, transmission, and perception.

2. Three Major Research Fields of Phonetics

(1) Articulatory Phonetics studies how speech sounds are produced.

(2) Acoustic Phonetics is the study of physical properties of the sounds produced in speech.

(3) Perceptual (Auditory) Phonetics studies the perception of speech sounds.

Ⅰ. 语音学和音系学的定义

1. 语音学

语音学研究语音的发生、传递和感知。

2. 语音学研究的三大领域

(1) 发音语音学研究语音的发生。

(2) 声学语音学研究语音的物质特征。

(3) 感知语音学(或听觉语音学)研究语音的感知。

3. Phonology Phonology is the study of sound systems and sound patterns of languages, in another word, it studies the way in which speakers of a certain language systematically use a selection of these sounds in order to express meanings.	**3. 音系学** 音系学研究的是语言的语音系统。换句话说，音系学研究的是说话人为表达意义而系统地选择语音的方法。
Ⅱ. Speech Organs	**Ⅱ. 发音器官**
▼1. Gestures Gestures are movements of the tongue and the lips, through which most speech sounds are made.	**1. 音姿** 大多数的语音都是通过舌头和嘴唇的动作发出的，而这些动作被称为音姿。
2. Speech organs 【考点：根据图指出发音器官名称】 Speech organs (vocal organs) are those parts of human body (lungs, trachea, throat, nose and mouth) playing a role in the production of speech.	**2. 发音器官** 发音器官是人体参与语音发生的那部分，包括肺、气管、喉、鼻和口。
3. Voiceless sounds The sounds produced without causing vibration of the vocal cords.	**3. 清音** 在发音过程中，发音时声带不振动，这样所发出的音叫做清音。
4. Voiced sounds The sounds produced with causing vibration of the vocal cords.	**4. 浊音** 在发音过程中，发音时声带振动，这样所发出的音叫做浊音 。
5. IPA(International Phonetic Alphabet) (1) IPA is a standardized and internationally accepted system of phonetic transcription. (2) Its basic principle is using a different letter for each distinguishable speech sounds. (3) With minor modification it is now still used by phoneticians and linguists.	**5. 国际音标** (1) 国际音标是一个标准的、被国际上广泛接受的语音描述系统。 (2) 它的基本原则是用不同的字母符号来表示不同的发音。 (3) 经过几次修正，目前国际音标仍然被语音学家和语言学家广泛使用。
Ⅲ. Consonants and Vowels	**Ⅲ. 辅音和元音**
1. Definition (1) **Consonants** are sounds produced by constricting or obstructing the vocal tract at some places to divert, impede or completely shut off the flow of air in the oral cavity. (2) **Vowels** are sounds produced without obstruction, so no turbulence or a total stopping of the air can be perceived.	**1. 定义** (1) 发音时，声道的某些部位受到压缩或阻碍后，使得气流在口腔里转向、受阻或完全被阻塞，由此产生的音叫做辅音。 (2) 发音时，声道不受任何压缩或阻碍，因此不会有气流的紊乱或停滞，由此产生的音叫做元音。

2. Consonants	**2. 辅音**
(1) Manner of Articulation and Place of Articulation	**(1) 发音方式和发音部位**
①**Manner of Articulation** refers to the actual relationship between the articulators and the way the airstream is affected as it goes through certain parts of the vocal tract.	① 发音方式指发音器官之间的关系，以及气流经过声道的某些部位时的方式。
② **Place of Articulation** refers to the location at which the speech sound is produced.	②发音部位是指语音产出的位置。
(2) Classification of Consonants	**(2) 辅音的分类**
【考点：描述给定辅音 & 根据描述指出辅音名称】	
① In terms of manners of articulation, consonants can be grouped into stops, nasals, fricatives, approximants, lateral, trill, tap & flap and affricates.	① 按发音方式分类，辅音可分为爆破音、鼻音、擦音、近/通音、边音、颤音、触音和闪音以及塞擦音。
stops: [p, b, t, d, k, g]	爆破音：[p, b, t, d, k, g]
nasals: [m, n, ŋ]	鼻音：[m, n, ŋ]
fricatives: [f, v, θ, ð, s, z, ʃ, ʒ, h]	擦音：[f, v, θ, ð, s, z, ʃ, ʒ, h]
approximants: [w, ɹ, j]	近音：[w, ɹ, j]
lateral: [l]	边音：[l]
affricates: [tʃ, dʒ]	塞擦音：[tʃ, dʒ]
② In terms of place of articulation, the consonants can be grouped into bilabials, labiodentals, dentals, alveolars, postalveolars, palatal, velars and glottals.	② 按发音部位分类，辅音可分为双唇音、唇齿音、齿音、齿龈音、后齿龈音、硬腭音、软腭音和声门音。
bilabials: [p, b, m]	双唇音：[p, b, m]
labiodentals : [f, v]	唇齿音：[f, v]
dentals: [θ, ð]	齿音：[θ, ð]
alveolars: [t, d, n, s, z, ɹ, l]	齿龈音：[t, d, n, s, z, ɹ, l]
postalveolars: [ʃ, ʒ]	后齿龈音：[ʃ, ʒ]
palatal: [j]	硬腭音：[j]
velars: [k, g, ŋ, w]	软腭音：[k, g, ŋ, w]
glottals: [h]	声门音：[h]
3. Vowel	**3. 元音**
【考点：描述给定元音 & 根据描述指出元音名称】	
(1) Cardinal vowels	**(1) 基本元音**
The cardinal vowels are a set of fixed reference vowels used to provide a frame for the description of the actually used vowels.	基本元音是指一系列固定不变的元音特质，目的是为语言中实际存在的元音描述提供一个参照框架。
(2) Criteria of vowel description	**(2) 元音的划分标准**
The height of tongue raising (high, mid, low)	舌头抬起的高度——高、中、低

The position of the highest part of the tongue (front, central, back)

The length or tenseness of the vowel (tense vs. lax or long vs. short)

lip-rounding (rounded vs. unrounded)

舌头最高部分的位置——前、中、后

元音的长度或紧度

唇的圆展度——圆唇、非圆唇

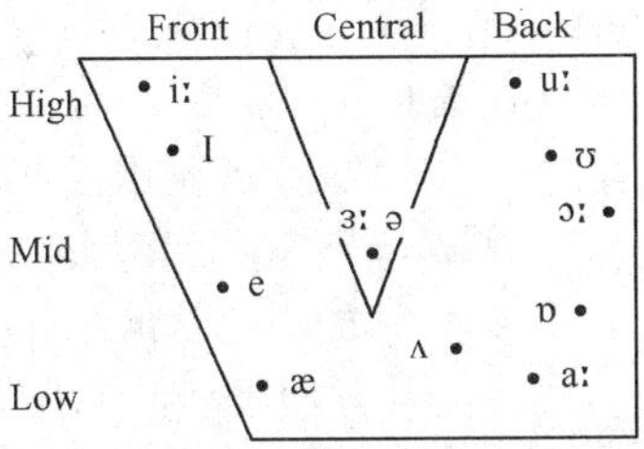

Diphthongs:

eɪ aɪ aʊ ɔɪ

əʊ ɪə ʊə eə

(3) Monophthongs, Diphthongs and Triphthongs

Monophthong: They are those pure vowels that have an unchanging quality, either from the number or the constant quality.

Diphthong: If a single movement from one element to a second element of the tongue is involved, the combining vowels are called diphthongs.

Triphthong: If two movements from one element to a second, then from the second to the third of the tongue are involved, the combining vowels are called triphthongs.

(3) 单元音，双元音，三元音

单元音指在数量上和性质上都恒定不变的纯元音。

如果在发音时通过舌头的一次运动，由第一个单元音滑向第二个单元音，所产生的音的组合就叫做双元音。

如果在发音时通过舌头的两次运作，由第一个单元音滑向第二个单元音，再由第二个单元音滑向第三个单元音，所产生的音的组合就叫做三元音。

Ⅳ. Coarticulation and Phonetic Transcriptions

*1. Coarticulation

The process of simultaneous or overlapping articulations when sounds show the influence of their neighbors, including anticipatory coarticulation and perseverative coarticulation.

(1) Anticipatory coarticulation: When the sound becomes more like the following sound, as in the case of lamb, it is called anticipatory coarticulation.

(2) Perseverative coarticulation: If the sound shows the influence of the preceding sound, it is a perseverative coarticulation, as in the case of map.

【考点：判断一单词包含哪种协同发音】

Ⅳ. 协同发音与语音转写

1. 协同发音

指在实际话语过程中话语持续受邻近音影响，发生同时或重合发音的过程，分前期协同发音和后滞协同发音。

(1) 如果发音的变化是倾向于后音的特质(如 lamb)，就称为前期协同发音。

(2) 如果发音显示出前面语音的影响(如 map)，则称之为后滞协同发音。

*2. Phonetic Transcription

(1) When we try to symbolize all the possible speech sounds, including even the minutest shades of pronunciation, it is called narrow transcription.

2. 语音转写

(1) 当我们用复杂的符号精确地标记语音所有可能的细小变化时，我们称之为“严式转写”。

(2) When we use a set of simple symbols in our transcription, trying to indicate only those sounds capable of distinguishing one word from another in a given language, it is called broad transcription.	(2) 当我们用一套简单的符号记音，试图把一个词与其他的词区别开来时，我们称之为“宽式转写”。
V. Phonemes and Allophones 【考点：区分 phone，phoneme，allophone】	**V. 音位和音位变体**
1. Phoneme Phoneme is a basic unit of phonological study, and it is an abstract collection of phonetic features which can distinguish meaning.	**1. 音位** 音位是音系学研究的一个基本单位，是一组语音特征的抽象集合体，具有区别意义的作用。
① Minimal Pair: When two different forms are identical in every way except for one sound segment in the same place in strings, the two words are said to form a minimal pair.	① 当两个词，除了出现在同一位置上的一个音外，其余的音都一样，那么这两个词就构成了一个最小的对立体。
② Phone: It is a basic unit of phonetic study, and it is a minimal sound segment that human speech organ can produce.	② 音素是语音学研究的一个基本单位，是人类的发音器官所能发出的最小语音片段。
2. Allophones The different realizations of the same phoneme in different phonetic environments are called allophones.	**2. 音位变体** 同一个音位在不同语音环境中的实现方式被称为该音位的音位变体。
① Complementary distribution: When two or more than two allophones of the same phoneme do not distinguish meaning and occur in different phonetic environments, then the allophones are said to be in complementary distribution.	① 当同一个音位的两个或两个以上的音位变体不区别意义，并且出现在不同的语音环境中，那么它们被称作处于互补分布。
* ② Free variation: If two sounds occurring in the same environment do not contrast; that's to say, if the substitution of one for the other does not generate a new word form but merely a different pronunciation of the same word, the two sounds then can be seen as in free variation.	② 如果两个音素出现在一个相同的语音环境中，并不区别意义，即用一个音素替换另一个音素不产生一个新词，仅仅产生同一个词的不同读音，那么这两个音素就可被视为自由变体。
③ Phonemic contrast: If the phonetically similar sounds are two distinctive phonemes, e. g. [p] and [b] in "pit" and "bit", they are said to form a phonemic contrast.	③ 如果最小对立体中的两个音位出现在同一位置并且能够区别意义，例如[pit]和[bit]，那么这两个音位就构成了音位对立。
VI. Phonological Processes and Distinctive Features	**VI. 音系过程和区别特征**
1. Phonological processes Phonological processes are the processes of structural changes of targeted or affected segment in a specific environment (context), which include (1) a set of sounds to undergo the process, (2) a set of sounds produced by the process and (3) a set of situations in which the process applies. 【考点：用公式法描述一音系过程】	**1. 音系过程** 音系过程是“目标”或“受影响的音段”在特定环境中(语境中)发生结构上的变化的过程。任何音系过程包括：(1)一套会产生音系过程的语音；(2)一套经历了音系过程的语音；(3)音系过程得以发生的条件。

2. Assimilation

The assimilation rule assimilates one sound to another by copying a feature of a sequential phoneme, thus making the two phonemes similar, which includes nasalization, dentalization and velarization.

It includes progressive assimilation and regressive assimilation.

Progressive assimilation refers to the process in which a following sound is influenced by a preceding sound, making the two sounds similar.

Regressive assimilation refers to the process, in which a preceding sound is influenced by a following sound, making the two sounds similar.

*3. Distinctive features

They are those features which are phonologically relevant properties and can distinguish meaning, for example, plosiveness, bilabiality, and voicelessness in English phonology.

Ⅶ. Suprasegmentals

1. Suprasegmental features

The features that occur above the level of the segments and can distinguish meanings are called suprasegmental features, which include syllable, stress, intonation and tone.

2. The Syllable Structure

A syllable can be divided into two parts, the rhyme and the onset. As the vowel within the rhyme is the nucleus, the consonant(s) after it is the coda. All syllables must have a nucleus but not all of them have an onset and a coda. A closed syllable has a coda, while an open syllable has no coda. Take the word *cracked* for example. Its syllable can be shown as follows:

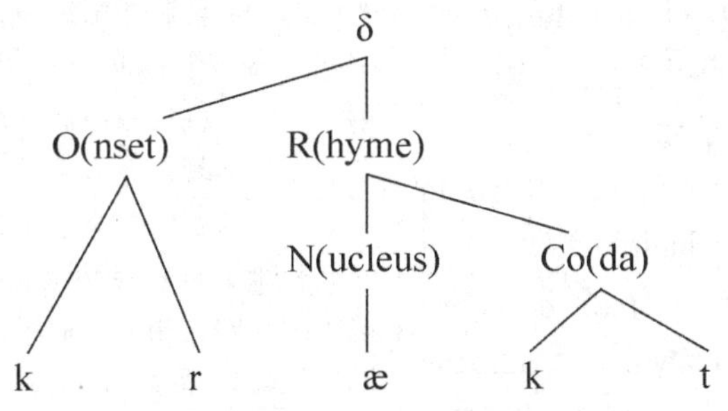

【考点：判断一个音节的节首、韵基和节尾】

2. 同化

同化指一个音具有邻近音的一部分或者全部特征的这一过程，包括鼻化、齿化、腭化。

同化主要包括顺同化和逆同化。

顺同化是指在这个过程里前面的相邻音影响了其后音素的发音，使两者相似。

逆同化是指这样一种过程，在这个过程中后面的相邻音影响了其前面音素的发音，使两者相似。

3. 区别性特征

区别性特征是指和音系有关的，即能够区别意义的语音特征，如英语音系中的爆破、双唇、清音等特征。

Ⅶ. 超音段特征

1. 超音段特征

指的是大于切分层面上的，能够区别意义的特征，其主要包括音节、重音、声调和语调。

2. 音节结构

一个音节可以分成两个部分，韵基和节首。韵基中的元音是核心，它后面的辅音用术语韵尾来表示。所有音节必须有结核，但不是所有的音节都有节首和节尾。有节尾的音节叫做“闭音节”，没有节尾的音节叫做“开音节”。

▼ 3. Sonority Scale

In English, there are many combinations of consonants that are not allowed at the position of onset and coda, which is explained by the work of sonority scale. The degree of the sonority of sounds affects their positions within the syllable.

▼ 4. Stress

It refers to the degree of force in producing a syllable.

(1) Change of the stresses due to suffixes

Some suffixes may change the position of the stress except the suffix *-ive*, e. g. *com'municate*, *communi'cation*, *com'municative*.

(2) Stresses in compounds and phrases

Besides, stress changes also occur in compounds and phrases. For example, a *'blackboard* is used by teachers to write on whereas a *black'board* is just a board with black color.

5. Intonation and Tone

(1) Intonation

Intonation refers to the occurrence of recurring fall-rise patterns, each of which is used with a set of relatively consistent meanings, either on single words or on word groups.

(2) Tone

Tones are pitch variations, which are caused by the different rates of vibration of the vocal cords.

▼① Tone change

Tones in tone language may change because same adjacent tones could produce tone changes. For example, in Mandarin Chinese, if two syllables with the same 214 tone occur continuously, then the first syllable should change to the 35 tone. This phenomenon is called tone sandhi.

▼② OCP in tone change

Tone sandhi leads to a general rule covering epenthesis in segmental phonology: Obligatory Contour Principle (OCP) is the opposite of assimilation and it applies to changes in supersegment characteristics caused by adjacent voices with the same characteristics.

3. 响音阶

在英语中，有很多辅音组合在音节的节首和节尾部分是不允许的，这是由于响音阶的作用。语音的不同音阶会影响它们在音节中的位置。

4. 重音

重音指在音节发音时所用的力度。

(1)后缀对重音的影响

后缀有时也会改变单词的重音，但有的后缀例外，如后缀-ive。

(2)复合词和词组中的重音

重音的改变也出现在复合词和词组中。例如单词 blackboard，当重音在词首时，特指教室的黑板；而当重音在第二个音节处时，泛指颜色是黑色的板。

5. 语调和声调

(1) 语调

语调涉及重复出现的升降模式，每个模式都应用于一套相对一致的意义，要么以词为单位，要么以各种长度的词群为单位。

(2) 声调

声调是指声带振动的频率不同引起的音高变化。

①音调变化

音调语言中的音调并不总是固定不变的，因为相同的相邻音调会产生音调变化。例如，在普通话中，如果两个音节(中文字符)有相同的 214 音调即第三声，那么规则就是第一个音节变为 35 音调即第二声。这种现象叫做变调。

②必异规则

变调与音段音系学中的增音都遵循一个共同的原则：必异规则。该规则与同化相反，适用于具有相同特征的相邻语音所引起的超音段特征的变化。

2.2 考研真题与典型题详解

I. Fill in the blanks.

1. The sound /p/can be described with "__________, bilabial, stop". (北二外 2007 研)
2. The sound /b/can be described with "__________, bilabial, stop". (北二外 2004 研)
3. Consonant articulations are relatively easy to feel. And as a result are most conveniently described in terms of __________ and manner of articulation. (北二外 2004 研)
4. __________ are produced by constricting or obstructing the vocal tract at some place to divert, impede, or completely shut off the flow of air in the oral cavity. (中山大学 2006 研)
5. The present system of the __________ derives mainly from one developed in the 1920s by the British phonetician, Daniel Jones (1881 - 1967), and his colleagues at University of London. (中山大学 2008 研)
6. Voicing refers to the __________ of the vocal folds. (北二外 2016 研)
7. The sound /k/ can be described with "voiceless, __________, stop". (北二外 2003 研)
8. __________ transcription should transcribe all the possible speech sounds, including the minute shades. (北二外 2004 研)
9. __________ refers to the change of a sound as a result of the influence of an adjacent sound. (中山大学 2005 研)
10. Stress refers to the degree of __________ used in producing a syllable. (中山大学 2006 研)
11. The syllable structure in Chinese is __________ or __________ or __________. (清华 2000 研)
12. The different members of a phoneme, sounds which are phonetically different but do not make one word different from another in meaning, are __________. (北二外 2009 研)
13. In English, the two words cut and gut differ only in their initial sounds and the two sounds are two different __________ and the two words are a __________ pair. (北二外 2010 研)
14. Phonetic similarity means that the __________ of a phoneme must bear some phonetic resemblance. (中山大学 2011 研).
15. In English there are a number of __________, which are produced by moving from one vowel position to another through intervening positions.
16. According to __________, when there is a choice as to where to place a consonant, it is put into the onset rather than the coda.
17. In phonological analysis the words fail-veil are distinguishable simply because of the two phonemes/f/ - /v/. This is an example for illustrating __________.
18. Most speech sounds are made by movements of the tongue and the lips, and these movements are called __________, as compared to those made by hands. These movements of the tongue and lips are made __________ so that they can be heard and recognized.
19. In English, consonant clusters in onset and coda positions disallow many consonant combinations, which is explained by the work of __________.

II. Multiple Choice

1. Of the three cavities, __________ is the most variable and active in amplifying and modifying speech sounds. (北二外 2004 研)

A. nasal cavity B. pharynx cavity C. oral cavity

2. Of the consonants /p/, /t/, /k/, /f/, /m/, /z/ and /g/, which has the features of voiceless and velar?（对外经贸2005研）

A. /k/ B. /p/ C. /g/ D. /t/

3. The consonant /s/ in the word "smile" can be described as:（对外经贸2006研）

A. voiceless oral alveolar fricative

B. voiceless nasal bilabial liquid

C. voiced oral alveolar plosive

D. voiced oral bilabial fricative

4. The vowel ________ is a low back vowel.（西安外国语学院2006研）

A. /iː/ B. /u/ C. /e/ D. /aː/

5. Which of the following is true of an allophone?（对外经贸2005研）

A. A phone can be the allophone of all English vowel phonemes.

B. There are no restrictions on the distribution of an allophone.

C. There is no possibility of an allophone becoming a phoneme.

D. An allophone changes the meaning of the word.

6. Which of the following is not a minimal pair?（对外经贸2006研）

A. /liːf/ /fiːl/ B. /sip/ /zip/ C. /sai/ /sei/ D. /keit/ /feit/

7. A sound which is capable of distinguishing one word or one shape of word from another in a given language is a ________.（北二外2003研）

A. allophone B. phone C. phoneme

8. Which of the following CANNOT be considered as minimal pair?（大连外国语学院2008研）

A. /ai/ - /ɔi/ B. /p/ - /b/ C. /s/ - /θ/

9. Point out which item does not fall under the same category as the rest, and explain the reason in ONE sentence.（南京大学2007研）

A. resolution B. resident C. restart D. resignation

10. ________ is one of the suprasegmental features.

A. Voicing B. Stop C. Deletion D. Tone

11. Classification of English speech sounds in terms of manner of articulation involves the following EXCEPT ________.

A. fricatives B. lateral C. affricates D. bilabial

12. An aspirated *p*, an unaspirated *p* and an unreleased *p* are ________ of the *p* phoneme.

A. analogues B. tagmemes C. morphemes D. allophones

13. Which branch of phonetics concerns the production of speech sounds?

A. Acoustic phonetics B. Articulatory phonetics.

C. Auditory phonetics D. Neither of them.

14. Which one is different from the others according to manners of articulation?

A. [f] B. [v] C. [z] D. [w]

15. Which one is different from the others according to places of articulation?

A. [n] B. [m] C. [b] D. [p]

16. What kind of sounds can we make when the vocal cords are vibrating?

A. Voiceless B. Voiced C. Glottal stop D. Consonant

17. The most recognizable differences between American English and British English are in __________ and vocabulary.

A. usage B. grammar C. pronunciation D. structure

18. Which of the following is the correct description of [v]?

A. voiceless labiodental fricative B. voiced labiodental fricative

C. voiceless labiodental stop D. voiced labiodental stop

Ⅲ. True or False

1. In the sound writing system, the reference of the grapheme is the phoneme. (清华 2001 研)
2. A phoneme in one language or one dialect may be an allophone in another language or dialect. (清华 2001 研)
3. The speech sounds which are in complementary distribution are definitely allophones of the same phoneme. (北二外 2010 研)
4. Broad Transcription is intended to symbolize all the possible speech sounds, including the minute shades. (北二外 2003 研)
5. The initial sound of "peak" is aspirated while the second sound of "speak" is unaspirated. They are in free variation. (北二外 2005 研)
6. Phonetic similarity means that the allophones of a phoneme must bear some morphological resemblance. (大连外国语学院 2008 研)
7. The last sound of "top" can be articulated as an unreleased or released plosive. These different realizations of the same phoneme are not in complementary distribution. (北二外 2007 研)
8. The speech sounds we hear and produce during linguistic communications are all phonemes. (对外经贸 2006 研)
9. A syllable can be divided into two parts, the NUCLEUS and the CODA. (大连外国语学院 2008 研)
10. All syllables contain three parts: onset, nucleus and coda. (北二外 2003 研)
11. In English, we can have the syllable structure of CCCVCCCC. (清华 2001 研)
12. The last sound of "sit" can be articulated as an unreleased or released plosive. These different realizations of the same phoneme are not in complementary distribution. (北二外 2009 研)
13. The assimilation rule assimilates one sound to another by copying a feature of a sequential phoneme, thus making the two phones similar.
14. The airstream provided by the lungs has to undergo a number of modifications to acquire the quality of a speech sound.
15. Two sounds are in free variation when they occur in the same environment and do not contrast, namely, the substitution of one for the other does not produce a different word, but merely a different pronunciation.
16. [p] is voiced bilabial stop.
17. Sound [p] in the word "spit" is an unaspirated stop.
18. Tones in tone language are not always fixed. For example, tones in Chinese never change.
19. All the suffixes may change the position of the stress.

20. Speech sounds are those sounds made by human beings that have become units in the language system. We can analyze speech sounds from various perspectives.

Ⅳ. Explain the following terms.

1. Assimilation（南开大学 2010 研；武汉大学 2008 研；中国海洋大学 2021 研）
2. Distinctive features of speech sounds（中山大学 2008 研；北师大 2003 研；北交大 2005 研，浙江大学 2007 研）
3. Syllable（四川大学 2006 研）
4. Cardinal vowel（四川大学 2006 研；暨南大学 2021 研）
5. Voiceless（西安交大 2008 研）
6. Minimal pairs（武汉大学 2005 研；浙江大学 2004 研；四川大学 2007 研；上海交大 2006 研；北航 2008 研；北二外 2006 研）
7. Coarticulation（武汉大学 2008 研；四川大学 2006 研；南开大学 2007 研；南京师范大学 2021 研）
8. Broad and narrow transcription（中山大学 2006 研）
9. Complementary distribution（武汉大学 2008 研；南开大学 2007 研）
10. acoustic phonetics（南开大学 2011 研）
11. SPEAKING（中山大学 2011 研）
12. sonority scale
13. OCP

Ⅴ. Short answer questions

1. For the following words, state the conditions under which the different forms of the past tense appear. What determines whether /t/, /d/, or /id/ is used? What distinctive features define conditioning environment?（南开大学 2004 研）

1. crushed	2. heaped	3. kicked	4. pitted
5. deeded	6. bagged	7. killed	8. nabbed
9. thrived	10. breathed	11. turned	12. hissed
13. plowed	14. climbed	15. singed	16. hanged
17. cinched	18. played	19. hated	20. branded

2. How are the vowels described usually?（北二外 2009 研）
3. Why do we say language is primarily vocal?（厦门大学 2009 研）
4. What are the criteria used in phonetic description of vowels?（厦门大学 2010 研）
5. In English, the phoneme /p/ is pronounced differently in pat, spat, and tap, can you form a rule that can generalize this linguistic phenomenon?（南开大学 2010 研）
6. What are the differences between voiced sounds and voiceless sounds in terms of articulation?（南开大学 2004 研）
7. Phoneme is the smallest meaningful unit of sound and morpheme is the smallest meaningful unit in grammar.（中山大学 2011 研）
8. In the African language Manika, the affix, the meaning of which is similar to that of the suffix -ing in English, has two phonetic forms, as shown in the data given below. You are required to
   (1) give the two phonetic forms of the affix;
   (2) give the underlying form of the affix;

(3) write a formal phonological rule to derive the underlying form of the affix to its phonetic forms, using the words [dumuni] "eating" and [sungoli] "sleeping" to illustrate the process of derivation(南开大学 2011 研)

bugo	*hit*	bugoli	*hitting*
dila	*repair*	dilali	*repairing*
don	*come*	donni	*coming*
dumu	*eat*	dumuni	*eating*
gwen	*chase*	gwenni	*chasing*
da	*lie down*	dali	*lying down*
famu	*know*	famuni	*knowing*
men	*hear*	menni	*hearing*
sungo	*sleep*	sungoli	*sleeping*`

9. What are suprasegmental features? How do the major suprasegmental features of English function in conveying meaning?
10. What is free variation?
11. What are vowels glide about? What differentiates pure or monophthong vowel from vowel glides?
12. What is assimilation? Is it similar to coarticulation? What dose it include?
13. Please explain why *lkaps, *hlpe are not allowed in English.
14. What is stress and what factors may influence stress?

Ⅵ. Essay questions

1. Is English a language that uses a phonetic alphabet system? Explain briefly why or why not with examples.(北外 2004 研)
2. What are the differences between voiced sounds and voiceless sounds in terms of articulation?(南开大学 2004 研)
3. What are phonemes, phones and allophones? Explain their relationship with examples from English or Chinese.(北外 2005 研)
4. What are suprasegmental features?(西安外国语学院 2006 研)

参考答案及解析

Ⅰ. Fill in the blanks

1. voiceless

   (/p/是双唇音，爆破音，清音。)

2. voiced

   (/b/是双唇音，爆破音，浊音。)

3. place

   (辅音根据发音方式和发音部位进行分类。)

4. Consonants

   (发音时，声道的某些部位受到压缩或阻碍后，使得气流在口腔里转向、受阻或完全被阻塞而产生的音叫做辅音。)

5. cardinal vowels

（基本元音是指一系列约定俗成、固定不变的元音特质，目的是为语言中实际存在的元音描述提供一个参照框架。）

6. vibration

（本题考查辅音发音过程中的清浊特征的定义。若发音过程中，声带振动，则为浊辅音，反之则为清辅音。）

7. velar

（/k/是清音，软腭音，爆破音。）

8. Narrow

（当我们用复杂的符号精确地标记语音所有可能的细小变化时，我们称之为“严式转写”。）

9. Assimilation

（同化指一个音具有邻近音的一部分或者全部特征的这一过程，包括鼻化、齿化、鄂化。）

10. force

（重音指在音节发音时所用的力度。）

11. CVC，CV，V

（普通话的音节中节首位置最多有一个辅音，结尾只能是鼻音/n，ŋ/，所以汉语的音节可以写为(C)V(C)。）

12. allophones

（同一个音位在不同语音环境中的实现方式被称为该音位的音位变体。因为变体是互补分布的，而且发音相似。）

13. phonemes；minimal

（/k/、/g/在 cut 和 gut 是两个不同的音位，这两个词，除了出现在同一位置上的一个音外，其余的音都一样，因此这两个词就构成了一个最小的对立体。）

14. allophones

（语音相似性指的是承担一些语音的相似的音位变体。）

15. diphthongs

（如果在发音时通过舌头的一次运动，由第一个单元音滑向第二个单元音，这样产生的音的组合就叫做双元音。）

16. the maximal onset principle

（当一个辅音既可放在节首也可放在节尾时，根据最大节首原则应将其放在节首。）

17. minimal pairs

（如果有两个词，它们除了出现在同一位置上的一个音外，其余的音都一样，那么这两个词就构成了一个最小的对立体，所以 fail-veil 是最小对立体。）

18. gestures；audible

（大多数的语音都是通过舌头和嘴唇的动作发出的，而这些动作被称为音姿。与手势相比较，舌头和嘴唇的动作都是可以听到的，这样它们就能被识别。）

19. sonority scale

（在英语中，有很多辅音组合在音节的节首和节尾部分是不允许的，这是由于响音阶的作用。语音的不同音阶会影响它们在音节中的位置。）

Ⅱ. Multiple Choice

1. C （在三大发音器官中，气流在口腔中受挤或转向从而产生不同的声音。）
2. A （/k/是清音，软腭音，爆破音；/t/是齿龈音，爆破音，清音；/g/是浊音，软腭音，爆破音，/p/是双唇音，爆破音，清音。）
3. A （/s/是清音，摩擦音，齿龈音。）
4. D （/a/是低元音，后元音，紧音。）
5. C （音素是语音学研究的一个基本单位，是人类的发音器官所能发出的最小语音片段，音位是一组语音特征的抽象集合体，并不是所有的因素都是音位。音位变体必须互补分布，且不会改变词义。）
6. A （根据最小对立体的定义，只有 A 不符合，因为 A 中的音不是在同一个位置上。）
7. C （音位是音系学研究的一个基本单位，是一组语音特征的抽象集合体，具有区别意义的作用。）
8. C （/s/是齿龈音，而/θ/是齿音，所以二者不能构成最小对立体。）
9. C （/s/ 在 restart 中位于清辅音前，所以被轻音化。）
10. D （超音段特征包括音节，重音，声调和语调。）
11. D （bilabial 是根据发音部位划分的。）
12. D （送气的/p/和不送气的/p/是同一个音位/p/在不同语音环境中的实现方式，所以被称为该音位的音位变体。）
13. B （发音语言学研究语音的发生。）
14. D （选项 A、B、C 都是摩擦音，/w/是近音。）
15. A （[m]，[b]，[p]都是双唇音，[n]是齿龈音。）
16. B （声带振动产生浊音。）
17. C （英音和美音最大的区别就是发音和词汇，比如发音方面，美音有儿化音。）
18. B （[v]是唇齿音，擦音，浊辅音。）

Ⅲ. True or False

1. T （字形是根据音位的表达写出来的。）
2. T （同一个音位在不同语音环境中的实现方式被称为该音位的音位变体。同一个音位在不同的语言中有不同的实现方式，所以在另一语言中是音位变体。）
3. F （音位变体要满足两个条件：互补分布和语音相似性。）
4. F （当我们用一套简单的符号记音，试图把一个词与其他的词区别开时，我们称之为宽式转写，宽式转写不包括一些细小变化。）
5. F （“peak”和“speak”中的发音不同的“p”是同一个音位的音位变体，而不是自由对立体。）
6. F （语音相似性指一个音位的音位变体必须具有语音相似点。）
7. T （如果两个音素出现在一个相同的语音环境中，且不区别意义，这两个音素可被看作自由变体。）
8. F （我们所听见和说出的声音并不总是音位，有可能是音素，只有那些有区别意义的才是音位。）
9. F （音节中必不可少的就是结核，即元音。节首和节尾可有可无。）
10. F （所有音节必须有结核，但不是所有的音节都有节首和节尾。）

11. T （英语的节首最多包括三个辅音，节尾最多包括四个辅音，而且必须有一个元音。）
12. T （这种情况下这两个音素就可被视为自由变体。）
13. T （同化规则通过“拷贝”序列音位的一个特征来将一个音同化为另一个，从而使两个音素相似。）
14. T （气流从肺部产生，而后穿过声道经过一些变化比如转向，受阻等发出不同的音。）
15. T （自由变体是指两个音素出现在一个相同的语音环境中，并不区别意义，即用一个音素替换另一个音素不产生新词，只产生同一个词的不同读音。）
16. F （[p]是双唇爆破音，是清辅音。）
17. T （/p/在/s/之后是不送气的。）
18. F （音调语言中的音调并不总是固定不变的，因为相同的相邻音调会产生音调变化。例如，在普通话中，如果两个音节（中文字符）有相同的 214 音调即第三声，那么规则就是第一个音节变为 35 音调即第二声。这种现象叫做变调。）
19. F （后缀有时也会改变单词的重音，但有的后缀例外，如后缀-ive。）
20. T （语音是人类发出的已经在语言系统中成为语音单位的声音。我们可以从不同的角度分析语音，如方言、社会变体、言语障碍、语音识别等。）

Ⅳ. Explain the following terms

1. It is a process by which one sound takes on some or all the characteristics of a neighboring sound. It is often used synonymously with coarticulation. Nasalization, dentalization and velarization are all instances of assimilation. There are two possibilities of assimilation: if a following sound is influencing a preceding sound, it is regressive assimilation; the converse process, in which a preceding sound is influencing a following sound, is known as progressive assimilation. For example, in “mink”, “n”, which is originally pronounced as /n/, will be velarized by the following “k”/k/, and therefore the word will be pronounced as /miŋk/.
2. The distinctive feature is a property which distinguishes one phoneme from another. For example, “voicing” is a distinctive feature, since it plays an important role in distinguishing obstruents in English.
3. Syllable: It refers to a unit of spoken language that is bigger than a speech sound. It consists of one or more vowel sounds alone or of a syllabic consonant alone or of either with one or more consonant sounds preceding or following.
4. Cardinal vowel: The cardinal vowels are a set vowel qualities arbitrarily defined, fixed and unchanging, intended to provide a frame of reference for the description of the actual vowels of existing languages.
5. When the vocal folds are apart, the air can pass through easily and the sound produced is said to be voiceless. For example, consonants (p, s, t) are produced this way, so they are voiceless consonants. “Voiceless” is defined in contrast with “voiced”. Consonants (b, z, d) are voiced consonants.
6. The two words which are identical in every way except for one sound segment that occurs in the same place in the string. For example, the English words bear and pear constitute a minimal pair as they differ in meaning and in their initial phonemes /b/ and /p/.
7. Coarticulation refers to the phenomenon of sounds continually show the influence of their neighbors. For example, as in lamb, when *a* is followed by *m*, the velum will begin to lower itself

during the articulation of *a* so that it is ready for the following nasal. When such simultaneous or overlapping articulations are involved, we call the process coarticulation. If the sound becomes more like the following sound, it is known as anticipatory coarticulation. If the sound displays the influence of the preceding sound, it is preservative coarticulation.

8. Broad and narrow transcription: In broad transcription, one letter symbol is used for one sound. In narrow transcription, there are diacritics added to the one letter symbols to show the finer differences between sounds.
9. When two sounds never occur in the same environment, they are in complementary distribution. For example, the aspirated English stops never occur after (s), and the unaspirated ones never occur initially. Allophones of the same phoneme are usually in complementary distribution. The allophones of /p/, for instance, are also in complementary distribution. The unaspirated($p^{=}$) occurs after /s/, while the aspirated(p^{h}) occurs in all other environments except after /s/.
10. Acoustic phonetics: It is one of the three branches of phonetics, it is the study of the physical properties of speech sounds.
11. SPEAKING is a mnemonic way of summarizing certain components of speech which make possible the description and analysis of communicative behavior: S = Situation, P = Participants, E = Ends, A = Act sequence, K = Key, I = Instrumentalities, N = Norms, and G = Genres.
12. In English, consonant clusters in onset and coda positions disallow many consonant combinations, which is explained by the work of sonority scale. The degree of sonority of different classes of sound affects their possible positions in the syllable.
13. Tone sandhi leads to a general rule that also covers epenthesis in segmental phonology: Obligatory Contour Principle (OCP), which is the opposite of assimilation and applies to many cases involving phonological change due to adjacent occurrences of identical sound segments or suprasegmentals like tone and stress patterns.

V. Short answer questions

1. /t/ appears after these sounds: /ʃ, p, k, s, tʃ/, /id/ is found after /t, d/, and /d/, and /d/ occurs after /g, l, b, v, ð, n, au, m, ŋ, ei/. The general factor to determine whether /t/, /d/, or /id/ is used is the distinctive feature of voicing. Therefore, /t/ occurs after a voiceless sound, except /t/; /d/ occurs after a voiced sound, except /d/; and /id/ occurs after either the consonant /t/ or /d/.
2. Usually, the description of the vowels needs to fulfill four basic requirements:
   (1) The height of tongue raising (high, mid, low);
   (2) The position of the highest part of the tongue (front, central, back);
   (3) The length or tenseness of the vowel (tense vs. lax or long vs. short), and
   (4) lip-rounding (rounded vs. unrounded).
3. Language is system of arbitrary vocal symbols used for human communication. Language is primarily vocal, because sound or speech is the primary medium for all human languages, developed or "new". Writing systems came much later than the spoken forms. The fact that small children learn and can only learn to speak (and listen) before they write (and read) also indicates that language is primarily vocal, rather than written. The term "human" in the definition is meant to

specify that language is human specific.

4. As the vowels can not be described in the same way as the consonants, a system of cardinal vowels has been suggested to get out of this problem. The cardinal vowels are a set of vowel qualities arbitrarily defined, fixed and unchanging, intended to provide a frame of reference for the description of the actual vowels of existing languages. The cardinal vowels are abstract concept. The cardinal vowel diagram is a set of hypothetical positions for vowels used as reference points.

   The description of English vowels needs to fulfill four basic requirements: (1) the height of tongue raising(high, middle or low); (2) the position of the highest part of the tongue (front, central , back); (3) the length or tenseness of the vowel(tense vs. lax or long vs. short); (4) lip-rounding(rounded vs. unrounded). For example,

   [i:]: high, front, tense, unrounded vowel.

   [u]: high, back, lax, rounded vowel.

5. In English, there is a rule that /p/ is unaspirated after /s/ but aspirated in other places. So /p/ in *pat*, *tap* is aspirated but unaspirated in *spat* since it is after /s/. To bring out the phonetic difference, an aspirated sound is transcribed with a raised "h" after the symbol of the sound. So a phonetic transcription for peak is [p^hi: k] and that for speak is [spi: k]. So [p, p^h] are two different phones and are variants of the phoneme /p/. Such variants of a phoneme are called allophones of the same phoneme. The allophones are said to be in complementary distribution because they never occur in the same context: [p] occurs after [s] while [p^h] occurs in other places. We can present this rule as:

   /p/ : [p] / [s]__________

   [p^h] elsewhere

   (note: __________ is the position in which /p/ appears.)

   In addition, sometimes a phoneme may also have free variants. The final consonant of *tap* may not be released by some speakers so there is no audible sound at the end of this word. Such phenomenon is called free variation.

6. When the vocal cords are spread apart, the air from the lungs passes between them unimpeded. Sounds produced in this way are described as voiceless, consonants [p, s, t] are produced in this way; but when the vocal cords are drawn together, the air from the lungs repeatedly pushes them apart as it passes through, creating a vibration effect. Sounds produced in this way are described as voiced [b, z, d] are voiced consonants.

7. A phoneme is a phonological unit; it is a unit that is of distinctive value. It is an abstract unit. It is not any particular sound, but rather it is represented or realized by a certain phone in a certain phonetic context. For example, the [p] sound in peak is called an aspirated [p], and the [p] sound in speak is an unaspirated [p]. Its distinctive features of a phoneme are capable of distinguishing meaning.

   Morpheme is the smallest unit of language in terms of the relationship between expression and content, a unit that cannot be divided into further smaller units without destroying or drastically altering the meaning, whether it is lexical or grammatical. For example, the word "tourists" contains three morphemes. There is one minimal unit of meaning, tour, another minimal unit of meaning -ist (meaning "person who does something"), and a minimal unit of grammatical function -s (indicating plural).

Therefore, phoneme is the smallest meaningful unit of sound and morpheme is the smallest meaningful unit grammar.

(此题考查音素与词素的概念。)

8. (1) The two phonetic forms are: [ni] and [li].

(2) The underlying form is [ni].

(3) [ni] → [ni] / [- vowel]

[ni] → [li] / [+ vowel, - u]

In the word sungo, the last sound [o] is vowel so -ing form of the word is sungoli. While the last sound of the word dumu is [u], which is quite an exception, the -ing form of the word is dumuni.

9. A suprasegmental feature refers to the phonemic features that occur above the level of sound segment. The major suprasegmental features in English include word stress, sentence stress, tone, and intonation. The location of stress in English distinguishes meaning.

For example, a shift of stress may change the part of speech of a word from a noun to a verb although its spelling remains unchanged. Tones are pitch variations, which are caused by the differing rates of vibration of the vocal cords. Pitch variations can distinguish meaning just like phonemes. When pitch, stress and sound length are tied to the sentence rather than the word in isolation, they are collectively known as intonation. Intonation plays an important role in the conveyance of meaning in almost every language, especially in a language like English.

10. Free variation is a linguistic term used both in phonology and sociolinguistics. In phonology, if two sounds occurring in the same environment do not contrast. For example, the substitution of one for the other does not generate a new word but merely a different pronunciation of the same word, the two sounds are said to be in "free variation".

For instance, both *either* and *direction* are pronounced differently in British English and American English without changing their meaning, which are often caused by the regional differences.

11. When pure or monophthongs are pronounced, the quality remains constant throughout the articulatioin. In contrast, those where there is an audible change of quality are called vowel glides. Vowel glides are produced by moving from one vowel position to another through intervening positions. If a single movement of the tongue is involved, the glides are called diphthongs. A double movement produces triphthongs.

12. Assimilation is a process by which one sound takes on some or all the characteristics of a neighboring sound. It is often used synonymously with coarticulation. Nasalization, dentalization and velarization are all instances of assimilation. There are two possibilities of assimilation: if a following sound is influencing a preceding sound, it is regressive assimilation; the converse process, in which a preceding sound is influencing a following sound, is known as progressive assimilation.

13. In English, consonant clusters in onset and coda positions disallow many consonant combina-

tions, which can be explained by the work of sonority scale. The degree of sonority of different classes of sound affects their possible positions in the syllable. According to the sonority scale, the most sonorous sounds are vowels, the least sonorous ones are stops, and between them are approximates, nasals and fricatives from the more sonorous to less sonorous. In * *lkaps* and * *hlpe*, it is clear that the vowels are put behind the stops which do not follow the normal sequence of the sonority scale, thus they are not acceptable in English.

14. Stress refers to the degree of force in producing a syllable. The stresses may change in different situations. First, some suffixes may change the position of the stress. For example, the stresses change in words like 'chaos, cha'otic, com'municate, communi'cation, and 'humid, hu'midity. But the suffix -ive does not make such a change, so we have com'municative, not communi'cative. Second, alternations of stress also occur between compounds and phrases as well. A 'blackboard is used in the classroom for teachers to write on whereas a black'board is any piece of board that is black in color, so different stresses can influence the meanings of the words.

Ⅵ. Essay questions

1. The Phonetic Alphabet is a system of letters and symbols that are used to represent the individual sounds of a language. English is a language that uses a phonetic alphabet system because it is a phonographic language by nature.

   There are mainly three types of language concerning its writing system: ideographic language which uses symbols (ideograms) to represent whole words or concepts (ideas), with Chinese as an example; syllabic language which word or concepts are represented by syllable, with Japanese syllabic system as an example; phonographic language which uses special alphabetic or other typographical characters to express the sounds of an actual spoken utterance in writing, with many European languages as examples. English uses alphabetic script to represent certain single type sound. For example, the sound which is written sh in English can be expressed by symbols of (ʃ) *ship*; and the sound that is written in c can be expressed by the symbol of (k) *cup*.

2. When the vocal cords are spread apart, the air from the lungs passes between them unimpeded. Sounds produced in this way are described as voiceless, consonants(p, s, t)are produced in this way; but when the vocal cords are drawn together, the air from the lungs repeatedly pushes them apart as it passes through, creating a vibration effect. Sounds produced in this way are described as voiced(b, z, d)are voiced consonants.

3. A phoneme is a minimally distinctive set of sounds in a language that can signal a difference in meaning. It is an abstract phonological unit represented or realized by a certain phone in a certain phonetic context.

   A phone is an individual phonetic unit or segment that occurs in speech. The speech sounds we hear and produce during linguistic communication are all phones. Each of the set of phones which correspond to a single phoneme of a language is called an allophone.

   Phonemes are placed between slant lines (/ /) and phones are placed between square brackets ([ ]). Allophones of the same phoneme generally occur in different contexts and never distinguish one word from another.

   For example, when we pronounce the two words *peak* and *speak*, we are aware that the sound [p] is pronounced differently, in the word *peak*, the sound [p] is pronounced with a strong puff of air stream; but the same stop sound is pronounced slightly differently in the word *speak*, the puff of air is withheld a little. The [p] sound in *peak* is called an aspirated [p^h] and the[p] sound in speak is an unaspirated[$p^=$].

There is a slight difference in the way they are pronounced, but such a difference dose not give rise to difference in meaning. So /p/is a phoneme in the English sound system, and it can be realized differently as aspirated or unaspirated in different contexts. The phoneme /p/ in English can be realized as aspirated [p^h] and unaspirated [$p^=$], which are allophones of the phoneme /p/.

4. Suprasegmental features refer to the phonological features above the sound segment level. They are the phonological properties of such units as the syllable, the word, and the sentence. The major suprasegmental features in English are syllable, stress, tone and intonation.

   The syllable refers to the phonological unit that is composed of one or more phonemes. Every syllable has a nucleus, which is usually a vowel. The nucleus may be preceded by one or more consonants called the onset and followed by one or more consonants called the coda.

   Stress refers to the degree of force used in producing a syllable. For words of more than one syllable, one is more stressed than the other. The more stressed syllable is the primary stress while the less stressed syllable is known as the secondary stress.

   Tones are pitch variations, which are caused by the differing rates of vibration of the vocal cords. Different rates of vibration produce what is known as different frequencies, and in auditory terms as different pitches. Pitch variations may be distinctive like phoneme, that is, when they may contribute to distinguish between different words.

   When pitch, stress and sound length are tied to the sentence rather than the word in isolation, they are collectively known as intonation. When we speak, we change the pitch of our voice to express ideas. The same sentence uttered with different intonation may express different attitude of the speaker. In English, there are four intonation patterns: the falling tone, the rising tone, the fall-rise tone, and the rise-fall tone.

第3章 词和形态学

3.1 复习笔记

本章要点：

1. Word Senses
   词的含义
2. Classification of Word
   词的分类
3. Word Formation
   词的形成
4. Lexical Change
   词汇的变化

常考考点：

词法的定义；屈折词与派生词；构词法(合成与派生)；词素的定义；词素变体；自由词素；黏着词素(词根，词缀和词干)；词的定义；语法词与词汇词；变词与不变词；封闭词与开放词。

本章内容索引：

Ⅰ. Word

1. Three Senses of "Word"

*2. Identification of Words

3. Classification of Words
   (1) Variable and invariable words
   (2) Lexical (content) words and grammatical (functional) words
   (3) Closed-class words and open-class words
   (4) Word class

Ⅱ. Morpheme and Morphology

1. Definition
2. Types of Morphemes
   (1) Free morpheme and bound morpheme
   (2) Root, affix and stem
   (3) Inflectional affix and derivational affix
3. Inflection and Word Formation
   (1) Inflection
   (2) Word Formation
4. Allomorph

***Ⅲ. The Counterpoints of Phonology and Morphology**

1. Sememe vs. Morpheme

2. Morpheme vs. Phoneme
3. Phonological Structure vs. Morpheme Structure
4. Morphophonology vs. Morphophonemics

Ⅳ. Lexical Change

1. Lexical Change Proper
   (1) Invention
   (2) Blending
   (3) Abbreviation (clipping)
   (4) Acronym
   (5) Back-formation
   *(6) Analogical creation
   *(7) Class shift
   *(8) Borrowing

*2. Semantic Change
   (1) Broadening
   (2) Narrowing
   (3) Meaning shift
   (4) Folk etymology

*3. Phonological Change
   (1) Loss
   (2) Addition
   (3) Metathesis
   (4) Assimilation

*** Ⅴ. Word Group and Phrase**

Ⅰ. Word Word is a unit of expression that native speakers may recognize by intuition, whether in spoken or written form.	**Ⅰ. 词** 词是语言表达单位，无论是在口语还是在书面语中，说母语的人都能够凭直觉识别这个语言单位。
1. Three Senses of "Word" (1) a physically definable unit; (2) both a general and specific term; (3) a grammatical unit.	**1. 词的三种含义** (1) 词是自然的有界限的对立单位； (2) 词既是一个普通术语又是一个专门术语； (3) 词是一个语法单位。
***2. Identification of Words**	**2. 词的识别**
(1) stability Words are the most stable of all linguistic units, in respect of their internal structure.	**(1) 稳定性** 就词的内部结构而言，词是所有语言单位中最稳定的。
(2) relative uninterruptibility The new elements should not be inserted into a word, even when there are several parts in a word.	**(2) 相对连续性** 连续性指的是一个词的几个成分之间不可介入新的成分，即使这个词由多个成分构成。

(3) a minimum free form Word is the smallest unit that can be used, by itself, as a complete utterance.	**(3) 最小的自由形式** 词是能够独立构成一个完整语句的最小单位。
3. Classification of Words 【考点：判断词的所属类型——可变 vs. 不变；语法 vs. 词汇；封闭 vs. 开放】	**3. 词的分类**
(1) Variable and invariable words Variable words have inflective endings, namely, part of the word remains constant while the other part changes regularly to fulfill different grammatical functions. Invariable words do not have inflective endings, such as *since*, *when*, *hello*.	**(1) 可变词和不变词** 可变词有形态变化，即词的一部分保持不变，另一部分有规则地变化以实现不同的语法功能。不变词没有形态变化。
(2) Lexical (content) words and Grammatical (functional) words ① Words that are mainly used to refer to substance, action and quality are lexical words, such as nouns, verbs, adjectives and adverbs. ② Words that are used for constructing groups, phrase, clause, clause complex, or even text are grammatical words, such as conjunctions, prepositions, articles, and pronouns.	**(2) 词汇词和语法词** 具有词汇意义(指代物质、动作和性质)的词称为词汇词，例如名词、动词、形容词和副词。 表达语法意义的词是语法词，例如连词、介词和代词。
(3) Closed-class words and open-class words Closed-class words refer to those whose membership is fixed or limited, such as pronouns, prepositions, conjunctions, articles, and others. It is hard for one to add or deduce a new member. Open-class words are those whose membership is in principle infinite or unlimited and can be added with the development of society, such as nouns, verbs, adjectives and many adverbs.	**(3) 封闭类词和开放类词** 封闭类词的成员数目固定，数量有限。像代词、介词、连词和冠词都属于封闭类词，一般不能轻易增加或衍生新的成员。 相比之下，开放类词的成员数目基本上是无限的，其数目会随着社会发展不断地、经常地增加。名词、动词、形容词和副词属于开放类词。
(4) Word class A more practical method of word class is to analyze their grammatical properties or group them into class based on their formal similarities. At first, word class was based on classical Latin and Greek analyses, but there are only two classes, which are similar to subject and predicate. Later, nine word classes were categorized, including noun, pronoun, adjective, verb, adverb, preposition, conjunction, interjection and article. Today, a few more word classes have been introduced into grammar. They are particles, auxiliaries, determiners.	**(4) 词类** 关于词汇分类的一种更为实际的方法就是根据他们的形式的相似之处分析词汇分类的语法属性或分组成类。词类划分最初见于拉丁语和希腊语的语法分析，但只有两类，类似今天的主语和谓语。之后，词汇被分成九种词类：他们是名词、代名词、形容词、动词、副词，介词，连词、感叹词和冠词。今天，几种词类被引入了语法。他们是小品词，辅助词，限定词。

Ⅱ. Morpheme and Morphology	**Ⅱ. 语素和形态学**
1. Definition Morpheme is the smallest unit of language, a unit that cannot be divided into further smaller units without destroying or drastically altering the meaning, whether it is lexical or grammatical. Morphology studies the internal structure of words, and the rules by which words are formed, including inflection and word formation.	**1. 定义** 语素是最小的语言单位，不能再进一步分成更小的单位而不破坏或彻底改变词汇意义或语法意义。 形态学研究词的内部结构以及词的构造规则，包括屈折变化和词的形成两个领域。
2. Types of Morphemes 【考点：判断语素所属类型—自由 vs. 黏着；词根 vs. 词缀 vs. 词干】	**2. 语素的类型**
(1) Free morpheme and bound morpheme ① Free morphemes are those which may occur alone or constitute words by themselves. All mono-morphemic words are free morphemes and poly-morphemic words, which consist wholly of free morphemes, are compounds. ② Bound morphemes cannot occur alone. They must appear with at least another morpheme.	**(1) 自由语素和黏着语素** ① 自由语素指能够单独出现或独立成词的语素。所有的单语素词都是自由语素，由自由语素构成的多语素词为复合词。 ② 黏着语素指不能单独出现，必须跟至少一个其他语素共同出现的语素。
(2) Root, affix and stem ① **Root** is the base form of a word that cannot be further analyzed without destroying its meaning. All words contain a root morpheme. It can either be a free morpheme or a bound morpheme. ② **Affix** is a collective term for the type of morpheme which can be used only when added to another morpheme (the root or stem), so affix is naturally bound. There are four main subtypes of affixes: prefix, suffix, infix and circumfix. ③ **Stem** is any morpheme or combination of morphemes to which an inflectional affix can be added. It can be equivalent to a root, or a root and a derivational affix. 【考点：词根与词干的区别】	**(2) 词根，词缀和词干** ① 词根是构成词的基础成分，不能再做进一步分析而不破坏其意义。每个词都包括一个词根语素，它可以是自由语素或黏着语素。 ②词缀是那些只能附着于另一个语素（词根或词干）上的一类语素的总称。词缀都是黏着语素，可分为前缀、后缀、中缀和环缀四种。 ③ 词干指能加屈折词缀的语素（组合），它相当于词根或词根加派生词缀。
(3) Inflectional affix and derivational affix Inflectional affixes do not change the word class of the word but only add grammatical function to the stem. Derivational affixes often change the lexical meaning and the word class. In English, inflectional affixes are mostly suffixes, but derivational affixes can be prefixes or suffixes. 【考点：屈折词缀与派生词缀的区别】	**(3) 屈折词缀与派生词缀** 屈折词缀不改变原词的词类，只在词干后面添加一个微小或微妙的语法意义。 派生词缀常常改变词汇的意义和词类。英语中屈折词缀多为后缀，但派生词组还可以是前缀或后缀。

3. Inflection and Word Formation (1) **Inflection** is the manifestation of grammatical relationships by adding inflectional affixes, such as number, person, finiteness, aspect and case, which do not change the grammatical class of the stems to which they are attached. (2) **Word Formation**: It refers to the process of word variation signaling lexical relationships. It can be further divided into compositional type (compound) and derivational type(derivation). ① **Compound**: It refers to those words which have more than one lexical morpheme, or the way to join two separate words to produce a single form. There are several different ways of classification of compounds. ⅰ. Compounds can be divided into noun compounds, verb compounds, adjective compounds and preposition compounds. ⅱ. Compounds can be further divided into the endocentric and the exocentric compound. Endocentric compound refers to a compound which has a center or a head word. Exocentric compound is one which has no center or a head word. ▼ⅲ. Besides, in terms of the relationship between the subcomponents of a compound, it can be divided into attributive compounds which is made of two lexemes with one modifying the other; coordinative compounds in which the two sub-components are equal without one modifying the other; and subordinative compounds with one of the sub-components being understood to be the argument of the other. Among these three kinds of compound, the first two are also called root compounds and the last synthetic compounds. ② **Derivation**: It refers to the process to add an affix to an already existing form to create a word, which includes prefixation, suffixation, and even both. Derivations, in contrast to inflections, can make the word class of the original word either changed or unchanged.	**3. 屈折变化与词的形成** (1) **屈折变化**是通过附加屈折词缀表现语法关系，如数、人称、有定性、体和格，不改变所附加词干的语法类别。 (2) **词的形成**指词形变化的过程，这些词形变化是标志词项之间关系的。词的形成可以进一步分为复合类(复合词)和派生类(派生词)两种。 ① **复合词**指那些由一个以上的词汇语素构成的词，或者由两个独立的词连接起来的构成新的形式。复合词有多种分类方式。 ⅰ. 复合词可以分为名词复合词、动词复合词、形容词复合词和介词复合词。 ⅱ. 复合词可以进一步分为向心复合词和离心复合词。 向心复合词指具有一个意义上的中心词的复合词。 离心复合词指没有一个意义上的中心词的复合词。 ⅲ. 根据组成复合词的子部分之间的关系，复合词还可以被分为修饰复合词，并列复合词和从属复合词。修饰复合词的特点是其中一个子部分修饰另一子部分；并列复合词的特点是两个子部分呈并列关系，这两种复合词又叫做根复合词。而从属复合词又叫做综合复合词，因为其中的一个子部分被视为另一个子部分的论元。 ② **派生法**指通过在词干上加上词缀而得到一个新词的方法，主要包括前缀化、后缀化或者两者同时发生。 派生和屈折变化相反，派生可改变原始词的词类，也可以不改变原始词的词类。

▼ Categorisation in derivation:

Derivational processes which involve the change of the base lexeme are called categorisation. In such a process, the attached affix with grammatical information is called a categoriser, which has no meaning and its only function is to change the category of the base lexeme. Among this process, the grammatical information is called categorical feature.

4. Allomorph

Those morphs which represent the same morpheme are called the allomorphs of the same morpheme. For instance, the noun plural morpheme {plural} in English has [-s], [-z], [-iz], [-ai], [-n], [-i], [Ø] and other morphs, such morphs are termed as the allomorphs of the morpheme {plural}.

Some morphemes have a single form in all contexts, some others may have considerable variations; some morphemic shapes represent different morphemes and thus have different meanings, for instance, the morphemic shapes {-s} can express plurality in *desks*, person/ finiteness in *speaks* and case in *girl's*.

* Ⅲ. The Counterpoints of Phonology and Morphology

1. Sememe vs. Morpheme

Sememe is the smallest component of meaning. For example, the morpheme *-s* has only one sememe: plurality, meaning more than one. Morpheme is the smallest meaningful unit of language, a unit which cannot be divided without destroying or drastically altering the meaning, whether it is lexical or grammatical.

As for the relationship between sememe and morpheme, there are five occasions.

(1) One morpheme vs. one sememe, such as the morpheme less has just one sememe WITHOUT.

(2) One morpheme vs. more than one sememe, such as *-a* has three sememes.

(3) One sememe vs. more than one morpheme. For example, there are other morphemes besides *a-* that also indicate the sememe of no or non.

(4) Morphemes that have no specific sememe, such as en-, that have no specific sememe, but may help change grammatical and semantic categories.

派生过程中的范畴化：

派生过程涉及原本词素的范畴变化，因此该过程也叫做范畴化过程(与认知语言学中的范畴化不同)。在这一范畴化的过程中，被添加的带有语法信息的词缀叫做分类标志，分类标志本身没有意义，其唯一功能就是改变原本词素的范畴。其中，语法信息叫做分类特征。

4. 语素变体

那些代表同一语素的不同形素叫做该语素的语素变体。例如，英语名词复数语素{plural}有[-s]，[-z]，[-iz]，[-ai]，[-n]，[-i:]，[Ø]等不同的形素，它们叫做复数语素{plural}的语素变体。

有些语素在任何语境中都只有一个形式，还有的有多个变化形式；有些语素形式能表示不同意义的语素，“s”可以表示复数、人称/有定性，也可以表示格。

Ⅲ. 音系学和形态学的对立

1. 义素与语素

义素是意义的最小单位，例如语素{-s}仅含有一个义素(复数)，意思是多于一个。语素是语言的最小意义单位，不能再进一步分成更小的单位而不被破坏或彻底改变词汇意义或语法意义。

语素和义素的关系有五种情况。

(1)一个语素对应一个义素，例如-less 只有一个意义即没有。

(2)一个语素对应多个义素，例如-a 有三种含义。

(3)一个义素对应多个语素，例如除了 a-还有其他的语素能表达否定含义。

(4)语素没有具体对应的义素，例如 en-没有具体的义素，但是能改变语法和语义范畴。

(5) Function changes in both sememe and morpheme without morpheme change. For example, when run is in run a company, it is a verb, but when run in a short run, it is a noun.

(5)语素没变，语素和义素的功能都变。例如 run 能作名词也能作动词用。

2. Morpheme vs. Phoneme

Morpheme is the smallest meaningful unit of language. It is the smallest unit in grammar. Phoneme is the smallest unit of sound. A single phoneme may represent a morpheme, but they are not identical, e. g. , the phoneme /z/ represents the plural morpheme in "caps" but nothing in "praise".

2. 语素与音位

语素是最小的语义单位，它是语法中的最小单位。音位是语音中的最小单位，单个音位可以代表一个语素，但它们不是同一的。例如音位 /z/ 在"cups"代表了复数的语素，但是在"raise"却与语素无关。

3. Morpheme Structure vs. Phonological Structure

Morphemes may be represented by phonological structures, which are monophonemic, monosyllabic or polysyllabic.

3. 语素结构与音系结构

语素可以通过音系结构呈现。语素可以是单音位的，也可以是单音节的或多音节的。

4. Morphophonology vs. Morphophonemics

Morphophonology or morphophonemics is a branch of linguistics referring to the analysis and classification of the phonological factors that affect the appearance of morphemes, and the grammatical factors that affect the appearance of phonemes. It studies the interrelationship between phonology and morphology.

4. 形态音系学或形态音位学

形态音系学又叫形态音位学，研究音位学和形态学的关系，对影响语素形式的音位要素或影响音位形式的语法要素进行分析和分类。它主要研究音系学与形态学之间的内部关系。

Ⅳ. Lexical Change

Apart from compound and derivation, lexical change includes invention, blending, abbreviation, acronym, backformation, analogical creation and borrowing.

Ⅳ. 词汇变化

词汇的变化除了复合词和派生词之外，还有新创词语、混成法、缩写法、缩略语、逆构词法、类推构法以及借词。

1. Lexical Change Proper

【考点：名词解释 & 指出一词的词汇变化方式】

(1) **Invention (coinage)**: It is also called coinage, which refers to the new lexical items which come directly from the consumer items, their producers or their brand names, such as Coke, nylon and others to cope with the invention of new entities.

(2) **Blending**: A process in which two words are blended by joining together the initial part of the first word and the final part of the second word, or by joining the initial parts of the two words, such as *alcopop* (*alcohol* + *pop*), *faction* (*fact* + *fiction*), *flare* (*flame* + *glare*), etc.

1. 特有词汇变化

(1) **新创词**又称造词，指直接用某一种商品的生产商或者商标的名字作为该类产品名称的造词方法，例如 Coke, nylon 等，它们都已成为了代表新事物的新创词语。

(2) **混成法**是指一个词由两个单词混合而成，一般把第一个单词的开头部分和第二个单词的最后部分连接起来，或者是把两个单词的开头部分连接起来。例如 *alcopop* (*alcohol* + *pop*), *faction* (*fact* + *fiction*), *flare* (*flame* + *glare*), 等。

(3) **Abbreviation(clipping)**: The way of shortening a longer word into a shorter form, e. g. *photograph-photo*, *gasoline-gas*, etc.

(4) **Acronyms** are words formed by combining the first letters of the words of a phrase or the name of an organization, which are pronounced as a separate word, such as *LASER*, *IELTS*.

【考点：指出 Acronym 与 Initialism 的区别】

(5) **Back-formation** refers to a word formed by subtraction of a real or supposed affix from an already existing longer word, e. g. *television-televise*.

*(6) **Analogical creation**: The principle of analogical creation can account for the co-existence of two forms, regular and irregular, in the combination of some English verbs.

*(7) **Class shift**: By shifting word class one can change the menning of a word from a concrete entity or notion to a process or attribution. This process of word formation is also known as ZERO – DERIVATION, or CONVERSION.

*(8) **Borrowing**: It is also called loan, which means the words have been borrowed from the other languages. There are several types of processes with regard to borrowing.

① **Loanwords**: It is a process in which both form and meaning are borrowed with only a slight change, in some cases, to the phonological system of the new language that they enter.

② **Loanblend**: It is a process in which part of the form is native and the rest has been borrowed, but the meaning is fully borrowed.

③ **Loanshift**: It is a process in which the meaning is borrowed, but the form is native.

④ **Loan translation**: It is a special type of borrowing, in which each morpheme or word is translated in the equivalent morpheme or word in another language.

【考点：区分四种借词方式并举例】

***2. Semantic Change**

【考点：简答—指出语义变化的主要方式并举例说明】

(1) **Broadening**: It is a process to extend or elevate the meaning from its originally specific sense to a relatively general one.

(3) **缩写法**(截断法)，是指把一个较长的词汇通过截断而得到的较短的词的构词方法。例如 *photograph-photo*，*gasoline-gas* 等。

(4) **缩略语**是由一个词组或者组织机构的首字母组成的，作为一个独立的单词来发音，例如 *LASER*，*IELTS*。

(5) **逆构词法**是把一个语言中已经存在的较长单词删去想象中的词缀，由此造出一个较短的单词，例如 *television-televise*。

(6) **类推构词**：某些英语动词同时具有规则的和不规则的两种变化形式，这可以用这类构词的原则来解释。

(7) **词类转换**：通过改变词的词类从而改变词的意义，词的意义从一个具体的实体或概念变成一个过程或一种属性。这种形成词的方法叫零派生或转换。

(8) **借词法**是指从其他语言中借来的词放在自己语言中使用。借词法有以下几种类型：

① **借词**：借词是指形式和意义都是借用的，有时为了适应新语言的音位系统，可以有些细小的改变。

② **混合借词**：混合借词是指借词的一部分来自本国语，另一部来自外来语，但是意义全都是借过来的。

③ **转移借词**：转移借词的意义是借用的，但是形式是来自本国语。

④ **翻译借词**：翻译借词是一种特殊的借用，每个语素或单词都是从另一种语言中的语素或对单词对等地翻译过来的。

2. 语义变化

(1) **词义扩大**：词义扩大是指把意义从原来具体的意思扩充到相对概括的意思。

(2) **Narrowing**: It is contrary to broadening; the original meaning of a word can be narrowed or restricted to a specific sense.

(3) **Meaning shift**: The change of meaning has nothing to do with generalization or restriction, what makes the meaning of a word different is its departure from its original domain as a result of its metaphorical usage.

(4) **Folk etymology**: It refers to the change of the form of a word or phrase, resulting from an incorrect popular notion of the origin or meaning of the term, or from the influence of more familiar terms mistakenly taken to be analogous.

(2) **词义缩小**：词义缩小是指与词义扩大相反的一个过程，原来的词义缩小或被限制到某个明确的意义上。

(3) **词义转移**：词义转移跟概括和限制没有关系，导致词义变化的原因是它在隐喻手法中离开了原来的语义领域。

(4) **俗词源**：俗词源是指由于对词源错误而又普遍的解释或对词义的错误理解，或者由于受到更熟悉的词汇的影响而进行了错误的类推，导致词或短语的形式有了新的意义。

* 3. Phonological Change

Phonological change refers to the change in sound leading to changes in form. It is related to language variations in the phonological system of language.

The factors contribute to the formation of new pronunciation:

(1) **Loss**: The loss of sound can refer to the disappearance of the very sound as a phoneme in the phonological system. It may also occur in utterances at the expense of some unstressed vowels.

(2) **Addition**: It refers to the addition of some sounds to the original sound sequence.

(3) **Metathesis**: It is a process involving an alternation in the sequence of sounds.

(4) **Assimilation**: It refers to the change of a sound by the influence of an adjacent sound, which is more specifically called "contact" or "contiguous" assimilation.

3. 音位变化

音位变化是指因为语音上的改变而导致的形式变化。音位变化跟语言学音位系统的各种变化有关。

导致新发音产生的因素：

(1) **脱落**：语音脱落是指音位系统中作为音位的某个语音的消失。语音脱落也可以在语句中发生，往往是某些非重读元音发生脱落。

(2) **添加**：添加是指把某些语音添加到语音原有的链条上。

(3) **换位**：换位是指语流中一种可供选择的方法。

(4) **同化**：同化是指由于邻近语音的影响而产生的语音变化，更明确的叫法是“接触”同化或“邻近”同化。

* V. Word Group and Phrase

Word Group is a group of words; it is an expansion of a word. Phrase is a contraction of a clause.

1. Nominal Group

In a typical nominal group, there are head, premodifier, postmodifier.

2. Other Groups

①Verbal group

②Adverbial group

V. 词组和短语

词组是一组词，它是一个词的扩展。短语是一个从句的缩写式。

1. 名词性词组

在一个典型的名词性词组中，有中心词，前修饰词和后修饰词。

2. 其他词组

①动词词组

②副词词组

③Conjunction group ④Preposition group **3. Prepositional Phrase** Any expression with a preposition followed with an item is a prepositional phrase.	③连词词组 ④介词词组 **3. 介词短语** 任何以介词跟随的表达式是介词短语。

3.2 考研真题与典型题详解

Ⅰ. Fill in the blanks.

1. As the lexical words carry the main content of a language while the grammatical ones serve to link its different parts together, the lexical words are also known as content words and grammatical ones ________. (中山大学 2008 研)
2. In traditional grammar, ________ is the only word class which can function as a substitute for another item. (中山大学 2006 研)
3. In terms of the meaning expressed by words, they can be classified into ________ words and ________ words. (南开大学 2007 研)
4. The ________ is the minimal distinctive unit in grammar, a unit which cannot be divided without destroying or drastically altering the meaning, whether lexical or grammatical. (北二外 2008 研)
5. There are two fields of morphology: the study of ________ and the study of ________. (人大 2006 研)
6. A ________ morpheme is one that cannot constitute a word by itself. (北二外 2003 研)
7. ________ is a branch of linguistics that studies the interrelationship between phonology and morphology. (南开大学 2007 研)
8. ________ is a relatively complex form of compounding in which a new word is formed by joining the initial part of one word and the final part of another word. For example, the English word smog is made from ________ and ________. (人大 2006 研)
9. Back-formation refers to an abnormal type of word-formation where a shorter word is derived by deleting an ________ affix from a longer form already in the language. (中山大学 2006 研)
10. ________ is a unit of expression that has universal intuitive recognition by native speakers, whether it is expressed in spoken or written form. It is the minimum free form. (中山大学 2005 研)
11. Affix is the collective term for the type of formative that can be used only when added to another morpheme. Affixes are limited in number in a language, and are generally classified into three subtypes, namely, prefix, suffix, and ________. (北京邮电大学 2010 研)
12. Words can be classified into variable words and invariable words. As for variable words, they may have ________ changes. That is, the same word my have different grammatical forms but part of the word remains relatively constant. (中山大学 2011 研)
13. Bound morphemes are classified into two types: ________ and ________ root.
14. A word formed by derivation is called a ________, and a word formed by compounding is

called a ＿＿＿＿＿.

15. Derivational processes which involve the change of the category of the base lexeme are also called ＿＿＿＿＿. In such a process, the attached affix is called a categoriser, which carries an important piece of grammatical information, the categorial feature.

16. ＿＿＿＿＿ is a type of function words which are used to connect words, phrases or clauses.

Ⅱ. Multiple Choice

1. Words like pronouns, prepositions, conjunctions, articles are ＿＿＿＿＿ items.（北二外 2003 研）

   A. open-class　　B. closed-class

   C. neither open-class nor closed-class

2. Nouns, verbs and adjectives can be classified as ＿＿＿＿＿.（西安交大 2008 研）

   A. lexical words　　B. grammatical words

   C. function words　　D. form words

3. Bound morphemes do not include ＿＿＿＿＿.（西安交大 2008 研）

   A. roots　　B. prefixes　　C. suffixes　　D. words

4. ＿＿＿＿＿ other than compounds may be divided into roots and affixes.（大连外国语学院 2008 研）

   A. Polymorphemic words　　B. Bound morphemes

   C. Free morphemes

5. ＿＿＿＿＿ refers to the way in which a particular verb changes for tense, person, or number.（西安外国语学院 2006 研）

   A. Affixation　　B. Inflection

   C. Derivation　　D. Conjugation

6. Which two terms can best describe the following pairs of words: table—tables, day + break—daybreak.（大连外国语学院 2008 研）

   A. inflection and compound　　B. compound and derivation

   C. inflection and derivation

7. Compound words consist of ＿＿＿＿＿ morphemes.（北二外 2003 研）

   A. bound　　B. free

   C. both bound and free

8. Which of the following words is formed by the process of blending?（对外经贸 2006 研）

   A. WTO　　B. Motel　　C. Bookshelf　　D. red-faced

9. Which of the following words are formed by blending?（对外经贸 2005 研）

   A. girlfriend　　B. television　　C. smog　　D. bunch

10. The word UN is formed in the way of ＿＿＿＿＿.（西安交大 2008 研）

    A. acronymy　　B. clipping

    C. initialism　　D. blending

11. Which of the following is NOT a process of the lexical change?（大连外国语学院 2008 研）

    A. INVENTION.　　B. ACRONYM.

    C. LEXICON.

12. Language has been changing, but such changes are not so obvious at all linguistic aspects except that of __________. （西安外国语学院 2006 研）

A. phonology　　B. lexicon　　C. syntax　　D. semantics

13. "Wife", which used to refer to any woman, stands for "a married woman" in modern English. This phenomenon is known as __________. （西安交大 2008 研）

A. semantic shift　　B. semantic broadening

C. semantic elevation　　D. semantic narrowing

14. It is true that words may shift in meaning, i. e. semantic.change. The semantic change of the word tail belongs to __________.

A. narrowing of meaning　　B. meaning shift

C. loss of meaning　　D. widening of meaning

15. A prefix is an affix which appears __________.

A. after the stem　　B. before the stem

C. in the middle of the stem　　D. below the stem

Ⅲ. True or False

1. Some linguists maintain that a word group is an extension of word of a particular class. （清华 2001 研）
2. Words are the most stable of all linguistic units in respect of their internal structure. （大连外国语学院 2008 研）
3. Nouns, verbs, adjectives and many adverbs are content words. （北二外 2008 研）
4. Pronouns, prepositions, conjunctions and articles are all open class items. （清华 2001 研）
5. The words "loose" and "books" have a common phoneme and a common morpheme as well. （北二外 2007 研）
6. Free morpheme may constitute words by themselves. （大连外国语学院 2008 研）
7. Root also falls into two categories: free and bound. （北二外 2006 研）
8. A stem is the base form of a word which cannot be further analyzed without total loss of identity. （对外经贸 2006 研）
9. The words "water" and "teacher" have a common phoneme and a common morpheme as well. （北二外 2006 研）
10. The words "boys" and "raise" have a common phoneme and a common morpheme as well. （北二外 2008 研）
11. Analogic change refers to the reduction of the number of exceptional or irregular morphemes. （对外经贸 2005 研）
12. The smallest meaningful unit of language is allomorph.
13. Affixes are generally classified into three subtypes, namely, prefix, suffix and infix, depending on their position around the root or stem of a word.
14. A preposition is often used to express the relationship between an object or an event and a location, although sometimes the relationship denoted by a preposition c is very abstract.

Ⅳ. Explain the following terms.

1. Open-class words （浙江大学 2007 研）

2. Lexical word（武汉大学 2005 研）
3. Morpheme（武汉大学 2008 研）
4. Stem（四川大学 2007 研）
5. inflectional morpheme（南开大学 2004 研）
6. Free morphemes（西安交大 2008 研）
7. Bound morpheme（上海交大 2007 研）
8. Inflection（四川大学 2007 研）
9. Compound（四川大学 2007 研）
10. Allomorph（四川大学 2006 研）
11. Back-formation（四川大学 2008 研；北外 2010 研；中国海洋大学 2021 研）
12. Prefix（北外 2010 研）
13. cognate(南开大学 2011 研)
14. Categorisation
15. Circumfix

Ⅴ. Short answer questions

1. What is the distinction between inflectional affixes and derivational affixes?（四川大学 2007 研）
2. What does the concept morphophoneme mean? What is the relationship between phoneme and morphophoneme?（南开大学 2004 研）
3. What are phonologically conditioned and morphologically conditioned form of morphemes?（武汉大学 2005 研）
4. How are affixes classified?（四川大学 2008 研）
5. A number interesting word-formation processes can be discerned in the following examples. Can you identify what is going on in these?
   (a) The deceased's cremains were scattered over the hill.
   (b) He's always taking pills, either uppers or downers. （上海交通大学 2007 研）
6. How to distinguish root and stem?
7. Illustrate the relationship between morpheme and allomorph by examples.
8. What are closed-class words and open-class words?
9. What are compounds? And how can they be divided according to different standards?

Ⅵ. Essay questions

1. Illustrate lexical change proper with the latest examples in English, covering at least four aspects.（大连外国语学院 2008 研）
2. Semantic change plays a very important role in widening the vocabulary of a language. （中山大学 2008 研）
3. Illustrate the ways of lexical change. （武汉大学 2005 研）
4. What are the major types of semantic Changes?（人大 2006 研）

参考答案及解析

Ⅰ. Fill in the blanks.

1. function words

（词可分为词汇词和语法词。具有词汇意义的词称为词汇词，例如名词、动词、形容词和副词。表达语法意义的词是语法词，例如连词、介词和代词。）

2. pronoun

（在传统语法中，代词是唯一一种可用来代替其他语言项目的词性。）

3. lexical，grammatical

（从词所表达的意义划分，词可分为词汇词和语法词。）

4. morpheme

（语素是最小的语义单位，是语法中的最小单位。它不能被分割成更小的单位而不改变它的意义。）

5. inflection 或 inflectional morphology；word-formation 或 derivational morphology

（在形态学中，有两大主要研究方面，一是词的屈折变化，一是词的派生。）

6. bound

（黏着语素指不能单独出现，必须跟至少一个其他语素共同出现的语素。）

7. Morphophonology

（形态音系学是语言学的一个分支，主要研究形态学与音系学的关系。）

8. Blending；smoke；fog

（混成法是指一个词由两个单词混合而成，一般把第一个单词的开头部分和第二个单词的最后部分连接起来，或者是把两个单词的开头部分连接起来。）

9. imagined

（逆构词法是一种不规则的构词类型，即把一个语言中已经存在的较长单词删去想象中的词缀，由此造出一个较短的单词。）

10. Word

（词是个语言表达单位，无论是在口语还是在书面语中，说母语的人都能够凭直觉识别这个语言单位。它是最小的自由形式词，是能够独立构成一个完整语句的最小单位。）

11. infix

（词缀是那些只能附着于另一个语素（词根或词干）上的一类语素的总称。词缀都是黏着语素，可分为前缀、中缀和后缀三种。）

12. inflective

（可变词有屈折变化。）

13. affix；bound

（黏着语素指不能单独出现，必须跟至少一个其他语素共同出现的语素。词缀和黏着词根都是黏着语素。）

14. derivative；compound

（词汇的变化方式主要有复合和派生两种。派生而成的词叫派生词，复合而成的词叫合成词。）

15. categorisation

（派生过程涉及原本词素的范畴变化，因此该过程也叫做范畴化过程。在这一范畴化的过程中，被添加的带有语法信息的词缀叫做分类标志，其所代表的语法信息叫做分类特征。需要注意的是分类标志本身没有意义，其唯一功能就是改变原本词素的范畴。）

16. Conjunction

（连词是功能词的一种，主要用于连接词，词组和从句。）

Ⅱ. Multiple Choice

1. B （封闭类词的成员数目固定，数量有限，像代词、介词、连词和冠词都属于封闭类词。）
2. A （具有词汇意义(指代物质，动作和性质)的词称为词汇词，例如名词，动词，形容词和副词。）
3. D （黏着语素指不能单独出现，必须跟至少一个其他语素共同出现的语素。词根，词缀都可能是黏着词素。）
4. A （多语素词可被分为词根和词缀，而合成词是不可以被这样分的。）
5. B （屈折变化是通过附加屈折词缀表现语法关系，如数、人称、有定性、体和格。它并不改变所附加词干的语法类别。）
6. A （屈折变化是通过附加屈折词缀表现语法关系，如 tables。合成词是由词根语素按一定的规则组合起来构成的，如 daybreak。）
7. B （合成词是由自由词素组合而成的。）
8. B （混成法是指一个词由两个单词混合而成，一般把第一个单词的开头部分和第二个单词的最后部分连接起来，或者是把两个单词的开头部分连接起来。Motel 是由 motor 与 hotel 二词的缩合。）
9. C （smog 是由 smoke 和 fog 二词缩合而成的。）
10. C （acronymy 和 initialism 均是由几个词的首字母组成，区别是 acronymy 可以连起来读成一个词，如 NATO，NASA，AIDS 等；而 initialism 是一个字母一个字母分别读出来，如：the FBI，the US，the BBC。本题答案应为 C。）
11. C （词的变化方式很多，新创词和缩略语都属于其中，而选项 C 不属于。）
12. B （语言总在不断的变化，其在词汇方面的发展和变化尤为明显。）
13. D （词义缩小是指原来的词义缩小或被限制到某个明确的意义上。）
14. D （“tail”它曾经表示马的尾巴，现在可表示任何动物的尾巴，属于词义的扩大。）
15. B （词缀根据它们与词干的位置可分为前缀、中缀和后缀三种。前缀指出现在词干前面的词缀。）

Ⅲ. True or False

1. T （词组是指一组具有一定词性的词的组合扩展，且此过程并不改变词原来的词性。）
2. T （就词的内部结构而言，词是所有语言单位中最稳定的。）
3. T （具有词汇意义(指代物质、动作和性质)的词称为词汇词，例如名词、动词、形容词和副词。）
4. F （封闭类词的成员数目固定，数量有限。像代词、介词、连词和冠词都属于封闭类词。）
5. F （这两个词中的/z/和/s/是同一个音位[z]的不同变体，所以有共同的音位，但 loose 中的语素是 se，books 中的语素是 s。）
6. T （自由语素指是能够单独出现或独立成词的语素。）
7. T （词根是构成词的基础成分，它可以是自由语素或黏着语素。）
8. T （词根是词的基本形式，不能再做进一步的分析而完全不损失同一性。）
9. F （有共同的音位，但语素不同，前者是 ter，后者是 er。）

10. F （有共同的音位，但音位/z/在前者中表示复数，而在后者中没有任何意义。）
11. T （依据类推构词的原理，人们往往更容易记住规则的变化形式，所以那些比较例外的不规则的形式就会被人遗忘。）
12. F （语言最小的有意义的单位是语素不是语素变体。）
13. T （词缀是那些只能附着于另一个语素（词根或词干）上的一类语素的总称。词缀都是黏着语素，一般分为前缀、中缀和后缀三种。）
14. T （介词是功能词的一种，通常用于表示宾语或事件与地点时间等之间的关系，但有时这种关系是抽象的。）

Ⅳ. Explain the following terms.

1. Open-class words refer to words whose membership is in principle infinite or unlimited and with the emergence of new ideas, inventions, and so on; new expressions are continually and constantly being added to the lexicon. For example, nouns, verbs, and adjectives all belong to this class.
2. Lexical word. lexical words are also called content words, referring to those which have lexical meanings, that is, those which refer to substance, action and quality, such as nouns, verbs, adjectives, and adverbs.
3. Morpheme is the smallest unit of language in terms of relationship between expression and content, a unit that cannot be divided into further smaller units without destroying or drastically altering the meaning, whether it is lexical or grammatical. For example, in *boys*, there are two morphemes: "boy" and "-s"; in *international*, there are three morphemes: "inter-" "nation" and "-al".
4. A stem is a morpheme or combination of morphemes to which an inflectional affix can be added. For example, "friend-" in *friends*, and "friendship-" in *friendships* are both stems. The former shows that a stem can be equivalent to a root, whereas the latter shows that a stem may contain a root and a derivational affix.
5. Inflectional morpheme: It is also called inflectional affixes, which attaches to the end of words. Inflectional affixes only add a minute or delicate grammatical meaning to the stem. The plural suffix is a typical example of this kind.
6. Free morpheme is an element of meaning which takes the form of an independent word. They may occur alone, that is, they may make up words by themselves. For example, "dog", "nation" and "close" are free morphemes. And such words are called mono-morphemic words. Thus all mono-morphemic words are free morphemes.
7. Bound morphemes refer to those morphemes that can not occur alone and must appear with at least another morpheme. For example, in the word "careless", "-less" is a bound morpheme since it could not occur by itself as a word.
8. Inflection is the manifestation of grammatical relationship through the addition of inflectional affixes, such as number, person, finiteness, aspect and case, which do not change the grammatical class of the stems to which they are attached. For example, the past form of the verb *work* is realized by the addition of the inflectional suffix: "-ed"; the plural form of the noun *child* is realized by the inflectional suffix: "-ren".

9. Compound refers to those words that consist of more than one lexical morpheme, or the way to join two separate words to produce a single form, such as the compound words "blackboard" and "well-known".

10. A morpheme may take various shapes or forms, and an allomorph is any of the variant forms of a morpheme as conditioned by position or adjoining sounds. For instance, the morpheme of plurality {-s} has a number of allomorphs in different sound context, as in "cats" /s/, in "bags" /z/, in "matches" /iz/.

11. Back formation refers to an abnormal type of word formation where a shorter word is derived by deleting an imagined affix from a longer form already in the language. For example, the word "television" appeared before "televise", and so does "editor" to "edit".

12. In linguistics, a prefix is a type of affix that precedes the morphemes to which it can attach. Prefixes are bound morphemes (they cannot occur as independent words). While most languages employ both prefixes and suffixes, prefixes are less common. Some languages employ mostly suffixes and almost no prefixes at all. The use of prefixes has been found to correlate statistically with other linguistic features, such as a verb-object word order and the use of prepositions.

13. Cognate: cognates are words that have a common etymological origin. For example, length, height, width, breadth and depth, are cognates of the cover terms.

14. Derivational processes which involve the change of the category of the base lexeme are also called categorisation. In such a process, the attached affix is called a categoriser, which carries an important piece of grammatical information, the categorial feature. It should be noted that many categorisers are semantically vacuous, the only function of which is to change the category of the base lexeme.

15. Circumfix is one type of the affixes, which exhibits the properties of both prefixes and suffixes. A circumfix is like an exponent of a prefix and a suffix simultaneously. For example, in Dutch, the past participle of *fiets* (to cycle) is *ge-fiets-t*, which shows that the affix to express the grammatical information of past participle consists two parts, one before the root verb and the other following it.

V. Short answer questions

1. The distinction between inflectional morphemes and derivational morphemes could be illustrated in the following four aspects.

   Inflectional affixes very often only add a minute or delicate grammatical meaning to the stem, for instance, those inflectional affixes in words such as *toys*, *walks*, *John's*, etc. Therefore, they serve to produce different forms of a single word. In contrast, derivational affixes often change the lexical meaning, e. g. *cite*, *citation*; *generate*, *generation*.

   Inflectional affixes do not change the word class of the word they attach to, such as *flower*, *flowers*; whereas derivational affixes might or might not, such as the relation between small and *smallness* for the former, and that between *brother* and *brotherhood* for the latter.

   Very often inflectional affixes are conditioned by non-semantic linguistic factors outside the word they attach to but within the phrase or sentence. Whereas, derivational affixes are more often based on simple meaning distinctions.

In English, inflectional affixes are mostly suffixes, which are always word final. But derivational affixes can be prefixes or suffixes.

2. Morphophoneme refers to the phoneme (or string of phonemes) that constitutes the various allomorphs of a morpheme.

   Relationship between phoneme and morphophoneme: Generally speaking, the concept of morphophoneme adds a grammatical meaning to the concept of phoneme. For example, as to the phoneme /s/, it is in fact a configuration of allomorphs of different morphemes, such as the plural morpheme and the 3rd person present simple morpheme. Therefore, we would regard this phoneme as a morphophoneme, represented as /s/.

3. Some phonological factors can affect the appearance of morphemes, namely, the form of a morpheme; and there could be assimilation, and dissmilation. For example, the negative morpheme could be realized as "in-" or "im-" followed by different phonological environments, as in "inefficient" and "imperfect", as a result of assimilation.

   Morphemes can also be conditioned by morphological factors; for example, the allomorphs of the plural morpheme, as could be seen in "oxen", "cows", and "feet".

4. Considering the free and bound morpheme, affix is the collective term for the type of formative that can be used only when added to another morpheme, so it is naturally bound.

   Depending on their position with reference to the root or stem of the word, affixes are generally classified into three subtypes, namely, prefix, suffix, and infix. For examples, "para-" as prefix, "-tion" as suffix, and "-bloomingly-" in word "abso-bloomingly-luty" as infix.

   Affix can also be classified depending on the distinction between inflectional affixes and derivational affixes. The *formal* often only add a minute grammatical function to the stem and do not change the word class of the word they attach to; while the latter are very productive in making new words and often change the lexical meaning. For instances, "-s" in words "toys", "walks" and "John's" is inflectional affixes, while "-tion" is a derivational affix in word "recitation".

5. The words "deceased" "upper" and "downer" have undergone a process of class shift. By shifting the word class one can change the meaning of a word from a concrete entity or notion to a process or attribution. This process of word formation is also known as zero-derivation, or conversion. In the sentences above, "deceased", "upper" and "downer" are originally adjectives, meaning "dead", "higher" and "lower" respectively; in the sentences above, however, they mean "dead people", "a drug used as a stimulant." and "a depressant or sedative drug", which are nouns.

6. Root is that part of a word-form that remains when all the inflectional and derivational affixes have been removed. Thus in the word *undesirables*, the root is *desire*. Stem is the part of a word-form that remains when all inflectional affixes have been removed. So in the word *undesirables*, the stem is *undesirable*. The stem of a word may be: a) a simple stem consisting of only one morpheme or root, e. g. work; b) a root plus a derivational affix, e. g. worker; c) two or more roots, e. g. workshop.

7. Morpheme is the smallest meaningful linguistic unit of language, not divisible or analyzable into

smaller forms. What is usually considered a single word in English may be composed of one or more morphemes. Take *disagreeable* for example, it contains three morphemes, dis-, agree and -able. A morpheme may take various shapes or forms. For instance, -ion, -tion, -sion and -ation are the positional variants of the same suffix. They do not differ in meaning or function but show a slight difference in sound depending on the final phoneme of the preceding verb. They are called allomorphs. So an allomorph is any of the variant forms of a morpheme as conditioned by position or adjoining sounds.

8. A word that belongs to the closed-class is one whose membership is fixed or limited. New members are not regularly added. Therefore, pronouns, prepositions, conjunctions, articles, etc. , are all closed items.

   The open-class is one whose membership is in principle infinite or unlimited. With the emergence of new ideas, inventions, etc. , new expressions are continually and constantly being added to the lexicon. Nouns, verbs, adjectives and many adverbs are all open-class items.

   However, the distinction between closed-class words and open-class words is not quiet as clear-cut as it seems. Preposition, though a closed-class, is relatively open one in English. Expressions such as "regarding", "throughout", "out of" are now recognized as prepositions or complex prepositions. In respect of open-class items, auxiliary verbs, which used to be ranked as open-class words, are relatively closed in number.

9. (1) Compounds refer to those words which have more than one lexical morpheme, or the way to join two separate words to produce a single form. There are several different ways of classification of compounds. (2) First, in terms of part of speech, compound can be divided into noun compounds, verb compounds, adjective compounds and preposition compounds. (3) Second, in terms of construction, Compounds can be further divided into the endocentric and the exocentric compound. Endocentric compound refers to a compound which has a center or a head word. Exocentric compound is one which has no center or a head word. (4) Last, according to the relationship between the sub-components of a compound, compounds can be divided into attributive compounds which are made of two lexemes with one modifying the other; coordinative compounds in which the two sub-components are equal without one modifying the other; and subordinative compounds with one of the sub-component being understood to be the argument of the other. Among these three kinds of compound, the first two are also called root compounds and the last synthetic compounds.

Ⅵ. Essay questions

1. New words or expressions are created through the following processes except compound and derivation, which are called lexical change proper.

   (1) Invention

   Technological and economic activities are the most important and dynamic in modern human life, many new lexical items come directly from them, such as Kodak, Coke, nylon, etc.

   (2) Abbreviation

   Many English words have come into being through abbreviation. This phenomenon is also called clipping: a new word can be created by:

① cutting the final part, for example, ad for advertisement.

② cutting the initial part, for example, plane for aeroplane.

③ cutting both the initial and final parts accordingly, for instance, fridge for refrigerator.

(3) Blending is a relatively complex form of compounding, in which two words are blended by joining together the initial part of the first word and the final part of the second word, or by only joining the initial parts of the two words, for example, emotion + icon → emoticon; car + hijacking→carjacking.

(4) Acronym is made up from the first letters of the name of an organization, which has heavily modified headword; an example is EU for European Union. This process is also widely used in shortening extremely long words of word groups in science, technology and other special fields, for example, SARS is short for "Severe Acute Respiratory Syndrome". What's more, people also use this process in internet chatting or e-mail communication, such as BTW for "by the way", ASAP for "as soon as possible".

2. Semantic change plays a very important role in widening the vocabulary of a language. Since language is symbolic, each word serves as a symbol in relation to a specific meaning. In this sense, we need infinite numbers of words or symbols to code the physical entities and our experiential concepts. But this is impossible for communication. Therefore, users give a new concept to an old form, thus the meaning of a form is multiplied. There are three kinds of semantic changes, namely, broadening, narrowing, and meaning shift. Class shift and folk etymology also contribute to change in meaning.

Semantic broadening refers to the process in which the meaning of a word becomes more general or inclusive than its historically earlier denotation. For example, the word holiday used to mean "holy day" in religious English. It means "a day for rest" today regardless of its religious nature, and hence its meaning is widened.

Semantic narrowing is a process in which the meaning of a word becomes less general or inclusive than its historically earlier meaning. For example, the Old English word "hund" ("hound") was once used for any breed of dog; whereas in Modem English its meaning has been narrowed to a particular kind of dog.

Semantic shift is a process of semantic change in which a word loses its former meaning and acquires a new, sometimes related, meaning. For example, the word "silly" meant "happy" in Old English, and "naive" in Middle English, but "foolish" in Modem English.

3. Lexical change includes invention, blending, abbreviation, acronym, back-formation, analogical creation, borrowing, compound and derivation.

a. Coinage: it is the invention of totally new terms. The most typical sources are invented trade names of one company's product that become general terms for any version of that product. Such as Kleenex, Teflon and Xerox.

b. Borrowing: it is the taking over of words from other languages. The English language has adopted a vast number of words from other languages, such as *encore*, which is borrowed from French.

c. Compounding: it is the process of a joining of two separate words to produce a single form. For example, "fingerprint" is composed of "finger" and "print".

d. Blending: blending is typically accomplished by jointing part of one word to the other whole word or other part of the word. For example, the word *smog* is formed by combining parts of two words "smoke" and "fog".

e. Clipping: it occurs when a word of more than one syllable is reduced to a shorter form. Common example is like ad ("advertisement").

f. Back-formation: it is a specialized type of word formation in which new words are coined from already existing words by "subtracting" an affix thought to be part of the old word. For example, the noun *television* first came into use and then the verb *televise* was created from it.

g. Analogical creation. It refers to the phenomenon that a new word or a new phrase is coined by analogy between a newly created one and an existing one. For example, "marathon" appeared at the First Olympic Games and by analogy modern English created such words as "telethon", "talkthon".

h. Acronyms: some new words, known as acronyms, are formed form the initial letters of a set of other words. These can remain essentially "alphabetisims" such as CD (compact disk) where the pronunciation consists of the set of letters. More typically, acronyms are pronounced as single words, as in NATO (North Atlantic Treaty Organization).

i. Derivation: it is the process of forming new words by adding prefixes, infixes or suffixes to the root. For example, the prefix un- is added to pleasant to form "unpleasant"; the suffix -able is used to form 'predictable'.

4. There are mainly three kinds of semantic changes, namely, broadening, narrowing, and meaning shift. Class shift and folk etymology also contribute to change in meaning.

(1) Broadening

Broadening is a process to extend or elevate the meaning from its originally specific sense to a relatively general one. For instance, the word holiday used to mean "holy day" in religious English. Today it means "a day for rest" regardless of its religious nature.

(2) Narrowing

Contrary to broadening, the original meaning of a word can be narrowed or restricted to a specific sense. A typical example is the word *meat* which originally meant "food". In the course of time, the range of meaning was narrowed to mean specifically "the flesh of animals used as food".

(3) Meaning shift

All semantic changes involve meaning shift. Yet, in its narrow sense, meaning shift refers to the change of meaning, which has nothing to do with generalization or restriction. What makes the meaning of a word different is its departure from its original domain as a result of its metaphorical usage. For instance, the word *bead* originally means "prayer", but later it refers to "the prayer bead", the visible manifestation of a prayer, finally "small, ball-shaped piece of glass, metal or wood".

(4) Class shift

By shifting the word class one can change the meaning of a word from a concrete entity or notion to a process or attribution. This process of word formation is also known as zero-derivation, or conversion. The word *engineer* as a noun means "a person trained in a branch of engineering", but it means "to act as an engineer" or "to plan, to maneuver" when used as a verb.

(5) Folk etymology

It refers to a change in form of a word or phrase resulting from an incorrect popular notion of the origin or meaning of the term or from the influence of more familiar terms mistakenly taken to be analogous. As a result of this modification, the word sparrowgrass in English derived from asparagus; the Spanish cucaracha changed into English cockroach.

第4章　句法：从语词到篇章

4.1　复习笔记

本章要点：

1. The traditional approach, the structural approach
   传统学派，结构主义学派
2. Immediate constituent analysis
   直接成分分析
3. Endocentric and exocentric constructions
   向心结构和离心结构
4. The generative approach
   生成语法
5. The functional approach
   功能学派
6. Systemic-functional grammar
   系统功能语法

▼7. Cohesion and Coherence
　衔接与连贯

常考考点：

句法的定义；句法关系；向心结构；离心结构；深层结构；表层结构；成分；直接成分分析法的定义；并列结构与从属结构；句子成分；范畴(性、数、格)。用实例进行分析，用直接成分分析法以及树形图分析句子的结构；衔接与连贯等。

本章内容索引：

Ⅰ. Syntax

1. Definition
2. Syntactic Relations
   (1) Positional Relation
   (2) Relation of Substitutability
   (3) Relation of Co-occurrence

Ⅱ. The Traditional Approach

1. Number, Gender, Case
2. Tense and aspect
3. Concord and government

Ⅲ. The Structural Approach

1. Syntagmatic and paradigmatic relations
2. Immediate constituent analysis(IC Analysis)

(1) Definition

(2) Advantages

(3) Problems

3. Endocentric and exocentric construction

(1) Endocentric construction

①Subordinate endocentric constructions

②Coordinate endocentric constructions

(2) Exocentric construction

Ⅳ. The Generative Approach

1. Deep structure and surface structure

2. Syntactic Movement

(1) NP-movement

(2) Wh-movement

(3) Aux-movement

3. Move-α rule

Ⅴ. The Functional Approach

Ⅵ. Systemic-Functional Grammar

▼Ⅶ. Beyond the Sentence

1. Discourse and Text

2. Cohesion and Coherence

Ⅰ. Syntax **1. Definition** Syntax is the study of the rules deciding how different constituents are combined to form sentence, or the study of the relationships between elements in sentence structures.	**Ⅰ. 句法** **1. 定义** 句法就是研究语言不同成分组成句子的规则或句子结构成分之间的关系。
2. Syntactic Relations **(1) Positional Relation** Positional relation refers to the order in which words are placed in a language. It is the basic syntactic relation, and also the requirement of grammatical acceptability and semantic intelligibility of human language.	**2. 句法关系** **(1) 位置关系** 位置关系或词序指的是一门语言中词语的排列顺序。 位置关系是任何人类语言中的基本句法关系，也是语言的句法可接受性和语义可理解性的要求。
(2) Relation of Substitutability The relationship of substitutability refers to classes or sets of words that can be replaced each other grammatically in the same sentence structure. It can also refer to a phrase composed of several words that can be replaced grammatically for a single word of a particular set.	**(2) 替代关系** 替代关系指在相同的句子结构中，语法上可以互相代替的词类或语词的集合，它还可指由多个词组成的词组，语法上代替特定集合中的单个语词。

(3) Relation of Co-occurrence It means that lexical sets of different classes allow words from another class or set to appear to form a sentence or a specific component of a sentence.	**(3) 同现关系** 共现关系指不同词类的不同词汇集合允许另一个词类或集合的词出现构成一个句子或句子的某一特定成分。
II. The Traditional Approach Traditionally, a sentence is seen as a sequence of words. The study of sentence formation involves a great deal of the study of the words such as the distinction of parts of speech, the identification of functions of words in terms of subject, predicate, etc. Sometimes these parts of speech and function are called categories.	**II. 传统语法学派** 传统语法认为句子是词的序列。因此句子构造的研究涉及了对词的大量研究，例如词类是对词进行的分类，主语、谓语是对词的功能的描写等。这些词类和功能有时叫做范畴。
1. Number, Gender, Case (1) Number is a grammatical category used to analyze word classes displaying such contrasts as singular, dual, plural, etc. In English, number can be mainly found in nouns, and it has only two forms: singular and plural. Number is also shown in the inflection of pronouns and verbs. (2) Gender is a grammatical category dividing nouns into classes basically characterized by sex. Gender is also a category of nouns and pronouns. In English, the gender distinctions are on the whole natural, determined by the biological gender of the creature. However, exactly speaking, the gender here means the grammatical gender, which includes feminine, masculine and neuter. (3) Case is an inflectional category, basically of nouns, which typically marks their roles in relation to other parts of the sentence. In English, pronouns have three cases of nominative (e. g. we, he, she), accusative (e. g. us, him, her) and genitive (e. g. our, your, his). But nouns have only two cases: general (e. g. Tom, girl) and genitive (e. g. Tom's, girl's).	**1. 数、性和格** (1) 数是用来分析词类的语法范畴，有单数、双数和复数等。在英语中，数主要是名词的范畴，包括两种形式：单数和复数。数还体现在代词和动词的屈折变化上。 (2) 性指的是依照性别把名词分成不同类别的语法范畴。性主要也是名词和代词的范畴。在英语中，性的差别是自然的，由动物本身的生理性别决定。然而准确地讲，性在这里指的是语法性，语法性主要有阴性、阳性和中性三种。 (3) 格主要是名词的屈折范畴，它典型地标识着它们和句子其他部分之间的关系。在英语中，代词一般有三种格。即：主格、宾格和属格；名词只有两种格：普通格和属格。
2. Tense and aspect 【考点：区分 Tense 和 Aspect 的区别】 Tense and aspect are two important categories of the verb, and they were not separated in traditional grammar. The distinction between tense and aspect lies in that the former is deictic, i. e. indicating time relative to the time of utterance; while the latter is not deictic, the time indicated is not relative to the time of utterance, but relative to the time of another event described, or implied, in the narrative.	**2. 时态与体** 时态与体是动词的两个重要范畴，传统语法没有对它们加以区分。时态与体之间的区别在于：时态是指示性的，也就是说指明的时间与说话的时间相关；体则不是指示性的，指明的时间与说话的时间没有关系，却与叙述中描写或暗示的另一个事件的时间相关。

3. Concord and government

Concord, also known as agreement, refers to the language phenomenon that the forms of two or more words in a syntactic relationship should agree with each other in terms of some categories.

Government is another type of control over the forms of some words by other words in certain syntactic constructions. It is different from concord in that this is a relationship in which a word of certain class determines the forms of others in terms of certain category.

3. 一致关系与支配关系

一致关系是指在一个给定的语言结构中，词和短语之间利用至少它们中的一个所携带的屈折形式互相匹配的句法关系。

支配关系是指句法结构中某些词的形式受另一种其他类型词的控制。它与一致关系有所不同，就某个范畴而言，它是指某类词决定其他词形式的关系。

Ⅲ. The Structural Approach

It is founded by Ferdinand de Saussure who regards linguistic units as interrelated with each other in a structure/system, not as isolated bits.

Ⅲ. 结构主义学派

结构主义学派的创始人索绪尔认为语言单位在结构（或系统）之中是互相关联的，不是孤立的单位。

1. Syntagmatic and paradigmatic relations

(1) The syntagmatic relation refers to a relation between one item and others in a sequence, or between elements which are all present. There are syntactic and semantic conditions the words in a syntagmatic relation must meet.

(2) The paradigmatic (or associative) relation is a relation between elements replaceable with each other at a particular place in a structure, or between one element present and the others absent. They can substitute for each other without violating syntactic rules. Words in a paradigmatic relation are comparable only in terms of syntax and semantic factors are not taken into consideration here. These words have the same syntactic features. But they are not replaceable with each other semantically.

(3) The syntagmatic and paradigmatic relations together, like the two axes of a coordinate, determine the identity of a linguistic sign. The syntagmatic relation is also be considered as the horizontal relation, or chain relation. And the paradigmatic relation is also known as the vertical relation. or choice relation.

1. 组合关系和聚合关系

(1) 组合关系是指一个词项和同一序列中的其他词项之间的关系或者说是共现的所有成分之间的关系。这些处于组合关系中的词，必须满足一些句法和语义条件。

(2) 聚合关系，或称联想关系，是指在结构的某个位置彼此可以互相替换的成分之间的关系。它们能够相互替换而不违反句法规则。处于聚合关系中词语只是在句法关系上可以比较。它们有共同的句法特征，但是在语义上不能相互替换。

(3) 组合关系和聚合关系就像坐标的两根数轴，共同决定语言符号的身份。组合关系也称为水平关系或链状关系。聚合关系也称为垂直关系或选择关系。

2. Immediate constituent analysis (IC Analysis)

【考点：简答——直接成分分析法的利弊】

2. 直接成分分析法

(1) Definition The immediate constituent analysis may be defined as: the analysis of a sentence in terms of its immediate constituents—word groups(or phrases), which are in turn analyzed into the immediate constituents of their own, and the process goes on until the ultimate constituents are reached. However, for the sake of convenience, in practice we usually stop at the level of word. The immediate constituent analysis of a sentence may be carried out with brackets or with a tree diagram.	**(1) 定义** 直接成分分析法先把句子分析为直接成分——词组(或短语),再把这些直接成分依次切分,得到各自的直接成分,层层切分,直到最终成分为止。实际操作中,为了方便,通常切分到词为止。直接成分分析法可以用括弧或树形图表示。
(2) Advantages Through IC analysis, the internal structure of a sentence may be demonstrated clearly, and ambiguities, if any, will be revealed.	**(2) 优点** 通过 IC 分析法,句子的内在结构可以清晰地展示出来,如果有歧义也会被揭示出来。
(3) Problems ① At the beginning, some advocators insisted on binary divisions. Any construction, at any level, will be cut into two parts. But this is not always possible. ② Constructions with discontinuous constituents will pose technical problems for tree diagrams in IC analysis. The most serious problem is that there are structural ambiguities which cannot be revealed by IC analysis.	**(3) 问题** ① 开始的时候,一些提倡者坚持二元切分。任何结构体在任何层面都分成两个部分。但实际上并不总是如此。 ② 含有不连续成分的结构体会给 IC 分析法的树形图造成技术困难。最严重的问题是有些结构的歧义不能用 IC 分析法来揭示和分析。
3. Endocentric and exocentric construction 【考点:判断一短语属于向心结构还是离心结构】	**3. 向心结构和离心结构**
(1) Endocentric construction It is a kind of construction whose distribution is functionally equivalent, or approaching equivalence, to one of its constituents, which serves as the center, or head, of the whole, therefore, a headed construction. Endocentric construction include two types: subordinate and coordinate constructions. ①Subordinate endocentric constructions: Those endocentric constructions where there is only one head, with the head dominant and the other constituents being modifiers are called subordinate endocentric constructions. ②Coordinate endocentric constructions: Those endocentric constructions where there are more than one head, with equal syntactic status and no one dependent on the other are called coordinate endocentric constructions.	**(1) 向心结构** 向心结构包含一个作为整体结构的中心或核心的成分,该中心或核心可以在最后,也可以在开头。从结构上可以划分为两类:主从结构和并列结构。 ① 主从向心结构:凡是结构中只有一个支配性主词,其他成分为该主词的修饰成分,这样的向心结构称为主从向心结构。 ② 并列向心结构:凡是结构中有一个以上句法地位相等的主词,互不依靠,这样的向心结构称为并列向心结构。

(2) Exocentric construction It refers to a construction whose distribution is not functionally equivalent to any of its constituents, none of which serves as a noticeable head or a center of the whole. Like the prepositional phrase on the desk, the whole construction has a different grammatical function from either its constituents on or the desk. They cannot substitute for each other.	**(2) 离心结构** 离心结构是指一个其成分功能不等于它的任何一个成分，没有明显的主词或中心词的结构。
Ⅳ. The Generative Approach The theory of generative approach originated from the ideas of American linguist Noam Chomsky. In 1957, he published *Syntactic Structures*, after that the theory has undergone a number of changes.	**Ⅳ. 生成语法** 生成学派是由美国语言学家乔姆斯基创立的。在 1957 年他发表了《句法结构》，之后这一理论经历了一系列的变化。
1. Deep structure and surface structure 【考点：绘制一句子的深层/表层结构树形图】 The deep structure is the abstract representation of the syntactic properties of a construction, i. e. the underlying level of structural relations between its different constituents. The surface structure is the final stage in the syntactic derivation of a construction, which closely corresponds to the structural organization of a construction people actually produce and receive.	**1. 深层结构和表层结构** 深层结构是对一个结构体的句法属性的抽象描述，即不同成分之间的结构关系的潜在层面。 表层结构是结构体句法派生过程的最后阶段，与人们实际发送、接受的结构组织相符合。
2. Syntactic Movement It refers to the movement of any constituent in a sentence out of its original place to a new position.	**2. 句法移位** 句法移位是指一个句子的任意成分从原来的位置移到另一个新位置。
(1) NP-movement It is relative to two constructions, i. e. passive sentence and raising construction. Generally, passive sentences are produced by the movement of the active sentences; in the raising construction, there are two kinds of raising which are raising verbs and raising adjectives.	**(1) NP 移位** NP 移位涉及两种结构：被动句和提升结构。一般认为，被动句是由主动句移位产生的。NP 移位不仅发生在被动句，而且发生在提升结构中，主要有两种提升结构：一类是含有提升动词的结构，另一类是含有提升形容词的结构。
(2) Wh-movement The movement mostly takes place in wh-question sentences, indirect wh-question sentences and relative clauses.	**(2) Wh-移位** 主要发生在 wh-问句，包括直接 wh-问句和间接 wh-问句以及关系分句中。
(3) Aux-movement It refers to the movement of such words as be, have, do, may, can, shall, should and so on, from the original position to the beginning of the sentence.	**(3) Aux-移位** 是指诸如 be, have, do, may, can, shall, should 之类的助动词从原来的位置移动到句首。
3. Move-α rule It is a general movement rule which accounts for the syntactic behavior of any constituent movement.	**3. Move-α 规则** 这个规则是指任何成分可以移动到任何位置。

V. The Functional Approach (the Prague School)

A sentence may be analyzed from the functional side or the grammatical side. Apart from the analysis of a sentence in terms of subject and predicate, there may also be a functional analysis in terms of theme and rheme. Theme refers to "that which is known or at least obvious in the given situation and from which the speaker proceeds". Rheme can be regarded as "what the speaker states about, or in regard to, the starting point of the utterance." The theme-rheme order is the usual one in unemotional narration, which is called objective order. In emotional narration, however, it may be possible to reverse the order, to put rheme before theme. And this is called a subjective order.

V. 功能学派（布拉格语言学派）

功能学派认为句子能从功能的角度分析，也可以从语法的角度分析，一个句子除了可以用主语和谓语来描述外，还可以用主位和述位来分析。主位指“已知的信息或至少在给定语境中明确的，话语起点前的信息”，述位指“说话者陈述的有关，或者涉及话语起点的内容”。主位－述位的顺序在非感情的叙述中是常见的，叫做客观顺序，而在感情叙述中，述位还可以放在主位的前面，叫做主观顺序。

Ⅵ. Systemic-Functional Grammar (Halliday's approach)

The characteristics of the theory are systemic and functional. It characterized Halliday's theory as more attention is paid to paradigmatic relations than to syntagmatic relations. And this is the main concern of Chomsky. What is new in Halliday is that he has tried to relate the functions of language to its structures. He argues that there are three general functions of language: ideational, interpersonal and textual. And they are related to three grammatical systems: transitivity, mood and theme.

Ⅵ. 系统功能语法

该理论的特色是系统的和功能的，对聚合关系的关注比对组合关系关注更多，而乔姆斯基更关注组合关系。创新之处是，努力把语言功能跟结构联系起来。认为有三种普遍的功能：概念功能、人际功能和语篇功能。它们跟三种语法系统相联系：及物性、语气和主位。

▼Ⅶ. Beyond the Sentence

1. Discourse and Text

Etymologically speaking, discourse refers to spoken language while text means the written documents. In contemporary linguistics, these two terms can be used interchangeably.

A text is regarded as a semantic unit, which is concerned with meaning rather than form and is realized in sentences. Therefore, a text is not an arbitrary combination of words, it is something that differs from a sentence in kind. To make it clearer, a text is more than a random set of words; it should be overtly connected and covertly cohered: it shows connectedness.

Ⅶ. 句子之上的结构

1. 语篇和篇章

从词源学上看，语篇指的是口头语言而篇章指的是书面语言，在当代语言学中，这两个词可以互换。

篇章被视为一个语义单位，关注的是意义而非形式，是通过句子实现的。因此篇章不是单词的随意组合，它本身具有意义的连接性。

2. Cohesion and Coherence	2. 衔接与连贯
①Cohesion is a concept to do with discourse or text rather than with syntax. It refers to the relationship of meaning existing in the text. Discourse /textual cohesiveness can be achieved through a variety of cohesive markers such as reference, substitution, ellipsis, conjunction and lexical collocation. ②The connectedness of a text not only depends on the cohesion of a text, but also requires the language user to connect different information units through coherence. The connectedness of discourse is a feature of the mental representation of the text rather than of the text itself. The connectedness conceived is often called coherence. Coherence may be have cognitive properties, but its reconstruction is often based on the linguistic signs of the text itself.	①衔接是一个与语篇和篇章相关的概念，与句法无关。它指的是存在于篇章中的意义关系。通过多种衔接标志词如参照，替代，省略，连词和词汇搭配等可以实现衔接。 ②文本的意义连接性不仅取决于衔接，也需要语言使用者通过连贯将不同的信息单位联系起来。话语的连通性是文本心理表征的一个特征，而不是文本本身。连贯具有认知属性，但其重建往往是基于文本本身的语言标志。

4.2 考研真题与典型题详解

Ⅰ. Fill in the blanks

1. IC is the short form of immediate ________ used in the study of syntax.（北二外 2003 研）
2. ________ refers to ties and connections which exist within texts. They are also called formal links between sentences and between clauses.（人大 2007 研）
3. Coordination and subordination belong to ________ construction.
4. A ________ sentence contains two clauses joined by a linking word, such as “and”, “but”, “or”.
5. A clause that takes a subject and a finite verb, and at the same time stands structurally alone is known as a ________ clause.
6. IC analysis emphasizes the ________ structure of a sentence, seeing it as consisting of word groups first.
7. Syntactic movement is dictated by rules traditionally called ________ rules, whose operation may change the syntactic representation of a sentence.
8. Syntactic relations include ________, ________ and ________.
9. Etymologically speaking, ________ refers to spoken language while ________ means the written documents. In contemporary linguistics, these two terms can be used interchangeably.
10. ________ is a concept to do with discourse or text rather than with syntax, it refers to relations of meaning that exists within the text, and defines it as a text.

Ⅱ. Multiple Choice

1. ________ refer to the relationship that linguistic units have with other units because they may occur together in a sentence.（西安外国语学院 2006 研）

A. Syntagmatic relations　　B. Hypotactic relations

C. Paradigmatic relations　　D. Paratactic relations

2. For structuralists, ________ is one whose distribution is functionally equivalent to that of one or more of its constituents. （西安外国语学院 2006 研）

A. coordinate construction　　B. subordinate construction

C. endocentric construction　　D. exocentric construction

3. Phrase structure rules allow us to better understand ________ . （西安交大 2008 研）

A. how people produce and recognize possible sentences

B. what constitutes the grammaticality of strings of words

C. how words and phrases form sentences

D. All of the above

4. Bloomfield introduced the IC analysis, whose full name is ________ Analysis. （北二外 2010 研）

A. Internal Component　　B. Innate Capacity

C. Internal Constituent　　D. Immediate Constituent

5. The phrase "on the shelf" belongs to ________ construction.

A. endocentric　　B. exocentric　　C. subordinate　　D. coordinate

6. ________ refers to construction where one clause is coordinated or conjoined with another.

A. Conjoining　　B. Embedding　　C. Concord　　D. Government

7. The criterion used in IC analysis is ________ .

A. transformation　　B. conjoining

C. grouping　　D. substitutability

8. The phrase "my small child's cot" is an ambiguous phrase, which can be revealed by ________ tree diagrams.

A. one　　B. two　　C. three　　D. four

9. ________ is a grammatical category used for the analysis of word classes displaying such contrast as singular, dual, plural, etc. ________ .

A. Category　　B. Number　　C. Gender　　D. Case

10. In English, ________ and ________ are often expressed by subject and object.

A. theme and rheme　　B. theme and predicate

C. predicate and object　　D. subject and predicate

11. Which one of them is not the cohesive device ________ .

A. ellipsis　　B. reference　　C. substitution　　D. subject

Ⅲ. Explain the following terms

1. Paradigmatic relations（北交大 2005 研；中山大学 2006 研）
2. Immediate constituent（武汉大学 2008 研；武汉大学 2006 研；南京师范大学 2021 研）
3. Endocentric construction（四川大学 2006 研）
4. IC analysis（四川大学 2010 研；人大 2006 研）
5. Concord (or: Agreement)（武汉大学 2008 研；中山大学 2008 研；上海交大 2007 研）
6. Embedding（武汉大学 2004 研）
7. Logical subject（中山大学 2011 研）
8. anaphor（南开大学 2011 研）

Ⅳ. Short answer questions

1. How does modern language define "object"? Provide an example.（清华 2001 研）
2. What's your understanding of "Gender"?（西安交大 2008 研）
3. What are the endocentric and exocentric constructions?（北交大 2007；武汉大学 2004 研；西安交大 2008 研）
4. What are the advantages of using tree diagrams in the analysis of sentence structures?（西安交通大学 2008 研）
5. How do you understand syntagmatic and paradigmatic relations?（北二外 2010 研）
6. Endocentric construction is one whose distribution is functionally equivalent to that of one or more of its constituents, i. e., a word or a group of words, which serve as a definable centre or head（中山大学 2011 研）
7. Analyze the morphemic structure of the English words *gentlemanliness* and *unlockable*, using a labeled tree diagram to illustrate the morphemic structure of the word under analysis（南开大学 2011 研）

   （1）*gentlemanliness*　　　（2）*unlockable*

8. What is move-α rule?
9. What are theme and rheme?
10. What are discourse and text?
11. What are cohesion and coherence? How to achieve them?

Ⅴ. Essay questions

1. Why is it important to know the relations a sign has with others, such as syntagmatic and paradigmatic relations?（北航 2008 研；四川大学 2008 研；北二外 2005 研）
2. Advantages and Disadvantages of Immediate Constituent Analysis (IC Analysis).（北交大 2006 研）
3. Disambiguate the following sentences, using the tree diagram with labels or analyzing their syntactic structures.（北交大 2006 研）
   1. Times flies like an arrow.
   2. We got down from the duck.
   3. Old men and women will be served first.
   4. John passed the hammer and saw through the window.
   5. Who would you like to visit?
4. Which of the following sentences are ambiguous? If you know how, use tree diagrams to show how these sentences are ambiguous.（南京大学 2006 研）

   （1）The children put the toy in the box.

   （2）The professor's appointment was shocking.

   （3）No smoking section is available.

   （4）Jack refused to change his decision.

5. What, in your view, makes a text a text, rather than a series of unconnected utterances? What are the implications of your answer for second language teaching?（北外 2006 研）
6. In interpreting utterances such as (1) and (2), the hearer generally treats the events described in the two sentences in each group as causally related even though such relationship is not enco-

ded in the meanings of the sentences. That is, the hearer tends to think that Helen fell on the ground because of Tom's pushing and that the vase broke because it was dropped. Explain why.（北外 2005 研）

（1）Tom pushed Helen. Helen fell on the ground.

（2）Peter dropped the vase. It broke.

7. What is the aim of IC（immediate constituent）analysis? Make an IC analysis of the following sentence by means of either brackets or a tree diagram?

My mother said Mary liked the handbag.（北外 2010 研）

8. For each of the following pairs of sentences, discuss how the two sentences are different from each other.（南京大学 2006 研）

（1）A. His carelessness I can't bear.

B. I can't bear his carelessness.

（2）A. A dagger killed the tourist.

B. The tourist was killed with a dagger.

（3）A. A hurricane killed eight people.

B. Eight people died in a hurricane.

9. In your opinion in what ways can corpus data contribute to lexical studies?（南开大学 2011 研）

参考答案及解析

Ⅰ. Fill in the blanks

1. constituent

（直接成分分析法是一种句法分析方法。它指先把句子分析为直接成分——词组（或短语），再把这些直接成分依次切分，得到各自的直接成分，层层切分，直到最终成分为止。）

2. Cohesion

（衔接不是一个句法概念，它指文本中存在的一种意义上的联系或关系，也包括句子或分句之间存在的一种形式上的联系。）

3. endocentric

（向心结构包含一个作为整体结构的中心或核心的成分，该中心或核心可以在最后，也可以在开头。从结构上可以划分为两类：主从结构和并列结构。）

4. coordinate

（并列从句是指一个句子由两个分句组成，这两个分句通常是由如 but, and ，or 这些并列连词来连接的。）

5. finite

（限定性从句通常有一个主语和一个限定性动词，且在结构上是独立的。）

6. Hierarchical

（参见第 1 题解析。）

7. Transformational

（句法移位是一种转换规则，指一个句子的任意成分从原来的位置移到另一个新位置。它可能会引起句子句法的变化。）

8. positional relation, relation of substitutability and relation of occurrence

（有三种句法关系，即（1）位置关系；（2）替代关系；（3）同现关系。）

9. discourse；text

（从词源学上看，语篇指的是口头语言而篇章指的是书面语言，在当代语言学中，这两个词可以互换。）

10. Cohesion

（衔接是一个与语篇和篇章相关的概念，与句法无关。它指的是存在于篇章中的意义关系。通过多种衔接标志词如参照，替代，省略，连词和词汇搭配等可以实现衔接。）

Ⅱ. Multiple Choice

1. A （组合关系是指一个词项和同一系列中的其他词项之间的关系或者说是共现的所有成分之间的关系。）
2. C （向心结构是指其整体在功能上等同于或者接近它的一个或多个成分的结构。）
3. D （乔姆斯基在其经典理论中提出短语结构规则，这个规则有助于我们更好的明白句子是如何产生与被理解的，以及单词和短语是怎样根据语法规则形成句子的。）
4. D （直接成分这一术语，最先是由布龙菲尔德在《语言论》中提出的。直接成分分析法，即 Immediate constituent analysis，简称 IC Analysis。）
5. B （离心结构是指一个其成分功能不等于它的任何一个成分，没有明显的主词或中心词的结构。在短语“on the shelf”中，没有明显的主词或中心词结构。）
6. A （当一个从句与另一个从句并列或结合时，这种句子结构就叫做“联合”。）
7. D （直接成分分析法的标准：替换性。看一个词语的序列是否可以被一个单词替换而结构保持不变。）
8. C （

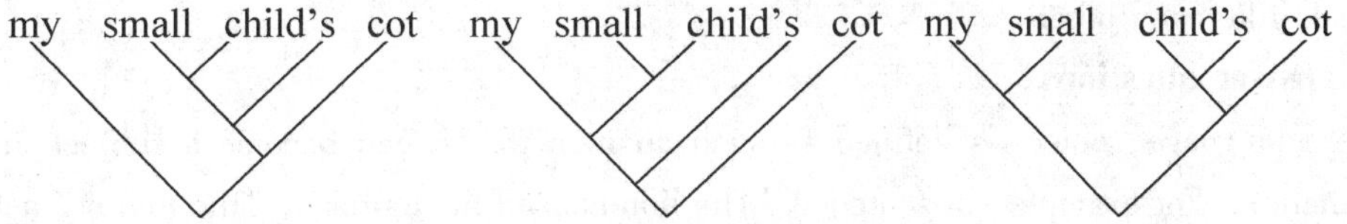

）

9. B （数是用来分析词类的语法范畴，有单数、双数和复数等。在英语中，数主要是名词的范畴，包括两种形式：单数和复数。）
10. A （较早提出主位和述位概念的是布拉格学派创始人之一马泰休斯。主位和述位通常指主语和谓语，但主位结构分析属于语义分析，而主语—谓语—补语分析属于结构分析。）
11. D （有很多衔接手段，例如，指称，替代，省略。主语不属于衔接手段。）

Ⅲ. Explain the following terms.

1. Paradigmatic relation, Saussure originally called associative, is a relation holding between elements replaceable with each other at a particular place in a structure, or between one element present and the others absent.
2. Immediate constituent: An immediate constituent is the constituent immediately, directly, below the level of a construction. For example, in the sentence “Poor John ran away”, the constituents “Poor John” and “ran away” are regarded as the immediate constituents of the sentence.
3. Endocentric construction: An endocentric construction is one whose distribution is functionally equivalent, or approaching equivalence, to that of one or more of its constituents, i. e. a word or a group of words, which serves as a definable center, or head. Hence an endocentric construc-

tion is also known as a headed construction. Noun phrases like "Lovely Lucy" are typical endocentric constructions.

4. IC analysis: IC analysis (immediate constituent analysis) refers to the analysis of a sentence in terms of its immediate constituents—word groups (or phrases), which are in turn analyzed into the immediate constituents of their own, and the process goes on until the ultimate constituents are reached. In practice, for the sake of convenience, we usually stop at the level of word.
5. It may be defined as the requirement that the forms of two or more words of specific word classes that stand in specific syntactic relationship with one another shall also be characterized by the same paradigmatically marked category (or categories). For example, the syntactic relationship between *that girl* and *she* in the following dialogue: A: Who is that girl? B: Oh, she is my sister.
6. Embedding refers to the means by which one clause is included in the sentence (main clause) in syntactic subordination, e. g., I saw man who had visited you last year.
7. Logical subject is the subject of a sentence that expresses the actual agent of an expressed or implied action. In passive voice such as "John was bitten by a dog", we have two terms "grammatical subject" and "logical subject". Since the core object noun (John in this case) sits in the slot before the verb in the passive, it is called grammatical subject, for the original object noun phrase occupies the grammatical space before a verb, the space that a subject normally occupies; the core subject (A dog), now the object of a preposition (by a dog), is called the logical subject, since semantically the core subject still does what a subject normally does: it performs an action.
8. Anaphor: The term anaphor is used in a narrow sense to include only reflexives like myself and reciprocals like each other.

Ⅳ. Short answer questions

1. In modern language, object is defined as such an item that it can become a subject in passive transformation. For example, in sentence "The lion chased the tourist", "the tourist" acts as the object. In the passive voiced sentence "The tourist was chased by the lion", "the tourist" acts as the subject of the sentence.
2. "Gender" displays such contrasts as "masculine", "feminine", "neuter", or "animate" and "inanimate", etc., for the analysis of word classes. When word items refer to the sex of the real-world entities, we are talking about natural gender. The opposite is grammatical gender. In English, the gender distinctions are on the whole natural, determined by the biological gender of the creature, e. g. actor, actress; hero, heroine; prince, princess; lion, lioness. In contrast, the gender distinctions in languages like French are grammatical. They may have nothing to do with the sex of the real-world entities at all. And all nouns have gender distinctions whether they refer to animate entities or not.
3. An endocentric construction is one whose distribution is functionally equivalent, or approaching equivalence, to that of one or more of its constituents, i. e. a word or a group of words, which serves as a definable center, or head. Hence an endocentric construction is also known as a headed construction. Noun phrases like Lovely Lucy are typical endocentric constructions.

   Opposite of endocentric constructions, the exocentric construction refers to a group of syntactically related words where none of the words is functionally equivalent to the group as a whole. There is no noticeable centre, or head in it. Prepositional phrases like "on the shelf" are typical examples of this type.

4. The tree diagram can not only reveal a linear order, but also a hierarchical structure that groups words into structural constituents. It can, in addition, show the syntactic category of each structural constituent, thus it is believed to most truthfully illustrate the constituent relationship among linguistic elements.
5. In Saussure's view, language is a system of signs, each of which consists of two parts: signified and signifier. And the relationships between these two parts are arbitrary. Syntagmatic relation is a relation between elements that form part of the same form, sequence, construction, etc. e. g. between s, p, and r in a form such as spring, or between a subject and a verb in constructions such as Bill hunts. The syntagmatic relation is also called horizontal relation or chain relation. Paradigmatic relation is a relation holding between elements replaceable with each other at a particular place in a structure. The paradigmatic relation is also called vertical relation or choice relation.
6. This sentence indicates the meaning of endocentric construction. Usually noun phrases, verb phrases and adjective phrases belong to endocentric types because the constituent items are subordinate to the head e. g. noun phrases like the three small children with children as its head, verb phrases like will have been leaving with leaving as its head, and adjective phrases like really very late with late as its head.

   Endocentric constructions fall into two main types, depending on the relation between constituents: coordination and subordination. In the coordinate construction, there are more than one head, e. g. boys and girls, coffee or tea, etc. The subordinate are construction words which modify the head, such as two dogs, swimming in the lake, etc.

   （考查向心结构概念。）
7. (1) *gentlemanliness*

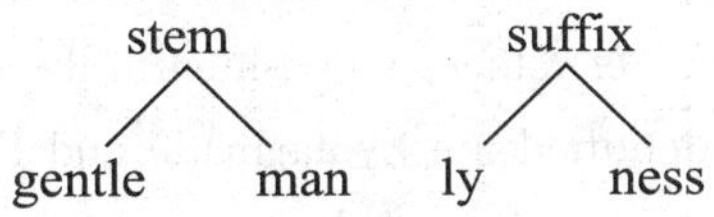

(2)

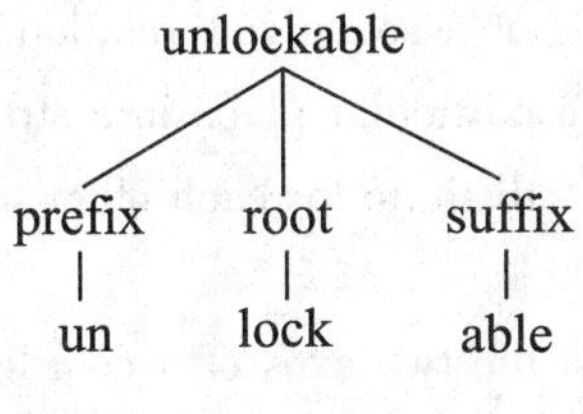

8. Move-α rule is a general movement rule accounting for the syntactic behavior of any constituent movement. It goes like this: any element may be moved to another place, or more generally changed in some way, as long as the relevant conditions (principles) are satisfied. That is to say, the movements are constrained by the other modules of grammar in order to rule out ungrammatical forms, such as the kissed boy girl and were kissed the girl by the boy. It is the interaction of move-α with other syntactic principles that results in grammatical strings. It is responsible for the mapping between active and passive.

9. Some linguists, who devoted considerable attention to problems of analyzing sentences from a functional point of view, believe that a sentence contains a point of departure and a goal of discourse. The point of departure is equally present to the speaker and to the hearer—it is their starting point, the ground on which they meet. This is called the theme. The goal of discourse presents the very information that is to be imparted to the hearer. This is called the rheme. For example, in the sentence The man is coming, The man is the theme, and is coming is the rheme.
10. Etymologically speaking, discourse refers to spoken language while text means the written documents. In contemporary linguistics, these two terms can be used interchangeably. A text is best regarded as a semantic unit: a unit not of form but of meaning, which is not composed of sentences but is realized in sentences. Therefore a text is not judged by its size, it is something that differs from a sentence in kind. To make it clearer, a text is more than a random set of words; it should be overtly connected and covertly cohered: it shows connectedness.
11. ①Cohesion is a concept to do with discourse or text rather than with syntax, it refers to relations of meaning that exists within the text, and defines it as a text. Discourse /textual cohesiveness can be realized by employing various cohesion markers such as reference, substitution, ellipsis, conjunction and lexical collocation. ②The connectedness of a text depends not only on the cohesion of a text, but also on language users establishing coherence by actively relating the different information units in the text. The connectedness of discourse is a characteristic of the mental representation of the text rather than of the text itself. The connectedness conceived is often called coherence. Coherence phenomena may be of cognitive nature, but that their reconstruction is often based on linguistics signals in the text itself.

V. Essay questions

1. In Saussure's view, language is a system of signs, each of which consists of two parts: "signified" (concept) and "signifier"(sound image). And the relationship between these two parts is arbitrary. Therefore the linguist cannot attempt to explain individual signs in a piecemeal fashion. Instead he must try to find the value of a sign from its relations to others, or rather, its position in the system.

   The two principal types of relations which Saussure identified are Syntagmatic and Paradigmatic relations. The syntagmatic relation is a relation between one item and others in a sequence, or between elements which are all present. The paradigmatic (or associative) relation is a relation holding between elements replaceable with each other at a particular place in a structure, or between one element present and the others absent. They can substitute for each other without violating syntactic rules.

   The syntagmatic and paradigmatic relations together, like the two axes of a coordinate, determine the identity of a linguistic sign. Syntagms and paradigms provide a structural context within which signs make sense; they are the structural forms through which signs are organized into codes.

2. Through IC analysis, the internal structure of a sentence may be demonstrated clearly, and if there is any ambiguity, it could be revealed. For example, how the sentence "Leave the book on the shelf" is ambiguous could be shown after the IC analysis.

   However, there are also problems in IC analysis. First, at the beginning, some advocators insisted on binary divisions, that is, any construction, at any level, will be cut into two parts. But this is not always possible. For example, in the phrase "men and women", it is not appropriate to combine "and" with only the preceding part or only the succeeding part. Second, constructions with discontinuous constituents will pose technical problems for tree diagrams in IC analysis. For example, in "make it up" the phrasal verb "make up" is separated by a pronoun. Third, which is also the most serious problem; there are structural ambiguities which cannot be revealed by IC analysis, as shown in "the love of God". In IC analysis, the different relations of "God" to the word "love" cannot be shown which makes the expression ambiguous.

3. (1) (a) Times flies like an arrow.

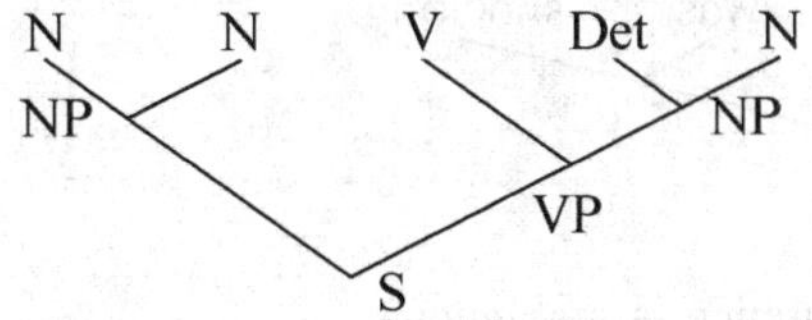

(b) Times flies like an arrow.

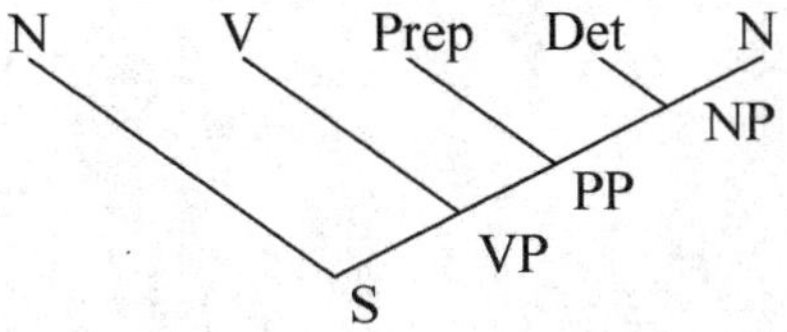

(2) (a) The word "down" could be seen as an adverbial, which means "from the higher position to a lower one".

(b) The word "down" could be also seen as a noun, which means "the fluffy feathers forming the first plumage of a young bird".

(3) (a) Old men and women will be served first.

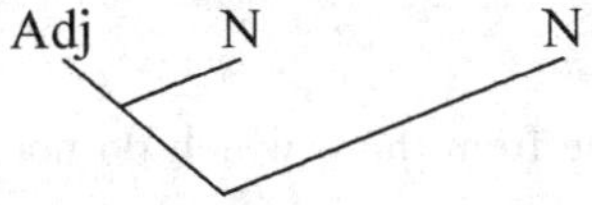

(b) Old men and women will be served first.

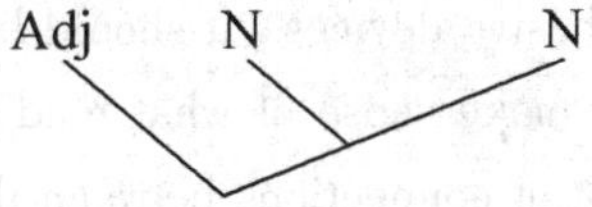

(4) (a) John passed the hammer and saw through the window.

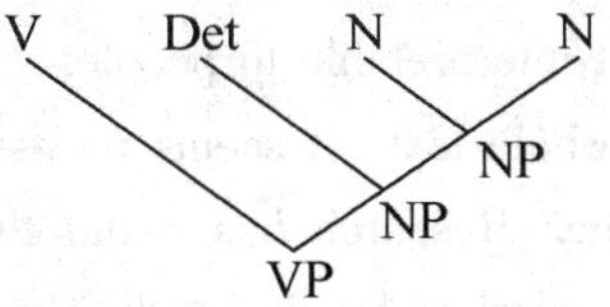

(b) John passed the hammer and saw through the window.

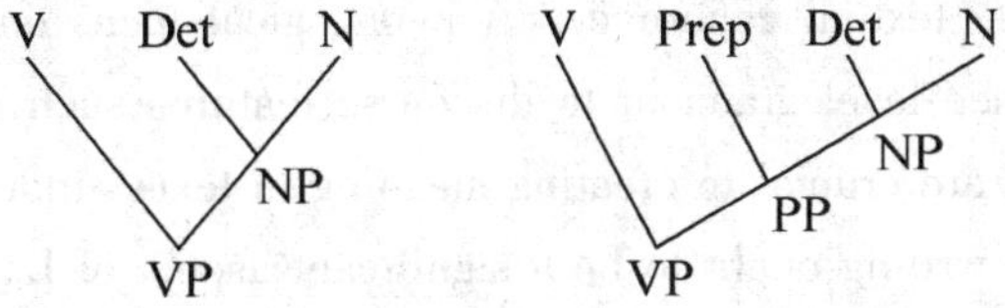

(5) (a) "Who" could be interpreted as the direct object of the verbal group "would like".

Therefore, the answer to this question could be "I would like John to visit".

(b) "Who" could also be interpreted as the direct object of the verb "visit". Thus, the answer to this question could be "I would like to visit John".

4. (1) This sentence is unambiguous since the structure can be illustrated as:

($_{NP}$ The children) ($_{VP}$put ($_{NP}$the toy) ($_{PP}$in ($_{NP}$the box.)))

(2)

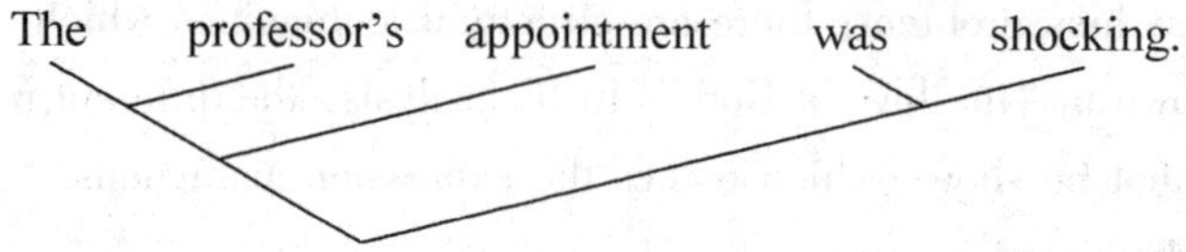

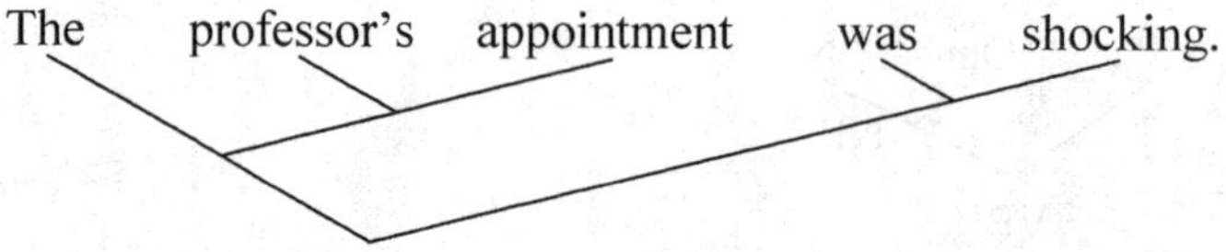

Therefore, it could be clear that the sentence is ambiguous.

(3)

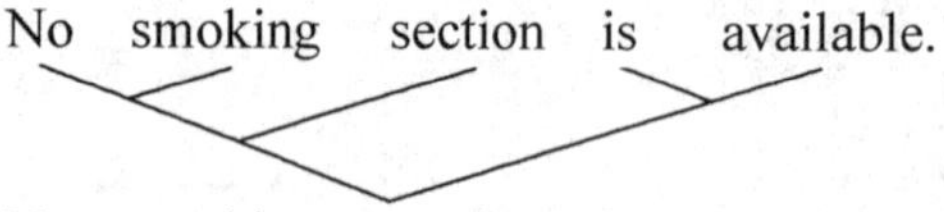

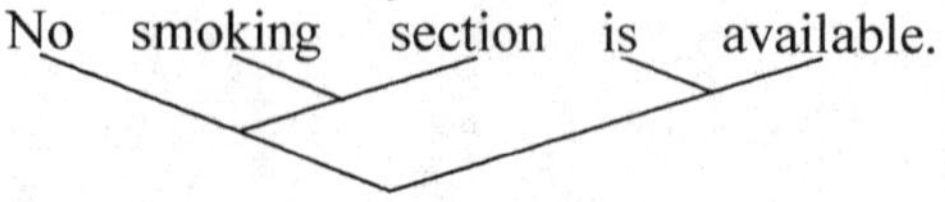

Thus, this sentence is ambiguous.

(4)

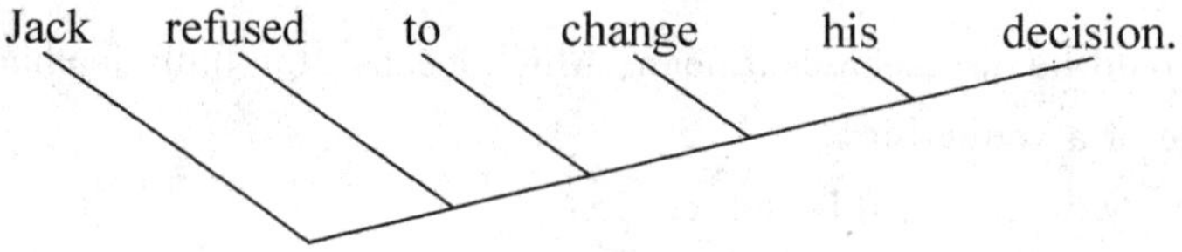

Thus, this sentence is unambiguous.

5. The factor to distinguish connected texts which make sense from those which do not is usually described as coherence. Coherence is traditionally described as the relationships that link the ideas in a text to create meaning for the readers, apart from cohesive devices. It should be noticed that cohesion by itself would not be sufficient to enable us to make sense of what read or hear; it is quite easy to create a highly cohesive text which has a lot of connections between the sentences, but which remains difficult to interpret. And coherence, as the invisible net of a text, performs a function of "connectedness" which makes the text interpretable to people.

Regarding the importance of coherence to a whole text, it seems necessary for a teacher of SFL to help students develop coherence in writing. Research has found that in their writing, ESL/EFL students focus almost exclusively on the word and sentence levels rather than the level of the whole discourse, that is, textual coherence. A pedagogical focus on coherence can shift students' attention from sentence-level grammar to discourse features such as textual structuring and propositional unity, which are crucial to creating meaning in texts. Indeed, helping students improve the coherence of their writing ought to be a significant aspect of L2 writing instruction.

To help students focus on coherence in writing, it is essential that teachers have a thorough understanding of what makes a text coherent. As is shown in the composition text books, it seems common to regard coherence simply as connectedness between sentences, use of explicit cohesive devices at the paragraph level, and use of connective devices such as pronouns, repetitive structures, and transitional markers. However, coherence should not be narrowed in terms of sentence-level connectedness and paragraph unity rather than discourse unity.

Thus, to help students create coherence in their writing, it is necessary for teachers to pay more attention in the broader sense of coherence.

6. The phenomenon described can be illustrated by the theory of cohesion and coherence in discourse analysis, especially the conjunctive kind of cohesive relation. Text processing requires inferences for establishing coherence between successive sentences. The achievement of coherence partly relies on the cohesive relationships within and between the sentences. Cohesion occurs where the interpretation of some elements in the discourse is dependent on that of another.

   It is realized partly through grammatical device and partly through lexical cohesion. Conjunction is one of the grammatically cohesive relations. It is based on the assumption that there are forms of systematic relationships between sentences in the linguistic system. Conjunction can be realized by some conjunctive words and some adverbs, such as *so*, *but*, *furthermore*, and so on. But in fact, the conjunctive relation between the discourses need not be realized by conjunctive words, as can be seen in these two examples.

   Yet it is not enough for the text to have connections between elements, there is also the coherence which distinguishes connected texts which make sense from those which do not. It enables people to make sense of what they read and hear, and then try to arrive at an interpretation which is in line with their experience of the way the world is. In fact, our ability to make sense of what we read is probably only a small part of that general ability we have to make sense of what we experience or perceive in the world.

   Therefore, by the coherence which helps us to connect the discourse with the world we experience, we the hearers will tend to make the discourse fit some situation which could accommodate all the details, and just as in the two examples, the causal conjunctive relations are established.

7. The goal of immediate constituent analysis is to analyze a linguistic expression into a hierarchically defined series of constituents. It is to break a syntactic unit and to describe these constitutes according to their forms and functions. Verbal structural descriptions, especially when we are dealing with longer syntactic units, such as sentences, can be rather lengthy and can vary in forms and styles. Therefore, linguists developed various ways to represent structural descriptions graphically, depicting constituent structure in a uniform and easily readable manner.

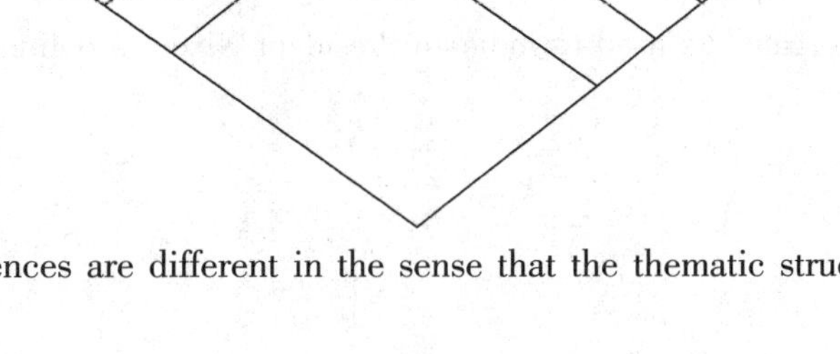

8. (1) These two sentences are different in the sense that the thematic structures are different. The

theme of a sentence is often the known information, which the sentence is mainly about. Sentence A provides some information about "his carelessness", since "his carelessness" serves as the theme. Whereas, Sentence B is a statement about "I", and from the remainder of the sentence the recipient could know some information about me.

(2) In sentence A, "A dagger" serves as the theme, with which the sentence could be seen as an answer of "What did the dagger do?" In sentence B, "The tourist" is treated as the given information, around which the sentence develops; thus, the corresponding question of this sentence as an answer could be "What happened to the tourist?"

(3) There are still differences of thematic structures between these two sentences, with the first one about "A hurricane" and the second one about "eight people". What's more, in sentence A, the verb "kill" emphasizes a direct relationship between the hurricane and the eight people, that is, it is the hurricane that caused the people to die. Whereas, in sentence B, a meaning like above is not entailed.

9. The most important use that we can make of corpora is that we can find very useful information about how language is actually used. Corpora usually provide a few types of information, and these types of information are helpful to our lexical studies.

(1) Frequency information.

Corpora can tell us how frequently certain language items or structures are used. This kind of information is useful when we try to select what to focus on, and decide what senses to focus on in lexical study.

(2) Context and co-text information.

Contexts are the situational environments in which language is used. Co-texts are the linguistic environments. Sometimes it is very difficult to tell the differences of two words or phrases which have similar meaning. However, if we look at the context and co-text in which they are used, the difference becomes clear.

(3) Grammatical information.

We usually refer to grammar books for grammatical information. However, what the corpora show is far more complicated than what grammar books tell about grammar. It helps to grasp lexical in a grammatical way.

(4) Collocation and phraseology information.

It is usually difficult for second and foreign language learners to learn which words are frequently used together, e. g. should we say make effort or take effort? A search in corpus will do the job. It's quick and efficient.

(5) Pragmatics information.

Information from corpora can tell us how language is actually used in communication. For example, "Watergate" is used to indicate President Nixon's political scandal.

第 5 章　意义

5.1　复习笔记

本章要点：

1. Meanings of “meaning”
   “意义”的意义
2. The referential theory
   指称理论
3. Sense relations
   涵义关系
4. Component analysis
   成分分析
5. Sentence meaning
   句子意义

常考考点：

语义学的定义；语义三角说；Leech 的七种意义分类；意义种类(传统、功能、语用)；词汇意义关系(同义、反义、下义)；识别各种实例中词与词的意义关系、以及句与句之间的蕴涵、前提、会话含义、同义、不相容、语义矛盾、语义反常等意义关系。用成分分析法分析同义词、反义词，句子意义的区别等。反义词的种类及举例。

本章内容索引：

Ⅰ. Semantics

Ⅱ. About Meanings

1. Meaning
2. Connotation
3. Denotation
4. Different types of meaning
   (1) Conceptual meaning
   (2) Associative meaning
   (3) Thematic meaning
5. Contextualism
6. Behaviorism

Ⅲ. The Referential Theory

1. Definition
2. Semantic Triangle
3. Sense and Reference
4. Sense Relations

(1) Synonymy
(2) Antonymy
(3) Hyponymy
(4) Polysemy
(5) Homonymy

Ⅳ. Componential Analysis

Ⅴ. Sentence Meaning vs. Utterance Meaning

Ⅵ. Semantic Relations between Sentences

1. Entailment
2. Presupposition
3. Synonymy
4. Inconsistency
5. Implicature

I. Semantics

Semantics is the study of meaning of linguistic units, especially the meaning of words and sentences.

II. About Meanings

1. Meaning

Meaning refers to what a language expresses about the world we live in or any possible or imaginary world.

2. Connotation

In the philosophers' usage, as opposed to denotation, connotation refers to the properties of the entity a word denotes.

3. Denotation

Denotation involves the relationship between a linguistic unit and the non-linguistic entity to which it refers. Thus it is equivalent to referential meaning.

【考点：名词解释 & 辨析——内涵与外延的区别，举例说明】

4. Different types of meaning (recognized by Leech, 1974)

(1) Conceptual meaning

Logical, cognitive, or denotative content.

(2) Associative meaning

① Connotative meaning: the communicative value an expression has by virtue of what language refers to.

② Social meaning: What a piece of language conveyed about the social circumstances of language use.

③ Affective meaning: the reflection of personal feelings of the speaker, including his attitude to something he is talking about.

I. 语义学

语义学是对语言单位，尤其是词和句子的意义的研究。

II. 意义

1. 意义

在语言学中，意义是指语言所表达的关于现实世界或者想象中的世界的想法。

2. 内涵

按照哲学界的用法，内涵和外延相对，指的是一个词所指称的实体的特性。

3. 外延

外延涉及语言单位跟非语言实体之间的关系。在这个意义上，它跟指称意义是一样的。

4. 意义的不同类型

(1) 概念意义

逻辑的、认知的、外延的内容。

(2) 联想意义

① 内涵意义：通过语言所指所传达的意义。

② 社会意义：所传达的关于语言使用的社会环境的意义。

③ 感情意义：所传达的关于说话人/作者感情、态度方面的意义。

④ Reflected meaning: It refers to what is communicated through association with another sense of the same expression. ⑤ Collocative meaning: The association a word has when it occurs in the environment of another word.	④ 反射意义：通过同一表达方式的其他意思所传达的意义。 ⑤ 搭配意义：通过词语的常用搭配而传达的意义。
(3) Thematic meaning What is communicated by the way in which the speaker or writer organize the message in terms of ordering, focus and emphasis. 【考点：简答——Leech 给出的七种意义及地位】	**(3) 主位意义** 通过顺序和重音这种组织信息的方式所传达的意义。主位意义是最边缘的意义，因为它只由单词的顺序以及它们的受强调程度决定。
5. Contextualism It is based on the presumption that one can derive meaning from, or reduce it to, observable context: the "situational context" and the "linguistic context". Utterances occur in particular spatiotemporal situations. The main components of the spatiotemporal situation include, apart from the place and time of the utterance, the speaker and the hearer; the actions they are performing at the time; the various external objects and events which exist in the situation. The "linguistic context" is sometimes called co-text. It is concerned with the probability of a word's co-occurrence or collocation with another word, which forms part of the meaning of the word. It is also concerned with the part of text that precedes and follows a particular utterance.	**5. 语境论** 语境论是建立在如下假设之上：意义源于语境，存在于语境。语境有两种：情景语境和上下文。所有的话语都是在特定的时空情景下产生的，除了话语产生的时间地点以外，情景因素还包括说话人和听话人、他们当时的行为以及情景中所存在的物与事。 上下文不仅涉及词与其他词的搭配，这种搭配构成词义的一部分，即搭配意义，它也涉及特定话语的前后部分。
6. Behaviorism Meaning is the "situation in which the speaker utters it and the response it calls forth in the hearer".	**6. 行为主义** 行为主义理论把意义定义为说话者说话的环境以及听者的反应。
Ⅲ. The Referential Theory **1. Definition** The theory of meaning that relates the meaning of a word to the thing it refers to or represent is called the referential theory.	**Ⅲ. 指称理论** **1. 定义** 把词语意义跟它所指称或所代表的事物联系起来的理论，叫做指称理论。
2. Semantic Triangle Ogden and Richards put forward this theory in *The Meaning of Meaning*. They believe that there is no direct relationship between a word and the things it refers to. It is mediated by concept, which is abstract with no existence in the material world and can only be sensed in our minds. The relation can be represented in a tree diagram as follows:	**2. 语义三角** 奥格登和理查兹在《意义的意义》一书中提出了语义三角的理论。他们认为词与所指事物之间没有直接的关系。它们是以概念为中介的。概念是抽象的，没有物质存在，只能通过我们的思维来感知。它们的关系可用图表表示如下：

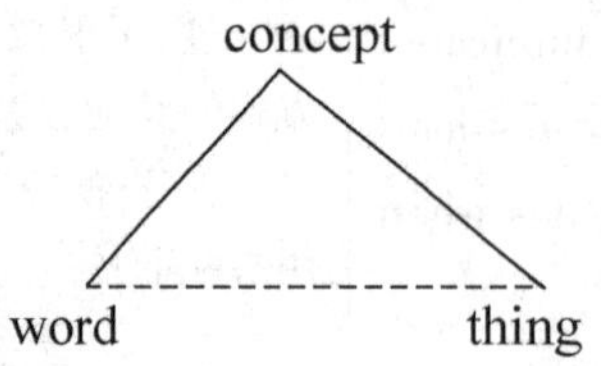

3. Sense and Reference

【考点：名词解释 & 辨析—Sense 和 Reference 的区别】

The distinction between sense and reference is similar to that between connotation and denotation. Sense refers to the abstract properties of an entity whereas reference refers to the concrete entities having these properties. That is to say, Leech's conceptual meaning includes two sides: sense and reference. Every word has a sense, but not every word has a reference.

4. Sense Relations

【考点：填空——判断两词的涵义关系：同义，反义，上下义】

(1) Synonymy

Synonymy is the technical name for the sameness relation. Total synonymy is rare. Synonyms are context-dependent, and they are always different in one way or another.

(2) Antonymy

Antonymy is the technical term for oppositeness relation. And it has main sub-types: gradable antonymy, complementary antonymy, and converse antonymy.

① Gradable antonymy. It is the commonest type of antonymy. They are gradable, namely, the members of a pair differ in terms of degree. The negation of one is not necessarily the assertion of the other.

② Complementary antonymy. In contrast to the gradable antonymy, the members of a pair in this type are complementary to each other. In other words, they cut a semantic field completely in half. Not only the assertion of one implies the denial of the other, but the denial of one also implies the assertion of the other.

【考点：简答——等级反义关系与互补反义关系的区别及特例】

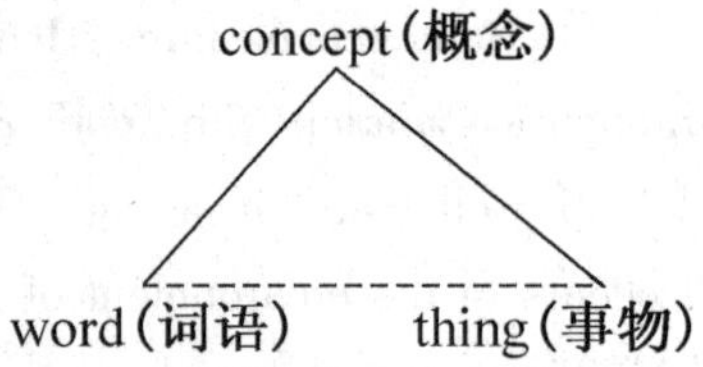

3. 涵义与指称

涵义与指称的区别类似于内涵和外延：前者指一个实体的抽象属性，后者指拥有这些属性的具体实体。换句话说，Leech 的概念意义包括两个方面：涵义和指称。然而涵义和指称还有其他的不同。在某种程度上，我们可以说每个单词都有涵义，但并非每个单词都有指称。

4. 涵义关系

(1) 同义关系

同义关系是相同关系的专业术语。完全的同义关系是很少的。所谓的同义词都是依赖语境的，它们总是在这方面或那方面有所不同。

(2) 反义关系

反义关系是对立关系的专业术语，它有三个主要次类：等级反义关系，互补反义关系和反向反义关系。

① 等级反义关系：等级反义关系是反义关系中最普通的一种。等级反义词是分等级的，也就是说，每个反义词的成员表示性质是程度上的差别。对一方的否定并不一定是对另一方的肯定。

② 互补反义关系：跟第一种反义词相反，这种反义词的成员彼此互补。也就是说它们把一个语义领域完全切分成两半。不但对一方的肯定意味着对另一方的否定，而且对一方的否定也意味着对另一方的肯定。

③ Converse antonymy. This is a special type of antonymy because its members do not constitute a positive or negative opposition. They show the reversal of a relationship between two entities. This type of antonymy is typically manifested in reciprocal social roles, kinship relations, temporal and spatial relations. It is in this sense that they are also called relational opposites. It always involves two entities, one presupposing the other. This is the main difference between this type and the previous two.

③ 反向反义关系：这是反义关系的一种特殊类型，因为其中的成员并不构成肯定或否定的对立，而只表现两实体间的一种反向关系。这种反义关系典型地表现在两两相对的社会角色、亲属关系、时间和空间系等方面；在这种意义上，它叫做关系对立。它总是涉及两个实体，一个预设了另一个。这是它和前面两种反义关系的主要区别。

(3) Hyponymy

Hyponymy is meaning inclusiveness or a matter of class membership. The upper term in this sense relation refers to superordinate, and the lower terms, the members, hyponyms. There are often several hyponyms in a superordinate and the members of the same class are co-hyponyms. Sometimes a superordinate may be a superordinate to itself. Superordinate or hyponyms may also be missing.

(3) 上下义关系

上下义关系是指意义内包关系或者说一种类和成员间的关系。位于这种意义关系上位的词语，即类名，叫做上坐标词；居于下位的是成员，叫做下义词。一个上坐标词通常有很多下义词。同类中的成员叫做同下义词。有时一个上坐标词同时是它自己的上坐标词，有时上坐标词会缺损。

(4) Polysemy

Different words can have the same or similar meaning, and the same word can have more than one meaning. This is what we call polysemy. A word having more than one meaning is called a polysemic word. Historically, polysemy can be regarded as the development or change of meaning.

(4) 多义关系

不同的词可以有相同或相似的意义，同一个词也可以有一个以上的意义，这就是我们所说的多义关系。具有多义关系的词叫做多义词。从历史上看，一词多义可以看作是词义的发展或变化。

(5) Homonymy

Homonymy refers to the phenomenon that words having different meanings have the same form, i. e. different words are identical in sound or spelling, or in both. When two words are identical in sound, they are called homophones. When two words are identical in spelling, they are homographs. When two words are identical in both sound and spelling, they are called complete homonyms.

(5) 同音/同形异义关系

同音/同形异义关系指的是不同意义的词具有相同的形式这样一种现象，即不同的词发音或者拼写相同，或者发音与拼写都相同。发音相同的词称为同音异义词；拼写相同的词称为同形异义词。发音和拼写都一样的词叫做完全同音同形异义词。

Ⅳ. Componential Analysis

Ⅳ. 成分分析法

【考点：填空——根据成分判定单词；简答——成分分析法的作用】

The meaning of a word is an analyzable unit. It can be regarded as a complex composed of different semantic features, with smaller semantic units than the word meaning. By analyzing the semantic components of a word in this way, sense relations can be better explained. Componential analysis is a

词义并非不可分析的整体。它可以看作由不同语义特征组成的复合体，有比词义更小的语义单位。通过这样来分析一个词的语义成分，能够更好地说明涵义关系。语义分析是词义分析法。这种方法所给予的观点是：词义可以分成不同

way proposed to analyze word meaning. The approach is based upon the belief that the meaning of a word can be dissected into meaning components, called semantic features. Plus and minus signs are used to indicate whether a certain semantic feature is present or absent in the meaning of a word, and these feature symbols are written in capitalized letters. For example, the word "woman" is analyzed as comprising the features of +HUMAN, +ADULT, +ANIMATE, +FEMALE.

的意义成分，叫做语义特征。这和把音位分析成更小的、被称之为区别性特征的成分的方法是一样的。加号或减号用来表示词义中是否具有某种语义特征，这些语义特征的标记通常以大写字母写出。例如"woman"这个词可以认为包含下列特征：

+HUMAN, +ADULT,
+ANIMATE, +FEMALE

V. Sentence Meaning vs. Utterance Meaning

A sentence is a grammatical concept, and the meaning of which is often studied as the abstract, intrinsic property of the sentence itself in terms of a predication. But if we think of a sentence as what people actually utter in the course of communication, it becomes an utterance, and it should be considered in the situation in which it is actually uttered (or used). So, the meaning of a sentence is abstract, and decontextualized, and that of an utterance is concrete, and context-dependent. Utterance meaning is based on sentence meaning; it is the realization of the abstract meaning of a sentence in a real situation of communication, or simply in a context. The utterance meaning of the sentence varies with the context in which it is uttered.

V. 句子意义与话语意义

句子是一个语法概念，句子意义经常被看作是句子本身所具有的抽象的内在特征。但是如果把句子看作是人们在交往过程中实际所说的话，它就成了话语，话语应在其实际运用的场景中予以考虑。因此句子意义是抽象的，是不依赖语境的；而话语意义是具体的，是依赖语境的。话语意义基于句子意义，是句子意义在特定交际情境或者语境中的具体体现。话语意义会随着语境的变化而变化。

▼ Cognitive Semantics

The idea that the meaning of a sentence depends on the meaning of the words that make it up and how they are combined is often referred to as the principle of compositionality. Cognitive semantics is a promising semantic theory along this line of thinking, though it is really a cluster of many partially overlapping approaches to semantics than a single well-defined theory.

Based on generative semantics, linguists adhere to the basic idea that language is all about meaning. There are four specific tenets: linguistic meaning is perspectival; linguistic meaning is dynamic and flexible; linguistics meaning is encyclopedic and non-autonomous; and linguistics meaning is based on usage and experience.

认知语义学

一个句子的意思取决于组成该句子的单词的意思以及它们的结合方式，这一观点通常被称为语义合成性原则。认知语义学的发展也是基于该原则。

以生成语义学为基础，认知语义学家坚持语言本身就是关于意义的这一基本观点。在认知语义学中，有四个基本原则：语言的意义是可透视的，语言的意义是动态灵活的；语言的意义是全面的，非自动的；语言的意义是基于用法和经验的。

Ⅵ. Semantic Relations between Sentences

【考点：分析句子的语义关系——蕴含，预设，同义，矛盾】

1. Entailment

If that one sentence is true gives us certain knowledge of the truth of the second sentence, then the first sentence entails the second. So entailment is a type of meaning-dependence between one sentence and another. Entailment is concerned with the meaning of the sentence itself. It does not depend on the context in which a sentence is used. In terms of truth value, the following relationships exist between the two sentences if a entails b:

When a is true, b is necessarily true;

When b is false, a is false;

When a is false, b may be true or false;

When b is true, a may be true.

2. Presupposition

【考点：根据所给句子推出其预设条件】

The speaker or writer always assumes that the hearer/reader already knows something of what he is going to say or write. This "something" often becomes the presupposition of a sentence. In terms of truth value, the following relationships exist between two sentences:

When a is true, b is necessarily true;

When a is false, b is still true;

When b is true, a can either be true or false;

When b is false, no truth value can be said about.

3. Synonymy

Two sentences may have the same meaning, that is, in terms of truth value, a has the same truth value as b: If a is true, b is true; also if a is false, b is false; and vice versa.

4. Inconsistency

We can have a complex but very clear definition of inconsistency like this: a is inconsistent with b: If a is true, b is false; also, if b is true, a is false. This relationship is called inconsistency or contradiction, because the truth of one sentence contradicts the truth of the other.

Ⅵ. 句子之间的语义关系

1. 蕴含

如果知道一个句子的真假能够判断另一个句子的真假，那么第一个句子就蕴含了第二个句子。蕴含只与句子自身的意义相关。它不依赖于句子所处的语境。从真值角度看，如果a蕴含b，那么它们存在着如下的真值关系：

当a为真时，b也一定为真；

当b为假时，a为假；

当a为假时，b或真或假；

当b为真时，a或真或假。

2. 预设

说话者或作者通常会假定听众或读者对其所讲的或所写的已经有了一定的了解。这种东西就成为了一个句子预设的部分。在真值方面，它们存在着如下关系：

当a为真时，b也一定为真；

当a为假时，b仍为真；

当b为真时，a或真或假；

当b为假时，无真假值可言。

3. 同义关系

两个句子拥有同样的意思，即在真值方面，a与b真值相同。若a为真，b亦为真；若a为假，b亦为假；反之亦然。

4. 自相矛盾

我们可以对自相矛盾有这样一个复杂但又非常清晰的定义：a与b自相矛盾，即若a为真，b为假；同样当b为真，a亦为假。这种关系就叫做不一致或自相矛盾，因为两个句子之间的真值互相矛盾。

5. Implicature	**5. 含意**
Implicature is also a type of semantic relations between two sentences. For example, if we can draw conclusion b from sentence a, here b is the implicature of a. This is generally understood to be a relation of pragmatic implication, defined in terms of the speaker's and the hearer's assumptions and beliefs.	会话含义是另一种句子之间的语义关系。例如，如果我们能从句子a中得到结论b，那b就是a的含意，通常是一种语用含义的关系。

5.2 考研真题与典型题详解

Ⅰ. Fill in the blanks.

1. According to G Leech, ________ meaning is the communicative value an expression has by virtue of what it refers to, over and above its purely conceptual content.（北二外 2006 研）
2. According to G Leech, ________ meaning refers to logic, cognitive, or denotative content.（北二外 2005 研）
3. According to G. Leech, ________ meaning refers to what is communicated of the feelings and attitudes of the speaker/writer.（北二外 2007 研）
4. The theory of meaning which relates the meaning of a word to the thing it refers to, or stands for, is known as the ________ theory.（中山大学 2008 研）
5. ________ is the technical name for the sameness relation.（北二外 2007 研）
6. Terms like "apple", "banana" and "pear" are ________ of the term "fruit".（北二外 2007 研）
7. "Mary gave a book to Jack" is synonymous with "Jack ________ a book from Mary."（北二外 2005 研）
8. Terms like "rolling pin" and "ladle" are ________ of the term "kitchen implements."（北二外 2005 研）
9. Antonyms like "husband" v. "wife" are ________ antonyms.（北二外 2003 研）
10. Terms like "desk" and "stool" are ________ of the term "furniture".（北二外 2003 研）
11. ________ = PARENT(x, y)&MALE(x)（北二外 2005 研）
12. ________ = CHILD (x, y) & MALE (x)（北二外 2006 研）
13. In their book ________ written in 1923, C. K. Ogden and I. A. Richards presented a "representative list of the main definitions which reputable students of meaning have favoured." There are 16 major categories of them, with sub-categories all together, numbering 22.（中山大学 2011 研）
14. Predication analysis is to break down predications into their constituents: ________ and ________.

Ⅱ. Multiple Choice

1. When the word "root" means "part of plant that keeps it firmly in the soil and absorbs water and food from the soil", the meaning is ________ meaning.（北二外 2004 研）
   A. connotative　　B. conceptual　　C. reflected
2. ________ deals with the relationship between the linguistic element and the non-linguistic world experience.（西安交大 2008 研）

A. Reference B. Concept C. Semantics D. Sense

3. Which of the following is NOT included in G. Leech's seven types of meaning?（大连外国语学院 2008 研）

A. Connotative meaning. B. Denotative meaning.

C. Conceptual meaning.

4. According to C. Ogden and I. Richards, ______ is regarded as the crucial intermediary between ______ and ______.（西安外国语学院 2006 研）

A. symbol ... referent ... thought

B. referent ... thought ... symbol

C. thought ... symbol ... referent

5. There are generally three kinds of sense relations recognized, sameness relation, oppositeness relation and inclusiveness relation. They are represented by ______ respectively.（大连外国语学院 2008 研）

A. synonymy, antonymy, and hyponymy

B. synonymy, hyponymy, and antonymy

C. antonymy, synonymy, and hyponymy

6. Bird and cuckoo have the sense relation of hyponymy. Which of the following pairs of words has the same sense relation?（对外经贸 2005 研）

A. Vowel and consonant B. Mouth and tongue

C. Lexicon and word D. Number and gender

7. By componential analysis, BECOME(x, (~ALIVE(x))) is an explanation of ______.（西安外国语学院 2006 研）

A. die B. dead C. kill D. killed

8. The sense relationship between "John plays the piano" and "John plays a musical instrument" is ______.（北二外 2004 研）

A. synonymy B. antonymy C. entailment

9. Which of the following are gradable antonyms?

A. good and bad B. male and female

C. apple and fruit D. buy and sell

10. Conceptual meaning is not ______

A. affective B. cognitive C. logic D. denotative

11. When the truth of sentence (a) guarantees the truth of sentence (b), and the falsity of sentence (b) guarantees the falsity of sentence (a), we can say that ______.

A. sentence (a) presupposes sentence (b)

B. sentence (a) entails sentence (b)

C. sentence (a) is inconsistent with sentence (b)

D. sentence (a) contradicts sentence (b)

12. "Socrates is a man" is a case of ______.

A. two-place predicate B. one-place predicate

C. two-place argument D. one-place argument

Ⅲ. True or False

1. In the sentence "Money is often said to be the root of all evil", "root" is used in its conceptual meaning.（北二外 2007 研）
2. After comparing "They stopped at the end of the corridor." with "At the end of the corridor, they stopped", you may find some difference in meaning, and the difference can be interpreted in terms of collocative meaning.（北二外 2006 研）
3. Conceptual meaning overlaps to a large extent with the notion of "reference".（北二外 2005 研）
4. When you use your own sentence with a meaning other than the conceptual, the meaning is sometimes referred to as speaker's meaning, or contextual meaning.（大连外国语学院 2008 研）
5. The theory of meaning which relates the meaning of a word to the thing it refers to, or stands for, is known as the referential theory.（北二外 2006 研）
6. Reference is one of the rarely used cohesive devices.（南开大学 2005 研）
7. Odgen and Richards argue that the relation between a word and a thing it refers to is not direct.（南开大学 2004 研）
8. "Tulip", "rose" and "violet" are all included in the notion of "flower". Therefore they are superordinates of "flower".（北二外 2006 研）
9. The idea that the meaning of a sentence depends on the meanings of the constituent words and the way they are combined is usually known as the principle of COMPOSITIONALITY.（大连外国语学院 2008 研）
10. The two words borrow and lend are antonyms but the two sentences "Jan lent some money to Jack" and "Jack borrowed some money from Jan" are synonymous.（北二外 2010 研）
11. All the words in a language can be used to refer, but only some have senses.（北二外 2010 研）

Ⅳ. Explain the following terms.

1. Conceptual meaning（四川大学 2010 研；武汉大学 2007 研；上海交大 2006 研）
2. Contextual meaning（浙江大学 2005 研）
3. Concatenation（四川大学 2006 研）
4. Denotation（南开大学 2004 研；中国海洋大学 2021 研）
5. Semantic Triangle（大连外国语学院 2008 研）
6. Lexical relations（上海交大 2006 研）
7. Homonymy（上海交大 2007 研）
8. Relational opposites（武汉大学 2005 研）
9. Synonymy（西安交大 2008 研）
10. Componential analysis（浙江大学 2005 研；北航 2008 研；南京师范大学 2021 研）
11. Entailment（武汉大学 2006 研）
12. Presupposition（武汉大学 2004 研）
13. Polysemy（北外 2010 研）
14. linguistic variable(北外 2011 研）

Ⅴ. Short answer questions

1. What is the referential theory of meaning?（北交大 2005 研）
2. What are the three kinds of antonyms?（武汉大学 2004 研）

3. What is your opinion on "true synonymy is non-existent"?（四川大学 2006 研）
4. How would you describe the oddness of the following sentences, using semantic features?（浙江大学 2004 研）
   (a) The television drank my water.
   (b) His dog writes poetry.
5. Do you think there are true synonyms in English? Why?（厦门大学 2010 研）
6. What is the difference between meaning, concept, connotation, and denotation?
7. What is sense and what is reference? How are they related?
8. How do you understand the cognitive semantics?

Ⅵ. Essay questions

1. Please list and explain the 7 types of meaning recognized by G. Leech.（南开大学 2004 研）
2. The British linguist F. R. Palmer argues that "there is no absolute distinction between gradable antonyms and complementary antonyms." Do you believe so? Support your view with examples.（南开大学 2007 研）
3. Words in our mental lexicon are known to be related to one another. Discuss the relationships between words, using examples from the English language.（北外 2003 研）
4. Categorize the following pairs: child-kid, alive-dead, big-small, husband-wife.
5. How many semantic relations are there among sentences? Give examples.

参考答案及解析

Ⅰ. Fill in the blanks.

1. Connotative
   （利奇认为内涵意义是指通过语言所指传达的意义，是位于纯粹的概念意义之上的。）
2. Conceptual
   （利奇认为概念意义是指逻辑的、认知的、外延的内容。）
3. Affective
   （利奇认为感情意义是指所传达的关于说话人/作者感情、态度方面的意义。）
4. Referential
   （把词语意义跟它所指称或所代表的事物联系起来的理论，叫做指称理论。）
5. Synonymy
   （同义关系是相同关系的专业术语，完全的同义关系是很少的。所谓的同义词都是依赖语境的，它们总是在这方面或那方面有所不同。）
6. hyponyms
   （上下义关系是指意义内包关系或者说一种类和成员间的关系。题中"苹果，香蕉，梨"都是"水果"的下义词。）
7. received
   （参考"同义词"的定义。）
8. hyponyms
   （"擀面杖"和"勺子"都属于"厨房用具"的下义词。）
9. converse

（反向反义关系是反义关系的一种特殊类型，典型地表现在两两相对的社会角色、亲属关系、时间和空间等方面；丈夫与妻子的关系属于此种反义关系。）

10. (co-)hyponyms

（在上下义关系中，一个上坐标词通常有很多下义词。同类中的成员叫做同下义词。题中“桌子”和“凳子”都是“家具”的下义词。）

11. father = PARENT(x, y)&MALE(x)

（同时满足“父母亲”和“男性”的条件的只能是“父亲”。）

12. Son

（同时满足“子女”和“男性”的条件的只能是“儿子”。）

13. The Meaning of Meaning

（C. K. Ogden and I. A. Richards 在《意义的意义》一书中展现了卓越的学生当时倾向的有代表性的定义。）

14. Argument; predicate

（述谓结构分析把述谓结构分析分割为论元和谓词。其中谓词是控制论元的主要要素。）

Ⅱ. Multiple Choice

1. B （概念意义指逻辑的、认知的、外延的内容，题中对“root”的解释正是此项。）
2. A （指称指拥有某些属性的具体实体，它处理的是语言元素与非语言世界的关系。）
3. B （利奇提出的 7 种意义分别为概念意义，内涵意义，社会意义，感情意义，反射意义，搭配意义和主位意义。）
4. C （奥格登和理查兹在《意义的意义》一书中提出了语义三角的理论。他们认为词与所指事物之间没有直接的关系。它们是以概念为中介的。）
5. A （有三种涵义关系，分别为同义关系，反义关系和上下义关系。）
6. B （布谷鸟是鸟的下义词，舌是口腔的下义词。）
7. A （表达式的意思是 X 变成无生命的，所以选项 A 是正确的。）
8. C （如果知道一个句子的真假能够判断另一个句子的真假，那么第一个句子就蕴含了第二个句子。题中如果第一个句子为真，则第二句为真；第一句为假，第二句或真或假。所以第一句蕴含第二句。）
9. A （等级反义词是分等级的，对一方的否定并不一定是对另一方的肯定。说一个事物不好，并不一定是说很坏。B、C、D 项分别为互补反义关系、上下义关系和反向反义关系。）
10. A （概念意义是逻辑的、认知的、外延的内容，而不是感情的。）
11. B （如果 a 蕴含 b，那么它们存在着如下的真值关系：当 a 为真时，b 也一定为真；当 b 为假时，a 为假。）
12. B （这句话中，谓词是 man，论元是 Socrates。可见只有一个论元，所以是一元谓词。）

Ⅲ. True or False

1. F （这里的“root”是用了它的联想意义中的内涵义，不是概念意义。）
2. F （搭配意义是通过词语的常用搭配而传达的意义。主位意义是通过顺序和重音这种信息的方式所传达的意义。显然这里用的是主位意义。）
3. T （概念意义是逻辑的、认知的、外延的内容。指称理论指把词语意义跟它所指称或所代表的事物联系起来，二者有其相似之处。）

4. T （有时句子的意思要根据说话人想表达的意思而定，这也可称为语境意。）
5. T （把词语意义跟它所指称或所代表的事物联系起来的理论，叫做指称理论。）
6. F （指称是一种常用的衔接手段。）
7. T （奥格登和理查兹在《意义的意义》一书中提出了语义三角的理论。他们认为词与所指事物之间没有直接的关系。它们是以概念为中介的。）
8. F （位于上下义这种意义关系上位的词语，即类名，叫做上坐标词；居于下位的是成员，叫做下义词。这里的上标词应该是“flower”。）
9. T （组合性原则是指句子的意思要由组成句子的各个成分和各成分的组合方式来决定。）
10. T （borrow 与 lend 是关系反义词。第一个句子的意思是 Jan 借给 Jack 一些钱，第二个句子是 Jack 借了 Jan 的一些钱，所以尽管这两个词是反义词，但这两个句子表达的是一个意思。）
11. F （一种语言中的所有词都有涵义但并不是每个词都有指称。）

Ⅳ. Explain the following terms.

1. According to Leech, conceptual meaning refers to the logical, cognitive, or denotative content of the meaning of a word. It is concerned with the relationship between a word and the thing it refers to. For example, the conceptual meaning of “human” is any person such as John and Mary.
2. It is also called speaker’s meaning, or utterance meaning, which is more closely related to the context. For example, when a person says “My bag is heavy”, what he actually means may be asking the hearer to help him carry the bag.
3. What makes a word separate from other words is that all the letters are lined up together with no intervening spaces. That is, in a word, all letters are concatenated. Sometimes new words can be made by concatenating two existing words—for example, “airline” is a concatenation of the words “air” and “line” into a new word.
4. It means the core sense of a word or a phrase that relates it to phenomena in the real world. In the case of linguistic signs, the denotative meaning is what the dictionary attempts to provide. It is the literal meaning of a word, the dictionary meaning, opposite to connotation.
5. Ogden and Richards presented the classic “Semantic Triangle” as manifested in the following diagram, in which the “symbol” or “form” refers to the linguistic elements (word, sentence, etc.), the “referent” refers to the object in the world of experience, and “thought” or “reference” refers to concept or notion. According to this view, there is no direct link between symbol and referent, that is, between language and the world. The link is via thought, the concept in our minds.

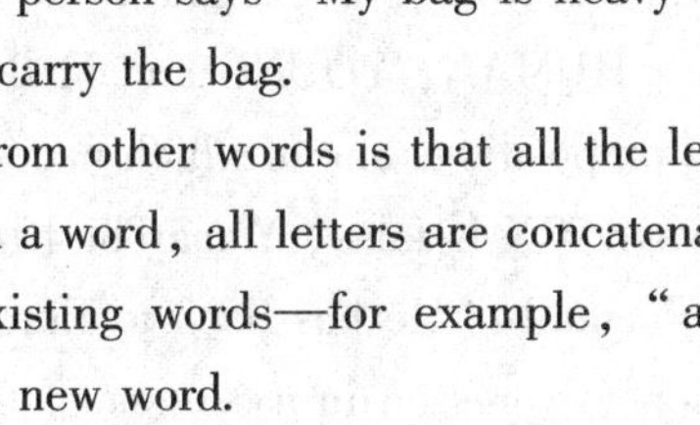

6. There are several types of lexical relations concerning the sense of the words. Those are synonymy, antonymy, hyponymy, polysemy, homonymy, and so on. (a) Synonymy refers to the sameness relation; “autumn” and “fall” are synonyms, for example. (b) Antonymy refers to the op-

positeness relation; for example, "buy" and "sell" are antonyms. (c) Hyponymy refers to the inclusiveness relation; for example, "apple" is a hyponym of "fruit". (d) Polysemy means one word that has more than one related meaning, and "bank", as an example, is a polysemous word. (e) Homonymy refers to the relation of two different words which are identical either in sound, or spelling, or both, such as "bow" (bau) and "bow" (bəu).

7. In any language there are words which have the same linguistic form but are different in meaning. These words are called homonyms. For example, bank (of a river), and bank (financial institution).
8. This is a type of antonymy, in which the members of a pair do not constitute a positive-negative opposition. They show the reversal of a relationship between two entities. For example, "buy/sell" is such a pair. X buys something from Y means Y sells something from X.
9. It is the technical name for the sameness relation. Two or more forms with very closely related meanings are synonyms, which are often, but not always, intersubstitutable in sentences. For example, in English "hide" and "conceal" in "He hid the money under the bed." and "He concealed the money under the bed". Often one word may be more appropriate than another in a particular situation, e. g. "conceal" is more formal than "hide".
10. It refers to a semantic approach which defines the meaning of a lexical element in terms of semantic components, or semantic features. For example, the meaning of the word *boy* may be analyzed into three components: HUMAN, YOUNG and MALE.
11. It refers to the relation between propositions one of which necessarily follows from the other. If X is true, Y is necessarily true, and if X is false, Y may be true or false. For example, the sentence "He has been to France" entails "He has been to Europe".
12. A presupposition is a proposition (expressed in a sentence) that is assumed to be true in order to judge the truth or falsity of another sentence. For example, John didn't pass chemistry presupposes that John took chemistry.
13. Polysemy means a single word having several or many meanings. According to Crystal: Polysemy is a term used in semantic analysis to refer to a lexical item which has a range of different meanings. Polysemic words are signs of an advanced culture. Polysemy is also an essential feature of a language's economy and efficiency.
14. Linguistic variables are those where the meaning remains constant but form varies like cat and pussy have the same social meaning but different from. So far as pronunciation is concerned house [h] and with [h] has same social meaning with different pronunciations. Here variables are just the tools to analyze the language to set social dimensional society.

V. Short answer questions

1. The theory of meaning which relates the meaning of a word to the thing it refers to, or stands for, is known as the referential theory. For example, when we say "M. A. K Halliday", we do use "M. A. K Halliday" to mean a particular person. This theory could explain the significance of expressions in terms of their having been conventionally associated with things or states of affairs in the world, and it could explain a human being's understanding a sentence in terms of that person's knowing what the sentence's component words refer to.

2. The three kinds of antonyms are gradable antonyms, complementary antonyms and converse antonyms. Gradable antonyms refer to antonyms that differ in terms of degree. For example, *good* and *bad*. Complementary antonyms are a pair of antonyms complementary to each other: not only the assertion of one means the denial of the other; the denial of one also means the assertion of the other, such as *male* and *female*. Converse antonyms do not constitute a positive-negative opposition; they only show the reversal of a relationship between two entities, such as *husband* and *wife*.
3. Generally speaking, synonyms are the words which have different forms but similar meaning. There are several types of synonyms: dialectal synonyms, such as *lift/elevator*, *flat/apartment*; synonyms of different styles, as shown in *gentleman/guy*; synonyms of different registers, such as *salt/sodium chloride*; synonyms differing in affective meaning, such as *attract/seduce*; synonyms differing in collocation, such as *beautiful/handsome*, *able/capable*.
4. (a) The verb *drink* represents a behavior of the animate beings, therefore, it is required that the subject of this verb should have a semantic feature as (+ANIMATE), however, the word *television*, which is in position of subject, has an opposite feature: (–ANIMATE). That's why such a collocation results in oddness.

   (b) The action of writing poetry is normally one which only human beings could do, therefore, the subject is required to have a semantic feature as (+HUMAN); however, the word *dog* in the subject position is featured as (–HUMAN). Therefore, the sentence is odd.
5. Synonymy is the technical name for the sameness relation. It is used to mean sameness or close similarity of meaning. Total synonymy is rare. The so-called synonyms are all context dependent. They all differ in one way or another.

   There are no real synonyms, because two or more words named synonyms are expected without exception to differ from one another in one of the following aspects:

   (1) in shade of meaning (finish, complete, close, conclude);

   (2) in stylistic meaning (buy, purchase);

   (3) in emotive (or affective) meaning (economical, stingy);

   (4) in range of use or collocative meaning (accuse, charge);

   (5) in British and American English usages (autumn, fall).

   For example, they may differ in style. In the context "Little Tom ________ a toy bear", here *buy* is more appropriate than purchase. Because *purchase* is more formal than *buy*.
6. Meaning refers to the association of language symbols with the real world. There are many types of meanings according to different approaches. Concept is the impression of objects in people's mind; connotation, meaning the properties of the entity a word denotes, is the implied meaning, similar to implication and implicature; denotation, like sense, is not directly related to objects, but makes the abstract assumption of the real world. For example, the denotation of human is any person such as John and Mary, and its connotation is "biped" "featherless" "rational" etc.
7. Sense is concerned with the inherent meaning of the linguistic form. It is the collection of all the features of the linguistic form; it is abstract and de-contextualized. For example the sense of the word "dog" is "a domesticated canine mammal, occurring in many breeds that show a great do-

mesticated canine mammal, occurring in many breeds that show a great variety in size and form". It does not refer to any particular dog that exists in the real world, but applies to any animal that meets the features described in the definition.

Reference means what a linguistic form refers to in the real, physical world; it deals with the relationship between the linguistic unit and the non-linguistic world of experience. If we say "The dog is barking", we must be talking about a certain dog existent in the situation. The word "dog" refers to a dog known to both the speaker and the hearer. This is the reference of the word "dog" in this particular situation.

It is a matter of the relationship between the form and the reality.

8. (1) The idea that the meaning of a sentence depends on the meanings of the constituent words and the way they are combined is usually known as the principle of compositionality. Cognitive semantics is a promising semantic theory along this line of thinking, though it is really a cluster of many partially overlapping approaches to semantics than a single well-defined theory. (2) Growing out of the tradition of generative semantics, linguists in this group maintain a foundational point that language is all about meaning. There are four specific tenets: linguistic meaning is perspectival; linguistic meaning is dynamic and flexible; linguistics meaning is encyclopedic and non-autonomous; and linguistics meaning is based on usage and experience.

VI. Essay questions

1. The seven types of meaning were first postulated by G. Leech. They are respectively illustrated as follows:

(1) Conceptual meaning, which refers to logical, cognitive, or denotative content. This type of meaning is "denotative" in that it is concerned with the relationship between a word and the thing it denotes, or refers to.

(2) Connotative meaning, what is communicated by virtue of what language refers to. It refers to some additional, especially emotive, meaning.

(3) Social meaning, referring to what is communicated of the social circumstances of language use.

(4) Affective meaning, which refers to what is communicated of the feelings and attitudes of the speaker/writer.

(5) Reflected meaning, which refers to what is communicated through association with another sense of the same expression.

(6) Collocative meaning, what is communicated through association with words which tend to occur in the environment of another word.

The five types of meanings from (2) to (6) are collectively known as Associative meaning in the sense that an elementary associated theory of mental connections is enough to explain their use.

(7) Thematic meaning, what is communicated by the way in which the message is organized in terms of order and emphasis. It is more peripheral since it is only determined by the order of the words in a sentence and the different prominence they each receive.

2. I would prefer not to agree with this argument that there is no absolute distinction between grad-

able antonyms and complementary antonyms. The common way to distinguish gradable antonyms and complementary antonyms could be to see the forms they could occur: adjective gradable antonyms could be modified by "very", and could have comparative forms and superlative forms; while the complementary counterparts could not. For example, we could say "very warm", "warmer", but we could not say "very absent" or "more absent" (absent here is opposed to present).

The expressions with "very" or "more" modifying complementary antonyms are in fact not true comparatives and have a clear indication of either this one or the other one in the pair of complementary antonyms. For example, expression like "He is more dead than alive" actually means "It is more correct to say that he is dead than to say he is alive". And this sentence could only be used when he is still alive; after all, we do not say someone is more dead than other.

3. Words are in different sense relations with each other in our mental lexicon. There are generally three kinds of sense relationships recognized, namely, sameness relation, oppositeness relation and inclusiveness relation. Synonymy refers to the sameness or close similarity of meaning, and words that are close in meaning are called synonyms. Total synonymy is rare, generally synonyms can be divided into several groups: dialectal synonyms like British English *autumn* and American English *fall*; stylistic synonyms like *child* and *offspring*; synonyms that differ in their emotive or evaluative meaning like *collaborate* and *accomplice*; collocational synonyms like *accuse* and *charge*; semantically different synonyms like *amaze* and *astound*. Antonymy refers to oppositeness of meaning. There are three main sub-types: gradable antonymy in which the members of a pair differ in terms of degree, like *long* and *short*; complementary antonymy which is a matter of either one or the other, like *alive* and *dead*; converse antonymy which shows the reversal of a relationship between two entities, like *teacher* and *student*. Hyponymy refers to the sense relation between a more general, more inclusive word and a more specific word. The word that is more general in meaning is called the superordinate, and the more specific words are called its hyponyms. Hyponyms of the same superordinate are co-hyponyms to each other. For example under the superordinate *flower* there are many hyponyms like *rose*, *tulip*, *lily*, etc. These members of the same flower class are co-hyponyms.

   Another common relationship is homonymy which refers to the phenomenon that words having different meaning have the same form, i. e. , different words are identical in sound or spelling, or in both. When two words are identical in sound, they are homophones, like *knight* and *night*; when two words are identical in spelling, they are homographs, like *lead v.* and *lead n.*; when two words are identical in both sound and spelling, they are complete homonyms, like *fast adj.* and *fast v.*

4. Child-kid can be categorized under synonymy, alive-dead complementary antonymy, old-young gradable antonymy, and husband-wife converse antonymy.

   Synonymy is the technical term for the sameness relation.

   The members of a pair of complementary antonymy are complementary to each other. They divide up the whole of a semantic field completely, which means not only the assertion of one means the denial of the other, and the denial of one also means the assertion of the other.

Pairs of words of gradable antonymy have three characteristics: (1) they are gradable—the members of a pair differ in terms of degree. As such, they can be modified by "very". And they may have comparative and superlative degrees. (2) Antonyms of this kind are graded against different norms. The criterion varies with the object described. (3) One member of a pair, usually the term for the higher degree, serves as the cover term.

Converse antonymy shows the reversal of a relationship between two entities. It is the same relationship seen from two different angles, and there is always two entities involved, which makes the major difference between this type and the above two types of antonymy.

5. There are basically six:

(1) Synonymy, e. g. X: "He was a bachelor all his life." Y: "He never married all his life."
X is synonymous with Y.

(2) Inconsistence, e. g. X: "Mark is married." Y: "Mark is a bachelor."
X is inconsistent with Y.

(3) Entailment, e. g. X: "Mark married a blonde heiress." Y: "Mark married a blonde."
X entails Y.

(4) Presupposition, e. g. X: "John's bike needs repairing." Y: "John has a bike."
X presupposes Y.

(5) Contradiction, e. g. X: "My unmarried aunt is married to a bachelor."
X is a contradiction.

(6) Anomaly, e. g. X: "The blackboard has a bad temper."
X is semantically anomalous.

第6章 语言与认知

6.1 复习笔记

本章要点：

1. Psycholinguistics
   心理语言学
2. Language acquisition, language comprehension, language production
   语言习得，语言的理解，语言的生成
3. First language acquisition
   第一语言习得
4. Cognitive linguistics
   认知语言学

常考考点：

语言习得；第一语言习得；语言的理解和生成；范畴；隐喻；整合理论等。

本章内容索引：

Ⅰ. Definition of cognition

Ⅱ. Definition of Psycholinguistics

Ⅲ. Language acquisition

1. The Behaviorist Approach
2. The Innateness Hypothesis

Ⅳ. Language comprehension

1. Sound Comprehension
2. Word recognition
3. Comprehension of sentences
4. Comprehension of text

Ⅴ. Language Production

1. Access to words
2. Generation of sentences
3. Written language production

Ⅵ. Cognitive Linguistics

1. Definition
2. Construal and Construal Operations
   (1) Attention/ Salience
   (2) Judgment/ Comparison
   (3) Perspective/ Situatedness
3. Categorization
   (1) Basic level

(2) Superordinate level
(3) Subordinate level
4. Image Schemas
5. Metaphor
(1) Ontological metaphors
(2) Structural metaphors
(3) Orientational metaphors
▼(4) Revision of the classification of metaphors
6. Metonymy
7. Blending Theory

I. Definition of cognition The term Cognition can be used in several different loosely related disciplines. In psychology, cognition refers to the mental processes of an individual, related to a concept which demonstrates that the mind has internal mental states (such as beliefs, desires and intentions). It can also be understood as information processing, especially when much abstraction or concretization is involved, or processes such as involving knowledge, expertise or learning for example are at work. Another definition of "cognition" refers to the capacity for mental process or knowledge, including aspects such as awareness, perception, reasoning, and judgment.	**I. 认知的定义** "认知"一词既可用于不同学科也可用于相关学科。在心理学中,"认知"是指个人的心理过程,即心智具有内部心理状态(比如信念、意志和意愿)。特别是在许多具象和抽象交织在一起时,如知识、技能和学习共同作用时,采用信息处理的方法可以理解心理过程。另外一种对"认知"的定义是指心理过程或知识的能力,包括意识、知觉、推理和判断等。
II. Definition of Psycholinguistics Psycholinguistics is the study of psychological aspects of language, which mainly does some research on the psychological states and mental activity related to language usage. A major focus of psycholinguistics is the study of the unconscious use of grammatical rules that enable people to understand and produce comprehensible sentences. Psycholinguists study the relationship between language and thought. It also pays attention to how languages are acquired and the roles they play in our thinking.	**II. 心理语言学的定义** 心理语言学是对语言心理方面的研究,通常研究的是与语言行为相关的心理状态和思维活动。心理语言学的一个重点是研究能够使人理解和产出可理解句子的语法规则的无意识运用。心理语言学家研究语言与思维的关系,心理语言学同时也还关注语言是如何习得的以及语言在思维运用中所发挥的作用。
III. Language acquisition Language acquisition refers to the learning and development of a person's language. The learning of a native or first language refers to first language acquisition (FLA), and the learning of a second or foreign language is called second language acquisition (SLA). Language acquisition is not only studied by linguists but also psychologists and applied linguists to enable them to understand the process, and to give a better understanding of the nature of language. There are basically two approaches to the question of first language acquisition: behaviorist approach and innateness approach.	**III. 语言习得** 语言习得指的是一个人语言的学习和发展。第一语言习得即一个人母语的学习和发展。语言学家、心理语言学家和应用语言学家通过研究语言习得来理解其形成和发展的全过程,更好的理解语言的本质。对于第一语言习得的问题存在两种说法:行为主义方法和天赋论。

1. The Behaviorist Approach Language is a learned behavior, learned by a process of habit-formation. This view of language learning is called behaviorism or behaviorist view. According to which, the language acquisition of children is a process of "stimulus-response-imitation-reinforcement". The internal linguistic knowledge of the individual is the direct outcome of combining the linguistic event that the individual has observed.	**1. 行为主义方法** 语言是一个学习的行为，是一个通过学习形成习惯的过程。对语言学习的这种观点称作行为主义或行为主义观点。根据这种观点，孩子的语言习得是一个“刺激—反映—模仿—强化”的过程。个人的内部语言知识是其对所观察的语言事件进行结合的直接结果。
2. The Innateness Hypothesis The innateness hypothesis says that the ability to acquire a human language is part of the biologically innate equipment of the human being, and that an infant is born with this ability.	**2. 天赋理论** 天赋论是说获取人类语言的能力是人类自身内在的机能之一，刚出生的婴儿就具备这种能力。
Ⅳ. Language comprehension	**Ⅳ. 语言的理解**
1. Sound Comprehension Sound comprehension is not a passive process. It often counts on the context from which listeners expect to hear. People understand the meaning as a whole, not in isolation. They do not listen to each word individually. The successful comprehension of speech sounds is a combination of the innate ability of humans to distinguish minor differences between speech sounds, and the ability to adjust to the acoustic categories of the language they are exposed to.	**1. 发音理解** 发音的理解不是一个被动的过程。它通常依赖于听话者所处的语境。人们需要从整体上来理解意思，而不是孤立地将其分开。并不是单独去听每一个词。对发音的成功理解要求人们具有区分细小的发音差别的内在能力，以及适应语言听觉种类的能力。
2. Word recognition Word comprehension is a quiet complex psycholinguistic process and is much more complex than the processing of speech sounds. Word plays a significant role in language comprehension because of its great importance in meaning transmission. Word recognition can be refer to the recognition of spoken words and written ones.	**2. 词语的识别** 词语的理解是一个非常复杂的心理过程，远比处理发音复杂得多。词汇由于其在传达意义过程中的极端重要作用而在语言理解中居于核心地位。单词辨识是指对口头词语和书面词语的识别。
3. Comprehension of sentences Besides decoding sounds and lexical meanings, comprehension also includes untangling the meaning of sentences. There are a few elements influencing the comprehension of sentences. The first is that the ambiguity of word meaning leads to difficulties in sentence understanding. The more complex information the word has, the more difficult the sentence is to be understood. The second factor is that the linguistic structure of the sentence affects the processing time.	**3. 句子理解** 语言的理解除了对发音、词汇意思的理解之外还包括对句子的理解。对句子理解的影响有以下几个因素：第一是存在歧义的词语使得句子难以理解。词语含有的信息越复杂，句子也就越难理解。第二是指影响处理时间的句子的语言结构。

4. Comprehension of text

Text can be seen as the net of propositions, making up the semantic interpretations of individual sentences. In the process of reading, readers abstract the main clues of a discourse and infer the background and relations underlying the text. This process of abstraction and inference is constrained by the limitation of short-term memory and guided by how arguments are mutually verified across propositions and by linguistic cues indicated by the text.

V. Language Production

Language production refers to the process involved in creating and expressing meaning through language.

1. Access to words

Words are generated via several processing steps and each step produces a particular type of representation. Through the spreading of activation, information is transmitted between representations. The first processing step refers to conceptualization, which is related to the decision on the notion to express. The following step starts with the retrieval of the words corresponding to the selected concept. The last step, called morpho-phonological encoding, is to choose the morphemes that corresponds to the selected word.

2. Generation of sentences

The first step to generate sentences is again conceptual preparation which means deciding what to say. A global plan is needed. Each part of the plan must be carefully prepared, perhaps via intermediate stages, so that a representational level is achieved that consists of lexical concepts. Theories of sentence generation demonstrates that speakers prepare utterances incrementally. As soon as the speakers have chosen the first few word concepts, they will initiate the language program and prepare the rest of the utterance later in the speech or between parts of the utterance.

4. 语篇理解

文本是命题的网络，这些命题构成单个句子的语义解释。读者在阅读过程中提炼出语篇的主要线索和思路并且推理出未出现在语篇中的背景和关系，这样的提炼和推理过程受读者短时记忆的时效的限制，也受论据在命题之间的互证方式和文本所表明的语言组织形式的指引。

V. 语言的生成

语言的生成是指通过语言来创造和表达意义的过程。

1. 词汇提取

词汇是经过几个处理步骤而计划成的。每个步骤产生一特定类型的表征，而且信息在各个表征之间通过激活的扩散而相互传递。第一个处理步骤叫做概念化，它决定着要表达何种概念。下一个步骤是选择能够和已确定的欲表达的概念相符合的词语。最后一个步骤是形态—音位编码，这个步骤开始于检索与被选择单词相对应的语素。

2. 句子的生成

在句子的生成过程中，第一步也是概念准备，也就是要确定想说出的内容。一个全局的计划也是必需的。计划的每一部分必须精心准备以使表征层面和词汇概念相一致，也许这需要通过一些中间阶段。这种表征形成输入而进入到语言计划，在语言计划开始以后，才能产生出含有多个句子的话语。语言生成理论假定说话者计划是呈递增状态的，说话者只要一做出了对最初几个词汇概念的选择，它们就会启动语言计划，稍后在说的时候或者在话语成分轮换时再准备其余的话语。

3. Written language production The process of written language production is similar to that of spoken language production. The main difference is that once a syntactic lexicon unit and its morphological representation have been achieved, orthographic form rather than the phonological form needed to be retrieved and produced. Phonology plays a significant part in this process, just as it does in deriving meaning from print in reading.	**3. 书面语的生成** 书面语的生成步骤和口头语的生成步骤很相似，主要的区别在于一旦句法词汇单位和它的形态表征得到提取，必须要被检索和产生的形式是正字法拼写形式而不是音位形式。音位在这一过程中起着很重要的作用，就像在阅读时从印刷体获取意义中它起的作用一样。
Ⅵ. Cognitive Linguistics **1. Definition** Cognitive linguistics is based on human experience of the world and how they perceive and conceptualize the world.	**Ⅵ. 认知语言学** **1. 定义** 认知语言学基于人类对世界的经验，对世界的感知和概念化。
▼ Basic principle of cognitive linguistics The basic principle of cognitive linguistics is that language is symbolic rather than automatic. Language is influenced by the way people use it and by their general cognitive abilities. Language, instead of developed on the back of Universal Grammar, has to be learned.	**认知语言学的基本原则** 认知语言学的基本原则是语言是象征性的，符号的而非自动的。语言受人类对其使用方式和人类普遍的认知能力的影响。语言不是基于普遍语法的，而是需要学得的。
2. Construal and Construal Operations Construal is the competence to conceive and portray the same situation in alternate ways through specificity, different mental scanning, directionality, vantage point, figure-ground segregation etc. Construal operations the process of conceptualization in human language processing. In other words, construal operations are the underlying psychological processes and resources used to understand linguistic expressions.	**2. 识解与操作** 识解是一种用交替的方式对同一场景进行构想和描述的能力，这种能力是通过详细程度、不同的心理扫描、指向性、有利位置、图形—背景分离等加以实现的。识解操作是人类语言处理过程中概念化的过程，或者说，识解操作是理解语言表达方式所使用的基本心理过程和来源。
(1) Attention/ Salience The operations grouped under salience are related to our allocation of attention to something that shows salience to us. In perception, we focus our attention on parts of the perceived scenery. In cognition, we allocate attention to the activation of conceptual structures.	**(1) 注意力/突显** 突显下的识解操作与我们关注突显事物所需注意力有关。在知觉中，我们把注意力集中在感知到情景部分。在认知中，我们把注意力关注于概念结构的激活。
(2) Judgment/ Comparison The construal operations of judgment/comparison is related to the judgement of something by comparing it to something else. This is the basic cognitive capacity. And it is also the foundation of human experience.	**(2) 判断/对比** 判断/对比识解操作与把一物比作另一物的判断相关。它是人类基本的认知能力，也是人类经验的基础。

(3) Perspective/ Situatedness Another construal operation in cognitive linguistics can be considered as perspective, in which we view a scene in terms of our situatedness. Perspective generally depends on two things. (1) It depends on where we are situated in relation to the scene we're viewing. (2) It depends on how the scene is arranged in relation to our situatedness.	**(3) 视点/观察者位置** 认知语言学的另外一个识解操作为视点，我们以所处的位置来观察一个情景。视点取决于两个方面：其一，取决于观察者的位置与观察情景的关系；其二，取决于情景的安排与观察者位置的关系。
3. Categorization Categorization refers to the process by which human beings classify experience based on similarities and differences. There are three levels in categories: the basic level, the superordinate level, and the subordinate level.	**3. 范畴化** 范畴化是人类基于经验的异同对经验进行分类的过程，是人类知识的产生不可或缺的部分，它使人类能够把现在的经验与过去的经验结合起来。范畴划分为三个层次：基本层次范畴、上位范畴和下属范畴。
(1) Basic level The categories at the basic level are those that are most culturally salient and are required to meet our cognitive needs the best. Based on this level, human can perceive the greatest differences between "objects" in the world.	**(1) 基本层次范畴** 基本层次范畴是最能体现文化突显性、实现认知需求的范畴。基于这个层次，人类可以感知到"事物"的最大不同。
(2) Superordinate level Superordinate categories are the most general ones. Each member does not have enough features in common to constitute a common gestalt.	**(2) 上位范畴** 上位范畴是最具概括性的范畴，各成员没有足够的共性构成一个共同的完形。
(3) Subordinate level Subordinate level are those have clearly identifiable gestalts and many individual specific features. We can perceive the differences between the members of the basic level categories at this level. The names of subordinate level categories are usually complex and they are typical compound forms. 【考点：名词解释——范畴；辨析三种层次范畴的区别】	**(3) 下属层次范畴** 它们具有清晰可辨的完形和许多个性特征。在此层次，我们可以感知基本层次范畴成员间的区别。下属范畴的名称通常形态复杂，它们是典型的复合形式。
4. Image Schemas An Image schema can be defined as a recurring, dynamic pattern of our perceptual interactions and motor programs that gives coherence and structure to our experience. Image schematic structures contain two characteristics. One is the preconceptual schematic structures. They are derived from our bodily experience. The other is the constant operation of our perceptual interaction and bodily movement through space and physical manipulation of objects.	**4. 意象图式** 意象图式是一种通过相互作用以及动觉程序获得的对事物经验给以连贯和结构的反复出现的动态模式。意象图式结构有两个特点：一是前概念图示结构，来自身体的经验；另一是人的感觉互动的不断操作，通过空间和把握物体的身体运动。

5. Metaphor 【考点：简答——隐喻的分类及关于分类的修正】 Metaphor contains the comparison between two concepts in that one is construed in terms of the other. It's often described as a target domain and a source domain. The target domain is the experience that the metaphor describes and the source domain is the method that people use to describe the experience.	**5. 隐喻** 隐喻涉及两个概念的对比，一个概念识解另一概念。隐喻被描述为目标域与源域，目标域是隐喻所描述的经验，源域是人们用来描述经验的方法。
(1) Ontological metaphors Ontological metaphor refers to the transformation of abstract concepts such as events, activities, emotions, ideas, etc. into entities and substances based on human experience with physical objects.	**(1) 实体隐喻** 实体隐喻是指人类以自身经验和生理实体为基础，把事件、行为、情感、思想等抽象概念转换为实体。
(2) Structural metaphors Structural metaphor plays the most important role because it allows us to go beyond orientation and referring and gives us the possibility to structure one concept according to another. It means that structural metaphors are grounded in our experience. Structural metaphors imply how one concept is metaphorically structured in terms of another.	**(2) 结构隐喻** 结构隐喻起着重要作用，使我们超越指向性和所指，给我们根据另一概念构建一个概念的可能性。结构隐喻植根于我们的经验，它意味着一个概念是以另一个的概念隐喻构建起来的。
(3) Orientational metaphors Orientational metaphor provides a concept a spatial orientation. They are featured by building a concept out of another concept, but by a co-occurrence in our experience. The orientational metaphors, grounded on an experiential basis, connects the two parts of the metaphor. And this kind of metaphor are based on human physical and cultural experience.	**(3) 方位隐喻** 方位隐喻给概念一个空间方位，它们不是以另一个概念构建一个概念为特点，是以不断发生的经验为特点。方位隐喻以连接隐喻两部分的经验为基础，是基于人类身体和文化的经验。
▼(4) Revision of the classification of metaphors According to the corrected and clarified conception about the classification and division of metaphor, the above division is artificial, that is, all metaphors are structural in that they map structures to structures, and all metaphors are ontological in that they create target domain entities and many metaphors are orientational in that they map orientational image-schemas.	**(4) 隐喻分类的修订** 根据对隐喻概念分类和划分的修正及澄清，上面三种对于隐喻的分类是人为的，也就是说，所有的隐喻都是结构性的，因为它们将源域的结构映射到目标域；所有的隐喻都是本体论的，因为它们创造了目标域实体；许多，隐喻都具有方位性，因为他们映射了方位意象图式。
6. Metonymy Metonymy, in the cognitive literature, is defined as a cognitive process in which the vehicle provides mental access to the target within the same domain.	**6. 转喻** 认知语言学把转喻定义为认知过程。在认知过程中，源域为同一域中的目标域提供了心理通路。

7. Blending Theory Fauconnier & Turner propose and discuss blending or integration theory, a cognitive operation whereby elements of two or more "mental spaces" are integrated via projection into a new, blended space which contains its unique structure. They present examples of blending and analyze the blending process, provide taxonomy of blends, and argue for the ubiquity and importance of blending as a cognitive resource. Blending operates on two input mental spaces to produce a third space, the blend. The blend inherits partial structure from the input spaces and forms an emergent structure of its own.	**7. 整合理论** 法考尼埃和特纳提出并讨论了整合理论，一种认知操作即两个或更多的心理空间通过投射整合为一个新的、合成空间，这个空间有其独特的结构。法考尼埃和特纳介绍了整合的例子，分析了整合的过程，提供了整合的分类，并把普遍存在和具有重要性的整合视为认知的来源。 整合在两个输入空间操作产生第三个空间，即合成空间。合成空间部分地继承了两个输入空间的结构，形成自己的层创结构。

6.2 考研真题与典型题详解

Ⅰ. Multiple Choice

1. How does the top-down approach differ from the bottom-up approach in language processing?（对外经贸 2005 研）
   A. Bottom-up processing is more effective than top-down processing in speech synthesis.
   B. Bottom-up processing utilizes all information one has in speech perception.
   C. Top-down processing uses one's existing knowledge and the incoming speech signal.
   D. Top-down processing is more efficient than bottom-up processing in speech comprehension.
2. ___________ is defined as a conscious process of accumulating knowledge of a second language usually obtained in school settings.
   A. Competence　B. Performance　C. Learning　D. Acquisition
3. During language acquisition, children go through several stages, during which stage they begin to have sensitivity to the phonetic distinctions used in their parents' language.
   A. Holophrastic stage
   B. Two word stage
   C. Three word stage
   D. Fluent grammatical conversation stage
4. ___________ is the study of psychological aspect of language.
   A. language acquisition　B. applied linguistics
   C. psycholinguistics　D. pragmatics
5. ___________ does not belong to Construal Operations.
   A. Attention/ Salience　B. Judgment/ Comparison
   C. Metaphor and metonymy　D. Perspective/ Situatednesss

Ⅱ. True or False

1. Metonymy involves using the familiar to stand for the unfamiliar.（对外经贸 2005 研）
2. The utterance meaning of the sentence varies with the context in which it is uttered.

3. Language acquisition refers to the process involved in creating and expressing meaning through language.
4. Structural metaphor means that human experiences with physical objects provide the basis for ways of viewing events, activities, emotions, ideas, etc., as entities and substances.
5. Superordinate categories are the most general ones. The members of a superordinate category do not have enough features in common to conjure up a common gestalt at this level.

Ⅲ. Explain the following terms.

1. Language acquisition（浙江大学 2004 研）
2. government（南开大学 2011 研）
3. Psycholiguistics
4. The Innateness Hypothesis
5. Construal and construal operations
6. Categorization
7. Cognition

Ⅳ. Short answer questions

1. What is the purpose of studying language and mind?（南开大学 2004 研）
2. What is the cognitive interpretation of image schema?（北航 2010 研）
3. How to understand a sentence?
4. What is blending theory?

Ⅴ. Essay questions

1. In informal speech, people often omit sentence subjects because they are commonly understood. What are the omitted subjects in the following two sentences? Why do people know that these are the correct subjects?（南京大学 2008 研）
   a. Hope you like everything here.
   b. Just imagine what has just happened here.
2. Describe the process of language perception, comprehension and production.
3. Research has found that two-year-old English children produce negative sentences such as a) to d), but not e):
   a) He doesn't like cabbage.
   b) Doesn't like cabbage.
   c) Him no like cabbage.
   d) No like cabbage.
   e) * Him doesn't like cabbage.
   How can you account for this?（北外 2006 研）

参考答案及解析

Ⅰ. Multiple Choice

1. B （在语言处理加工过程中，有两种方法，即从一般到具体的自上而下的方法和从具体到一般的自下而上的方法。其中自下而上的方法会用到言语感知中的所有信息。）
2. C （在学校里我们会学到第二语言，对第二语言知识的这种有意识的积累，叫做“学习”。）

3. A （孩子们的语言习得要经历三个阶段，单词句阶段，双词句阶段，以及三词句阶段。在单词句阶段，孩子们会对其父母话语中的语音特征特别敏感。）

4. C （心理语言学是对语言心理方面的研究，通常研究的是与语言行为相关的心理状态和思维活动。）

5. C （识解操作是人类语言处理过程中概念化的过程，或者说，识解操作是理解语言表达方式所使用的基本心理过程和来源。包括（1）注意力/突显；（2）判断/对比；（3）视点/观察者位置。）

Ⅱ. True or False

1. T （转喻是一种一个词或词组被另一个与之有紧密联系的词或词组替换的修辞方法。）

2. T （话语意义随着话语情境的变化而不同。）

3. F （语言产出是一个通过语言来表达意义的过程。）

4. F （实体隐喻是指人类以自身经验和生理实体为基础，把事件、行为、情感、思想等抽象概念转换为实体。）

5. T （上位范畴是最具概括性的范畴，各成员没有足够的共性构成一个共同的完形。）

Ⅲ. Explain the following terms.

1. Language acquisition: It refers to the gradual development of ability in a language by using it naturally in communicative situations.

2. Government: In the traditional approach, it refers to a type of control over the form of some words by other words in certain syntactic constructions.

3. Psycholinguistics is the study of psychological aspects of language; it mainly studies the psychological states and mental activity associated with the use of language. An important focus of psycholinguistics is the largely unconscious use of grammatical rules that enable people to produce and comprehend intelligible sentences. Psycholinguists investigate the relationship between language and thought, Psycholinguistics is also concerned with how languages are learned, and the role they play in our thinking.

4. The innateness hypothesis was proposed by Chomsky. It says that the ability to acquire a human language is part of the biologically innate equipment of the human being, and that an infant is born with this knowledge of basic grammatical relations and categories, and this knowledge is universal.

5. Construal is the competence to conceive and portray the same situation in alternate ways through specificity, different mental scanning, directionality, vantage point, figure-ground segregation etc. Construal operations are conceptualizing processes applied in language process by human beings. That is, construal operations are the underlying psychological processes and resources employed in the interpretation of linguistic expressions.

6. Categorization is the process of classifying our experiences into different categories based on commonalities and differences. There are three levels in categories: the basic level, the superordinate level, and the subordinate level.

7. Cognition is, in psychology, used to refer to the mental processes of an individual, with particular relation to a concept which argues that the mind has internal mental states (such as beliefs, desires and intentions) and can be understood as information processing, especially when much

abstraction or concretization is involved, or processes such as involving knowledge, expertise or learning for example are at work. Another definition of "cognition" is the mental process or faculty of knowing, including aspects such as awareness, perception, reasoning, and judgment.

Ⅳ. Short answer questions

1. The study of language and mind aims to model the workings of the mind in relation to language; for example, it helps explain how the language production and perception is achieved. Since structures and connections in the mind are inevitably unobservable, researchers put forward hypotheses based on fragmentary clues. The label most usually given to the study of "language and mind" is psycholinguistics, a term which is often perceived as being trendy. Psycholinguistics is concerned primarily with investigating the psychological reality of linguistic structures.
2. Image schema is a recurring, dynamic pattern of our perceptual interactions and motor programs that gives coherence and structure to our experience.

   Image schema exists at a level of abstraction, operates at a level of mental organization between propositional structures and concrete image, and it can be subdivided into the following items: a center-periphery schema, a containment schema, a cycle schema, a force schema, a link schema, a part-whole schema, a path schema, a scale schema and a vertical schema.
3. Besides decoding sounds and lexical meanings, comprehension also includes untangling the meaning of sentences. There are a few elements influencing the comprehension of sentences. The first is that the ambiguity of word meaning leads to difficulties in sentence understanding. The more complex information the word has, the more difficult the sentence is to be understood. The second factor is that the linguistic structure of the sentence affects the processing time. Psycholinguists have addressed th phenomena of sentence comprehension in different ways. Firstly, serial models propose that the sentence comprehension system continually and sequentially follows the constraints of a language's grammar with remarkable speed. Secondly, parallel models emphasize the comprehension system is sensitive to a vast range
4. Fauconnier & Turner proposes and discusses blending or integration theory, a cognitive operation whereby elements of two or more "mental spaces" are integrated via projection into a new, blended space which contains its unique structure. They present examples of blending and analyze the blending process, provide taxonomy of blends, and argue for the ubiquity and importance of blending as a cognitive resource.

   Blending operates on two input mental spaces to produce a third space, the blend. The blend inherits partial structure from the input spaces and has emergent structure of its own. There are some conditions needed when two input spaces one and two are blended: cross-space mapping, generic space, blend and emergent structure. The blending theory suggests a new way of thinking about what constitutes a novel inference. Because the mapping operation involves integrated frames rather than isolated predicates, the choice of one particular framing over another necessarily results in a different set of attendant inferences.

Ⅴ. Essay questions

1. The omitted subject in sentence a is "I", and the omitted subject in sentence b is usually "You". This is a matter of sentence comprehension in language comprehension. Psycholinguists

have proposed principles interpreting sentence comprehension with respect to the grammatical constraints. The most popular principle is "Minimal attachment" which defines "structurally simpler", and it claims that structural simplicity guides all initial analyses in sentence comprehension.

In this view, the sentence processor constructs a single analysis of a sentence and attempts to interpret it. The first analysis is the one that requires the fewest applications of grammatical rules to attach each incoming word into the structure being built; it is the automatic consequence of an effort to get some analysis constructed as soon as possible. In the first sentence, when "hope" as a verb is used to express the speaker's desire and expectation for something to happen, it conveys the will of the speaker. So, the subject of "hope" is usually the speaker her/himself and can be omitted when the two are talking to each other. When the speaker is making a statement and using "hope" to express other's will, the subject will not be omitted.

Therefore, according to "minimal attachment" principle, when the hearer interprets this sentence, they automatically interpret "I"—the speaker, as the subject of "hope". Sentence b can be said to be an imperative sentence which is a sentence that gives advice or instructions or that expresses a request or a command. This instruction or request is always aimed to the hearer or the reader, so the subject of an imperative is always "you". When the hearer interpret this sentence, he/she will interpret the verb "imagine" as a request or advice through which the speaker tries to make he/she involved in this action, so it is easier for he/she to consider "you" as the subject.

Context is another important factor for people to understand the subjects. The subjects will be more clear in particular context although they are omitted.

2. From the perspective of psycholinguistic analysis, language use in terms of perception, comprehension and production follows a certain pattern which involves the coordination of various language centers.

   When we speak, words are drawn from Wernicke's area and transferred to Broca's area, which determines the details of their forms and pronunciation. The appropriate instructions are then sent to the motor area which controls the vocal tract to physically articulate the words.

   When we hear something and try to comprehend it, the stimulus from the auditory cortex is transmitted to Wernicke's area, where it is then interpreted.

   When we perceive a visual image, a message is sent to the angular gyrus, where it is converted into a visual pattern.

3. This founding firstly demonstrates one point that the acquisition of auxiliary verbs comes later than that of comparatively "simpler" morphemes such as pronouns. Therefore, it is unlikely for children to make mistakes as shown in e). The reason for this phenomenon could be explained by the fact that in the early stage of children's language acquisition, the speech at first only contains content words and lacks the function elements.

   This founding also shows that children have a certain process of learning the negative form. There are generally three stages.

   (1) At first, the negative element is not part of the structure of the sentences. It is simply

attached to the beginning, as shown in d).

(2) The negative element is inserted into the sentence. The additional negative forms *don't* and *can't* are used, and with *no* and *not*, begin to be placed in front of the verb rather than at the beginning, as shown in c).

(3) Children begin to produce the appropriate part of do, be or the model verbs, to suit the person or tense, as shown in b) and a).

第7章　语言 文化 社会

7.1　复习笔记

本章要点：

1. Language and culture
   语言与文化
2. Sapir-Whorf Hypothesis
   萨丕尔—沃尔夫假说
3. Language varieties
   语言变体
4. Cross-culture communication
   跨文化交流

常考考点：

语言与文化的定义及关系；社会语言学的定义；萨丕尔－沃夫假说；语言变体；分析跨文化交际中出现障碍的原因；中西文化的异同。

本章内容索引：

Ⅰ. Language and Culture

1. Interrelations between language and culture
2. Sapir-Whorf Hypothesis
3. Culture in Language Teaching Classroom

Ⅱ. Language and Society

1. Sociolinguistics
2. Language varieties
   (1) Standard Language
   (2) Dialects
   (3) Registers
   (4) Pidgins and Creoles
3. Choosing a Code
   (1) Diglossia
   (2) Bilingualism and multilingualism
   (3) Code-switching
4. Linguistic Taboos and Euphemisms

Ⅲ. Cross-cultural Communication

1. When in Rome do as the Romans do.
2. Put yourself in other's shoes.
3. One culture's meat is another culture's poison.

4. Honesty and sincerity are key points to mutual understanding.

Ⅰ. Language and Culture **1. Interrelations between language and culture** Language is an irreplaceable carrier of culture. Culture is better interpreted through language.	**I. 语言与文化** **1. 语言与文化的相互关系** 语言是文化不可替代的载体。文化通过语言的使用得到更好的诠释。
2. Sapir-Whorf Hypothesis Sapir-Whorf Hypothesis suggests that our language shapes our thinking patterns and consequently, different languages may lead to our unique ways of understanding the world. There could be two points implied in this theory. On the one hand, language may determine our way of thinking; on the other hand, similarities between languages are relative and the greater the structural differentiations, the more diverse our understanding of the world. Therefore, this hypothesis has also been referred to as linguistic determinism or linguistic relativity. 【考点：名词解释；指出该假说的两种版本】	**2. 萨丕尔—沃尔夫假说** 萨丕尔假说认为，语言塑造了我们的思维模式，相应地，不同的语言表达决定了人们认识世界方式的不同。从这个观点出发，可以得到两点知识：一方面，语言可以决定我们的思维方式；另一方面，语言之间的相似性是相对的，结构性差异越大，反映出对于世界认识的越不同。因此，这个假说也被称作“语言决定论”和“语言相对主义”。
3. Culture in Language Teaching Classroom There are at least three objectives for us to teach culture in language class: ① Encouraging learners to get familiar with cultural differences; ② Helping learners go beyond their own culture and see things from the perspective of the target culture; ③ Helping learners realize the inseparability of language and culture by various practices in class and thus enhances their English.	**3. 语言教学中的文化** 总体而言，在语言课程中教授文化知识至少有以下三个目的： ①有助于学生了解文化差异； ②有助于语言学习者跳出自身文化的圈子，从目标文化的角度考虑问题； ③有助于通过各种课堂练习，强调对语言与文化不可分离性的理解，促进外语学习。
II. Language and Society **1. Sociolinguistics** Sociolinguistics is the study of language in relation to society. In sociolinguistics we are interested in how social factors influence the structure and use of language. It is the field that studies the relationships between language and society, between uses of language and the social structures in which the language users live. 【考点：区分“研究社会的社会语言学”与“研究语言的社会语言学”】	**II. 语言与社会** **1. 社会语言学** 社会语言学是研究语言与社会关系的学科，研究社会因素是如何影响语言的结构和使用。社会语言学是研究语言与社会关系的领域，研究语言的使用与语言使用者所处的社会结构的关系。
2. Language varieties Language changes along social development. It also changes from region to region, from one social group to another,	**2. 语言变体** 语言随着社会的变化而变化。地域、社会群体和个人之间的差异也能产生语言的变化。这些变化的

and from individual to individual. The products of such changes are the varieties of languages. Every language has more than one variety, especially in the way in which it is spoken. Therefore, language varieties are related to region, social class, educational background, and the degree of formality of a situation to which language is applied. Such varieties of language include standard language, dialects, registers, pidgins, creoles, and so on.	结果就是语言的变体。每种语言都不只有一种变体，特别是在口语中。因此，语言变体是与地域、社会阶层、教育背景和被使用语言所处环境的正式程度是密切相关的。这些语言的变体包括标准语言、方言、语域、皮钦语、克里奥尔语等。
(1) Standard Language	**(1) 标准语言**
Standard language is the variety of a language which has the highest status in a community or nation and it is usually based on the speech and writing of educated native speakers of the language.	标准语言是指在群体或者国家拥有很高地位的语言变体。它也是当地受过教育的人口语和书面语的语言基础。
(2) Dialects	**(2) 方言**
A recognizable variety of a language used in a specific region or by a specific social class is called a dialect. A dialect is not necessarily less complete, less logical, less language than a standard language. It is a variation of language different enough to be classified into a separate entity, but not different enough to be classed as a separate language. Sometimes a dialect rises in status and becomes the standard variety of a country. The study of dialects is called dialectology. Dialects can be categorized into following types:	方言是指在一个特定的区域或一个特定的社会阶层内所使用的能够识别的语言变体。方言不一定不如标准语言完整、逻辑和更具语言特征。它是语言的一个变体，由于其不同之处能够划分为一个单独的实体，但是还不足以划分成为一门语言。有时候方言的地位也会得到提升成为一个国家的标准语言。对方言的研究称作方言学，方言学可以细分为以下几类：
①regional/geographical dialects: varieties of a language spoken in a geographical area.	① 地域方言：在一个地域范围内的语言变体。
② temporal dialects: varieties of a language used at particular stages in its historical development.	② 时间方言：在历史发展的特定阶段的语言变体。
③ social dialects or sociolects: varieties of a language used by people belonging to particular social classes.	③ 社会方言：特定社会阶层所使用的语言变体。
④ idiolects: varieties of a language used by individual speakers, with peculiarities of pronunciation, grammar and vocabulary.	④ 个人方言：单个的说话人所用的语言变体，往往带有独特的发音、语法和词汇。
(3) Registers	**(3) 语域**
It is a speech variety used by a particular group of people, usually sharing the same occupation (e. g. doctors, lawyers) or the same interests. A particular register often distinguishes itself from others by having a number of distinctive words, by using words or phrases in a particular way, and sometimes by special grammatical constructions (e. g. legal language). 【考点：Register 与 Dialect 的区别】	语域是特殊人群使用的言语变体，通常指具有相同职业或具有同样爱好的人。某一语域通常具有自己一些独特的词汇或使用词或短语的特殊方式，而使其与其他语域区分开来，有时也使用特殊的语法结构，比如法律语言。

(4) Pidgins and Creoles

A pidgin refers to a variety of a language that is not native language of anyone, but is learned on contact situations such as trading. When a pidgin develops beyond its role as a trade language and becomes the first language of a social community, it becomes a creole. The process by which a pidgin becomes a creole is called creolization.

【考点：名词解释 & 辨析—Pidgin 和 Creole 的区别】

(4) 皮钦语和克里奥尔语

皮钦语不是任何人的母语，是在交往联系的情况下(例如交易)学习的语言变体。当皮钦语得到发展不再是作为交易的语言而成为一个社会群体的第一语言时，它就成为克里奥尔语。由皮钦语转变成为克里奥尔语的过程就称作克里奥尔语化。

3. Choosing a Code

3. 选择语码

(1) Diglossia

When two languages or language varieties exist together in a community and each one is used for different purposes, this is called diglossia. Usually, the more standard variety can be called the high variety or H-variety, which is used in government, the media, education, and for religious services. The other one is usually a non-prestige variety, the low variety or L-variety used in the family, with friends, when shopping, etc.

(1) 双言现象

当两种语言或语言变体同时存在于一个社区，并且每一种语言都有不同的使用目的时，这种现象就叫做双言现象。通常情况下，更标准的语言变体被称作高标准语言，用于政府、新闻媒介、教育和宗教活动。另一种一般是无声望的语言，称低标准语言，用于家里、朋友之间、购物时等。

(2) Bilingualism and multilingualism

Bilingualism is a situation where two languages are used by an individual or by a group of speakers, such as the inhabitants of a particular region or a nation. Multilingualism refers to a situation where three or more languages are used by an individual or by a group of speakers such as the inhabitants of a particular region or nation.

【考点：名词解释 & 辨析—Diglossia 和 Bilingualism 的区别】

(2) 双语和多语

双语指的是个人或群体使用两种语言的情况，例如特定地区或国家的居民。多语则是指个人或群体使用至少两种语言的情况。

(3) Code-switching

Code-switching refers to a change made by a speaker or writer from one language or language variety to another one. There are two major kinds of code-switching, that is situational code-switching and metaphorical code-switching. The former occurs when thc language used changes according to the situation in which the participants find themselves; they speak one language in one situation and another in a different one. When a change in topic requires a change in the language used, this is called metaphorical code-switching.

(3) 语码转换

语码转换是指说话者或写作者从一种语言或语言变体转用另一种语言或语言变体的现象。语码转换又可以分为情景语码转换和隐喻语码转换。情景语码转换发生在所使用的语言随着参与者对他们自身认识的境况发生改变，他们在不同情境下使用不同的语言。当话题的转变要求语言也随之变化时就叫做隐喻语码转换。

4. Linguistic Taboos and Euphemisms

Taboo is a term that is avoided for religious, political, or sexual reasons and is usually replaced by a euphemism, e. g. rest room or bathroom for toilet.

Euphemism refers to the use of a word which is thought to be less offensive or unpleasant than another word.

Ⅲ. Cross-cultural Communication

【考点：分析短文中表现了跨文化交流的哪种特点】

Successful communication in a cross-cultural setting brings about more wealth, peace, and opportunity, however a failure in this respect likely entices more prejudice, conflict, and hostility. Some suggestive principles are provided below as basic guidelines to this difficult work.

1. When in Rome do as the Romans do.

Linguistic forms are different from one language to another. Semantic selections vary across separate language systems. Something you can conveniently say in a language may not be so in another language. This difference makes cross-cultural communication not an easy job to deal with.

2. Put yourself in other's shoes.

Successful communication in a cross-cultural setting depends much on a sensible interpretation and prediction of what the other party will think, feel, and behave when some crucial things occur.

3. One culture's meat is another culture's poison.

Proverbs epitomize the essence of culture and the value system of society. A cross-linguistic survey of proverbial expressions will capture another point of interest.

4. Honesty and sincerity are key points to mutual understanding.

Rich communicative knowledge, high cultural consciousness, and good linguistic performance are necessary prerequisites for becoming a good cross-cultural communicator. Honesty and sincerity are the bridge which will help you transcend cultural barriers and become a good communicator in cross-cultural communication.

4. 禁忌语和委婉语

禁忌语是由于宗教、政治或性别原因而避免使用的词汇，通常被委婉语所代替，例如用 rest room 或 bathroom 来代替 toilet。

委婉语是用一词代替比较唐突的令人不快的另一词的表达方法。

Ⅲ. 跨文化交流

在跨文化交际中，交际的成功带来财富、和平和发展机会；交际的失败导致偏见、冲突、敌对局面。以下是几点建设性意见用于解决跨文化交际中的难题：

1. 入乡随俗。

不同语言，表达不同；不同的语言系统，语义选择也不尽相同。在一种语言中可以随意言说某物，在另一种语言中不一定能找到相对应的事物。也正是这一点使得跨文化交流成为一项并不简单的工作。

2. 换位思考。

面对重要事件与重大抉择，成功的跨文化交际，很大程度上取决于能否正确把握对方此时此刻的想法、充分理解对方此时此刻的感受、准确预见对方将要采用的行动。

3. 萝卜青菜各有所爱。

谚语是集语言、文化、社会之大成。跨文化语境中的谚语研究有助于了解不同的价值观念。

4. 诚实和真诚是互相理解的关键。

丰富的交流经验、充分的文化知识、良好的语言水平是保证跨文化交际的前提条件。更为重要的是，在跨文化语境中，态度决定一切，真诚相待，是跨越文化鸿沟，通往理解彼岸的桥梁和纽带。

7.2 考研真题与典型题详解

Ⅰ. Fill in the blanks.

1. "Linguistic relativity" was proposed by ________ and ________.（清华 2001 研）
2. Psycholinguistics is a branch of linguistics which is the study of psychological aspects of language. As an interdisciplinary academic field, it investigates the following major subjects: ________, ________ and ________.
3. A ________ language is originally a pidgin that has become established as a native language in some speech community.
4. A linguistic ________ refers to a word or expression that is prohibited by the "polite" society from general use.
5. Taboo and ________ are two faces of the same communication coin.
6. Language itself is not sexist, but its use may reflect the ________ attitude connoted in the language that is sexist.
7. As Carter and Simpson (1989) observed that "if the 1960s was a decade of formalism in stylistics, the 1970s a decade of functionalism, and the 1980s a decade of ________ stylistics".（中山大学 2011 研）

Ⅱ. Multiple Choice

1. ________ is defined as a conscious process of accumulating knowledge of a second language usually obtained in school settings.

   A. Competence　B. Performance　C. Learning　D. Acquisition

2. ________ are language varieties appropriate for use in particular speech situations.

   A. Slang　B. Address terms
   C. Registers　D. Education varieties

3. ________ refers to a marginal language of few lexical items and straight forward grammatical rules, used as a medium of communication.

   A. Lingua franca　B. Creole
   C. Pidgin　D. Standard language

4. In sociolinguistic studies, speaker are regarded as members of social groups, the social group that is singled out for any special study is called ________.

   A. the speech community　B. the linguistic group
   C. the linguistic community　D. the speech variety group

Ⅲ. True or False

1. If a child is deprived of linguistic environment, he or she is unlikely to learn a language successfully later on.
2. When children learn to distinguish between the sounds of their language and the sounds that are not part of the language, they can acquire any sounds in their native language once their parents teach them.
3. Language reflects sexism in society. Language itself is not sexist, just as it is not obscene; but it can connote sexist attitudes as well as attitudes about social taboos or racism.

4. According to the strong version of the Sapir-Whorf hypothesis, speaker's perceptions determine language and pattern their way of life.

Ⅳ. Explain the following terms.

1. Linguistic relativity (四川大学 2010 研；人大 2006 研)
2. Sapir-Whorf hypothesis (武汉大学 2004 研；暨南大学 2021 研)
3. Linguistic determinism (上海交大 2007 研)
4. Intercultural communication (南开大学 2006 研)
5. Cross-cultural communication (浙江大学 2003 研)
6. Pidgins and Creoles
7. Speech community (北外 2010 研)
8. Diglossia (南开大学 2010 研)
9. Register (南开大学 2010 研)
10. linguistic variable(北外 2011 研)
11. conversational maxim (南开大学 2011 研)
12. Blog(中山大学 2011 研)

Ⅴ. Short answer questions

1. Eskimos have many different words for different types of snow, Aborigines for different types of sand, and in Arabic one must choose from a whole range of words which are subsumed under the Western category CAMEL. Can you explain these phenomena with your linguistic knowledge? (北航 2008 研)
2. What is linguistic determinism? (北航 2008 研)
3. What do you think of the Sapir-Whorf Hypothesis? (西安外国语学院 2006 研)
4. What will you say to a statement like "our language is our culture"? (四川大学 2006 研)
5. How would you comment on Sapir-Whorf hypothesis? (北航 2010 研)
6. Why do we need to teach culture in our language classroom? (四川大学 2010 研)
7. What are sociolinguistics of society and sociolinguistics of language? (武汉大学 2007 研)
8. It is claimed in sociolinguistics that you are what you say. How would you comment on this theoretical claim? (武汉大学 2011 研)
9. In Chinese tone changes are used in the way that affects the meanings of individual words. (中山大学 2011 研)
10. What distinction, if any, can you draw between bilingualism and diglossia?
11. How do the speech of women and the speech of men differ from each other?
12. Describe the process of language perception, comprehension and production.
13. What is Sapir-Whorf hypothesis?

Ⅵ. Essay questions

1. Some comments on the following statement based on your own experience:
   There exists a close relationship between language and culture. In other words, a successful master of a given language has much to do with an understanding of that culture. (武汉大学 2007 研)
2. Explain this statement and give at least two examples of it: " In studying other cultures, we do

so from the perspective of our own culture."（北外 2007 研）

3. What is linguistic relativity and why is it so important in linguistic studies?（中山大学 2006 研）
4. How much does our language influence the way we think? How deeply do language and culture interpenetrate and influence one another? These questions about language have fascinated thinkers throughout the ages. For example, Johann Gottfried Herder and Wilhelm von Humboldt in the German Romantic tradition regarded language as a prisma or grid spread over things in the world so that each language reflects a different worldview. Write a short essay to explain your position on this view.（北外 2004 研）
5. How do you understand the role of linguistic research in social and economic development?（南开大学 2004 研）
6. Why do you think that, all other things being equal, women use more standard variants of stable sociolinguistic variables than men?（北外 2006 研）
7. What is a "slip of the tongue"? What has research into "slip of the tongue" phenomena revealed about speech production process?（南开大学 2011 研）

参考答案及解析

Ⅰ. Fill in the blanks.

1. Sapir, Whorf

   （萨丕尔—沃尔夫假说认为，一方面，语言可以决定我们的思维方式；另一方面，语言之间的相似性是相对的，结构性差异越大，反映出对于世界认识的越不同。因此，这个假说也被称作“语言决定论”和“语言相对主义”。）
2. acquisition, comprehension , production

   （心理语言学作为语言学的一个分支，是从心理学的角度来研究语言，主要包括语言习得，语言理解和语言产生。）
3. creole

   （当皮钦语得到发展不再是作为交易的语言，而成为一个社会群体的第一语言时，它就成为克里奥尔语。由皮钦语转变成为克里奥尔语的过程就称作克里奥尔语化。）
4. taboo

   （禁忌语是由于宗教、政治或性别原因而避免使用的词汇，通常被委婉语所代替。）
5. euphemism

   （禁忌语是由于宗教、政治或性别原因而避免使用的词汇，通常被委婉语所代替。委婉语是用一词代替比较唐突的令人不快的另一词的表达方法。他们是同一交流过程的两个方面。）
6. social

   （语言本身是不存在性别歧视的，但当语言被不同的人使用时，则会反映出社会中存在的性别歧视现象。）
7. discourse

   （正如 Carter and Simpson 认为的那样，如果说 20 世纪 60 年代是形式主义文体学，70 年代是功能主义文体学，那么 80 年代就是话语文体学。）

Ⅱ. Multiple Choice

1. C （在学校里，通过有意识的学习而学到第二语言的过程叫做学习，这不同于儿童不自觉地自然的言语习得过程。）
2. C （语域是特殊人群使用的言语变体，通常指具有相同职业或具有同样爱好的人。某一语域通常具有自己一些独特的词汇或使用词或短语的特殊方式，而使其与其他语域区分开来。）
3. C （皮钦语不是任何人的母语，是在交往联系的情况下(例如交易)学习的语言变体。）
4. A （在社会语言学中，语言使用者都被看作是社会的成员。而具有相同的语言认同或至少共享一种语言变体的人群可称作语言社区。）

Ⅲ. True or False

1. T （如果一个孩子失去了语言环境，他或她是不可能成功地学好一种语言的。）
2. F （不论孩子们生活在何种语言环境中，他们首先获得的是世上所有语言的普遍性知识，之后他们才会学习更为复杂的语言。）
3. T （语言可以反映出社会的性别歧视现象，但语言本身并无性别歧视意义，语言可以表达出人们对性别的态度及对一些禁忌语和种族歧视的态度。）
4. F （根据萨丕尔—沃尔夫假说的强势版本，语言决定了说话者的感知能力和生活模式，而非说话者的感知能力决定了语言和生活模式。）

Ⅳ. Explain the following terms.

1. Linguistic relativity: This is one of two points in Sapir-Whorf hypothesis. It states that similarity between languages is relative, the greater their structural differentiation is, the more diverse their conceptualization of the world is. For example, not every language has the same set of words for the colors; in Spanish there is no word that corresponds to the English meaning of "blue".
2. Sapir-Whorf hypothesis consists of two parts: linguistic determinism and linguistic relativity. Linguistic determinism refers to the notion that a language determines certain nonlinguistic cognitive processes. Different languages offer people different ways of expressing around, they think and speak differently. Linguistic relativity refers to the claim that the cognitive processes that are determined are different for different languages. Thus, speakers of different languages are said to think in different ways. The hypothesis is now interpreted mainly in two different ways: a strong version and a weak one. The strong version believes that the language patterns determine people's thinking and behavior; the weak one holds that the former influence the latter. So far, many researches and experiments are conducted to provide support for the weak version.
3. Linguistic determinism, is one of the two points of Sapir-Whorf hypothesis, and has developed into the strong version of this hypothesis. It could be summarized as follows: (1) One's thinking is completely determined by his native language because one cannot but perceive the world in terms of the categories and distinctions encoded in the language. (2) The categories and distinctions encoded in one language system are unique to that system and incommensurable with those of other systems. Therefore, the following statement could represent this hypothesis "If Aristotle had spoken Chinese, his logic would have been different".
4. Intercultural communication: Intercultural communication, also known as cross-cultural communication, is communication between people whose cultural perceptions and symbols systems are

distinct enough to alter the communication event. It is frequently used to refer to communication between people from different cultures, which implies a comparison between cultures.

5. Cross-cultural communication is an exchange of ideas, information, etc, between persons from different cultural backgrounds. The cultural conventions of the participants may be widely different, and misinterpretation and misunderstanding can easily arise, even leading to a total communication breakdown.
6. A pidgin refers to a variety of a language that is not native language of anyone, but is learned on contact situations such as trading. When a pidgin develops beyond its role as a trade language and becomes the first language of a social community, it becomes a creole. The process by which a pidgin becomes a creole is called creolization.
7. Speech community is a group of people who share a set of norms and expectations regarding the use of language. Speech communities can be members of a profession with a specialized jargon, distinct social groups like high school students or hip-pop fans. In addition, online and other mediated communities, such as many internet forums, often constitute speech communities. Members of speech communities will often develop *slang* or *jargon* to serve the group's special purposes and priorities.
8. When two languages or language varieties exist together in a community and each one is used for different purposes, this is called diglossia. Usually, the more standard variety can be called the high variety or H-variety, which is used in government, the media, education, and for religious services. The other one is usually a non-prestige variety, the low variety or L-variety used in the family, with friends, when shopping, etc.
9. It is a speech variety used by a particular group of people, usually sharing the same occupation (e. g. doctors, lawyers) or the same interests. A particular register often distinguishes itself from others by having a number of distinctive words, by using words or phrases in a particular way, and sometimes by special grammatical constructions (e. g. legal language).
10. Linguistic variables are those where the meaning remains constant but form varies like cat and pussy have the same social meaning but different from. So far as pronunciation is concerned house [h] and with [h] has same social meaning with different pronunciations. Here variables are just the tools to analyze the language to set social dimensional society.
11. Conversational maxim: A conversational maxim is any of four rules which were proposed by Grice 1975, stating that a speaker is assumed to make a contribution that follows the four maxims of quantity, quality, relevance and manner.
12. Blog, which is the short form of weblog, is defined by Dan Gilmore as "an online journal comprised of links and postings in reverse chronological order, meaning the most recent posting appears at the top of the page". Matisse Enzer's Glossary of Internet Terms puts it this way: A blog is basically a journal that is available on the web. The activity of updating a blog is "blogging" and someone who keeps a blog is a "blogger." Blogs are typically updated daily using software that allows people with little or no technical background to update and maintain the blog.

V. Short answer questions

1. These phenomena can be explained from the following perspectives:

   (1) These phenomena show a relationship between language and society. Language changes from region to region, from one social group to another and from individual to individual. The living environment makes great impact on the changes of language. As Eskimo are always living in an environment of a snow world, they have made a good cognition to snow and classified it in different types. Human use language to describe the world they have cognized.

   (2) These phenomena can be explained from the Sapir-Whorf Hypothesis. This hypothesis suggests that: our language helps mould our way of thinking and, consequently, different languages may probably express speaker's unique ways of understanding the world. So Eskimos's different words for different types of snow reflect their different ways to understand snow.

2. Linguistic determinism, is one of the two points of Sapir-Whorf Hypothesis, and has developed into the strong version of this hypothesis. It could be summarized as follows: (1) One's thinking is completely determined by his native language because one cannot but perceive the world in terms of the categories and distinctions encoded in the language. (2) The categories and distinctions encoded in one language system are unique to that system and incommensurable with those of other systems. Therefore, the following statement could represent this hypothesis "If Aristotle had spoken Chinese, his logic would have been different".

3. Sapir-Whorf hypothesis consists of two parts: linguistic determinism and linguistic relativity. Linguistic determinism, or the strong version, has been criticized for its excessive concern with surface structures of individual languages. In fact, all languages are fundamental of the same universal human character, including the lexico-semantic and syntactic components of language and all normal human beings are gifted with the same linguistic faculty and cognitive capacity. The flaws of that hypothesis can be revealed through the following analysis.

   (1) Different grammatical structures do not mean that speakers of different languages differ in thinking logic or reasoning.

   (2) Equivalent translation is always possible in spite of the fact that in practice there are hardly any people in perfect control of two genetically different languages.

   (3) People who have good command of two genetic-unrelated languages do not have "double minds" or do not have to change their thinking logic when speaking foreign tongue.

4. This statement reveals a fact that language is part of the culture. Culture is the total pattern of beliefs, customs, institutions, objects and techniques that characterize the life of a particular society. It is regarded as a carrier of culture, because without language culture would be impossible. Language is the principal mean by which culture is passed down. Language is the symbolic representation of a people, and it comprises their historical and cultural backgrounds as well as their approach to life and their ways of living and thinking. People use language for the sake of communication, but language itself cannot fulfil the task of communication without the culture system behind the language. Language is a product of our social life.

5. This hypothesis suggests that our language will mould our view of the world. The hypothesis has two important points, linguistic determinism—language may determine our thinking patterns and

linguistic relativity—similarity between language is relative, the greater their structural differentiation is, the more diverse their conceptualization of the world will be. Thus, two versions of the Sapir-whorf hypothesis have been developed, a strong version and a weak version. The strong version of the theory emphasizes the decisive role of language as the shaper of our thinking patterns. The weak version of the hypothesis, however, is a modified type of its original theory, suggesting that there is a correlation between language, culture and thought, but the cross-culture differences thus produced in our ways of thinking are relative rather than categorical.

6. Language has a close relationship with culture. Language is an indispensible carrier of culture and culture finds a better representation through language use. When it comes to language teaching and learning, the influence of cultural knowledge on the linguistic performance of language learners has been identified and highlighted. It has repeatedly been found that learners who lack sufficient knowledge about the target culture can hardly become active and appropriate language users in their target language. For these reasons, the information concerning cultural differences has rightly been introduced in language classrooms of different kinds of enhancing learners' cultural consciousness and improving their performance in cross-cultural contexts of communication. So we need to teach culture in our language classroom.

7. If we want to know more about a given society or community by examining the linguistic behavior of its members, we are doing a sociolinguistic study of society. That is, we are doing sociolinguistics at a macro level of investigation. At this level of discussion, things that we are interested in include bilingualism or multilingualism, language attitudes, language choice, language maintenance and shift, language planning and standardization, vernacular language education, and so on.

   On the other hand, if we want to know more about some linguistic variations in language use by turning to potential socio-cultural factors for a description and explanation, we are doing a sociolinguistic study of language. Consequently, we are more interested in examining micro linguistic phenomena such as structural variants, address forms, gender differences, discourse analysis, Pidgin and Creole languages, and other more language related issues.

8. Everyone speaks differently. A personal dialect of an individual speaker combines elements regarding regional, social, gender, and age variations. In other words, an individual speaker's regional and social back ground, his/her gender and age jointly determine the way he/she talks. From this point, we can claim that "You are what you say".

   Following this claim, we may expand the scope of our observation by introducing some social factors that are believed to influence our language behavior in a social context. Among these factors, some major ones include a) class; b) gender; c) age; d) ethnic identity; e) education background, f) occupation, and g) religious belief. In our daily speaking, the potential selection of linguistic forms can reflect the above factors, which determine our identities.

   For example, women use more "fancy" color terms such as "mauve" and "beige"; use less powerful curse words; use more intensifiers such as "terrible" and "awful"; use more tag questions. On the other hand, your way of speaking, to some extent, reflect your identity.

(本题为开放式题目，围绕自语言与社会及文化之间的关系阐述自己对这句话的观点即可。)

9. Tones are pitch variations, which are caused by the differing rates of vibration of the vocal cords. Pitch variations can distinguish meaning just like phonemes; therefore, the tone is a suprasegmental feature. The meaning-distinctive function of the tone is especially important in what we call tone languages. English is not a tone language. Chinese is a typical tone language. It has four tones. The first tone is level(阴平), the second rise(阳平), the third fall rise(上声), and the fourth fall(去声). The role of the tone can be well illustrated by pronouncing the same sound combination such as [pa] in the four different tones and have different meanings:

   bā(八) High level 'eight'

   bá(拔) High rising 'pull out'

   bǎ(靶) Low falling rising 'target'

   bà(坝) High falling 'dam'

   (考查汉语为声调语言，在解释时一定要举例子说明声调是如何改变意义的。)

10. Bilingualism refers to a linguistic situation in which two standard languages are used in a speech community; whereas in a diglossia community, two varieties of language are used for different situations, one being more standard and higher, and used for more formal matters, and the other less prestigious, and used for colloquial situations.

11. Women tend to use more prestigious forms, more polite and indirect language, more tag questions, less powerful curse words, more statement questions, and more specific color terms than their male counterparts.

    In mixed-gender groups, at public gatherings, and in many informal conversations, men spend more time talking than do women. For example, in one experiment, the men with expertise talked longer than the women with expertise. Men initiate more interaction than do women.

12. From the perspective of psycholinguistic analysis, language use in terms of perception, comprehension and production follows a certain pattern which involves the coordination of various language centers.

    When we speak, words are drawn from Wernicke's area and transferred to Broca's area, which determines the details of their forms and pronunciations. The appropriate instructions are then sent to the motor area which controls the vocal tract to physically articulate the words.

    When we hear something and try to comprehend it, the stimulus from the auditory cortex is transmitted to Wernicke's area, where it is then interpreted.

    When we perceive a visual image, a message is sent to the angular gyrus, where it is converted into a visual pattern.

13. It is a belief that our language helps mould our way of thinking and, consequently, different languages may probably express our unique ways of understanding the world. On the one hand, language may determine our thinking patterns; on the other, similarity between languages is relative, the greater their structural differentiation is, the more diverse their conceptualization of the world will be. As this hypothesis was strongly put forward by the American anthropological linguists Sapir and Whorf, it has often been called the Sapir-Whorf hypothesis.

Ⅵ. Essay questions

1. Language use is heavily tinted with its culture. A language does not only expresses facts, ideas, or events which represent similar world knowledge by its people, but also reflects the people's attitudes, beliefs, world outlook, and so on. In a word, language expresses cultural reality. To dig it further, a language, as a system of signs with their own cultural substances and values, may be viewed as a symbol of social identity. People are identified via their use of language. In this sense, language symbolizes cultural reality.

   On the other hand, as people's language uses express the culture, to be more specific, their community culture represented by its social conventions, norms and social appropriateness, the culture both emancipates and constrains people socially, historically and metaphorically.

   Historically, each culture has its past and tradition. A culture consists both of its ways how a social group represents itself, its technological achievements, monuments and works of art and of its historical identity recorded and passed down by the pop culture. It is language that has played a major role in socializing the people and in perpetuating culture, especially in print form.

   In addition, culture also affects its people's imagination or common dreams which are mediated through the language and reflected in their life. Language is not only intrinsically related to what the culture is and what it was, but also related to the culture of imagination governing people's decisions as well as actions. The interplay between language and culture may result in various forms of socialization and people with different cultures may be socialized in different ways with different acculturation.

   Although language and culture are inextricably intertwined, this relationship is not analogous to that of structures and processes. Rather, culture is a wider system that completely includes language as a subsystem. Linguistic competence is one variety of cultural competence and speech behavior is one variety of social behavior. The relation of language to culture is that of part to whole.

2. Culture is a semiotic meaning system in which symbols function to communicate meaning from one mind to another. It is related to language in such a way that language is a part of culture and a part of human behavior, and also the primary medium for transmitting much of culture. Therefore, without language, culture would not be possible. Consequently, when studying a culture, we often rely on the language. Therefore, we may use our own language to describe the target culture, which may be the one interpretation of the statement "In studying other cultures, we do so from the perspective of our own culture".

   What's more, when studying other cultures, we will definitely come across the differences between the target culture and our own culture. We will subconsciously compare the two different cultures. Seeing from the perspective of our own culture, we find how the target culture is different from our own culture, and this makes the target culture more distinctive from our own.

3. Linguistic relativity is one of the two points in Sapir-Whorf hypothesis, which states that distinctions encoded in one language are unique to that language alone, and "there is no limit to the structural diversity of language". Therefore, similarity between languages is relative, the greater their structural differentiation is, the more diverse their conceptualization of the world will be.

For example, in English, the boundaries among the color spectrum are made in this way: red, orange, violet, blue, and yellow. In fact, these discriminations are arbitrary, and in other language the boundaries are indeed different. In neither Spanish, Italian nor Russian is there a word that corresponds to the English meaning of "blue".

Linguistic relativity is important in linguistic studies because it recognizes the fact of linguistic diversity, which stands as the base which descriptive linguistics lies on. Linguistic diversity also triggers out the study of the linguistic similarity.

The study of the linguistic relativity has shed light on two important insights: there is nowadays recognition that language, as a code, reflects cultural and preoccupations and constrains the way people think.

4. Humans have a unique linguistic system for communication that serves as the primary vehicle for expressing thoughts. Language and thought may be viewed as two independent circles that develop along two different routes but overlap in some parts, where language and thought are consistent with each other. But language is not the only means of expressing thought. As for the relationship between language and the thought, we think that language does not determine the way we think but influence the way we perceive the world and recall things, and affects the ease with which we perform mental tasks. That is, language may be used to provide new ideas, bring about a change in beliefs and values, solve problems, and keep track of things in memory. For example, a well-developed vocabulary may well assist us in learning the concepts the lexis covers. We recall things more easily when they correspond to readily available words or phrases. It is certainly easier for us to make a conceptual distinction if it neatly corresponds to a particular lexical item available in our language. When we label our experience with linguistic symbols, our language will influence how we remember and think about those experiences; otherwise the relationship between language and perception, memory or thinking will be greatly reduced.

   In terms of relationship between language and culture, we can infer that a language not only expresses facts, ideas, or events that represent similar world knowledge by its people, but also reflects the people's attitudes, beliefs, world outlooks, and etc. Language expresses cultural reality. On the other hand, as people's language uses express their culture represented by its social conventions, norms and social appropriateness, the culture both emancipates and constrains people socially, historically and metaphorically. Sharing a same community culture, people have acquired common ways of viewing the world through their speech interactions with other members of the same group. Although language and culture are inextricably intertwined, culture is a wider system that completely includes language as a subsystem. The knowledge and beliefs that constitute a people's culture are habitually encoded and transmitted in the language of the people. Language as an integral part of human being, permeates his thinking and way of viewing the world, language both expresses and embodies cultural reality.

   As for the relationship between language and world views, the language system does not necessarily provide specifics of one's world view. All humans share a general conceptualizing capacity; Speakers of different languages are capable of distinguishing and recognizing experiences according to their respectively different linguistic coding systems for the same objective world. On the one hand, people speaking the same language may have different world views, including political, social, religious, scientific and philosophical views. On the other hand, people speaking different languages may share similar world views on above aspects. Moreover, one language can describe many different worldviews, as is evident in the case of successful translation.

According to the theories shown above, we can infer that Johann Gottfried Herder and Wilhelm von Humboldt's view has both merits and limitations. First, they see clearly that there exists a relationship between language and thoughts. Second, they assume that language influences so much the way people think that people who think in different ways will have different world views. Based on the theoretical views above we think this view is not rational in this aspect.

5. To see the role linguistics plays in social and economic development, we could specifically consider the integration of linguistic research with other fields of social life, such as computational linguistics, psycholinguistics, applied linguistics, anthropological linguistics.

As to the applied linguistics, it is undeniable that linguistic research has greatly influenced the language teaching and learning. For example, various linguistic schools have shed insight into the methodology of language teaching, especially foreign language teaching. Those different models of language teaching are all aimed at a more successful and effective language teaching.

As is known, for a human being in the society, communication is very important. In the social communication, linguistic research also made some important interpretations and explanations. Such as Grice's Cooperative Principle, Brown& Levinson's face and politeness theory, etc, those theories have good inspirations as to how to create a successful communication, and how to avoid and deal with miscommunication

In a word, although without linguistic research society and economics could still develop in their own way, yet linguistics with its effort to explain what is the nature of the activities concerning language, and how these activities works, has undoubtedly made it easier for the social and economic development.

6. Language is a social, value-loaded practice, which reflects an intricate network of social, been explained in terms of a great political, cultural, and age relationships within a society.

Women's speech closely approaches the standard variety than the speech of men, this has consciousness of status on the part of women. Women are more usually more status-conscious than men in the English-speaking world, they are aware of their low status in society and, as a result, use more standard speech forms in their attempt to claim equality or achieve high social status. In a sense, they are up in arms against men's society. The status of men has been traditionally defined by their occupation and wealth, while women have had to find other ways of establishing their position and one of these has been their speech.

A second explanation relates to the ways in which society treats women. Women are expected to behave better than men, traditionally, just as society has been harsher on women with regard to such vices as promiscuity and drunkenness, a better standard of language may have been required.

A third explanation is that, by using standard or polite forms, a woman is trying to protect her face. In other words, a woman claims more status in society. Her greater use of standard forms may also imply that she does not attend solely to her own face needs but also to those of the people she is interacting with, thus avoiding disagreement and seeking agreement and rapport.

7. A slip of the tongue is a kind of speech errors, which is conscious or unconscious deviations from the apparently intended form of an utterance.

   In the process of speech sound production, a slip of sound is easily occurred. In the perspective of speech sound production, it refers to some phonological process.

   (1) Addition: something is added to the target utterance, e. g. "I didn't explain it *clarefully* enough" for "I didn't explain it *carefully* enough".

   (2) Anticipation: in anticipation of a forthcoming segment, we replace an earlier segment with the later segment, e. g. "*bake* my bike" for "take my bike".

   (3) Perseverance: an earlier segment replaces a later one (while also being articulated in its correct location), e. g. "...he pulled a pantrum." for "...he pulled a *tantrum*".

   (4) Blends: occur when more than one word is being considered, and the two blend into a single item, e. g. "Don't bother me in the sleast." for "Don't bother me in the *slightest.*"

   (5) Deletion: something is omitted, e. g. "...mutter *intelligibly.*" for "... mutter *unintelligibly.*"

第 8 章　语言的使用

8.1　复习笔记

本章要点：

1. Speech act theory
   言语行为理论
2. Cooperative principle and its maxims
   合作原则及其准则
3. Gricean theory of conversational implicature
   格赖斯会话含义理论
4. Politeness principle
   礼貌原则
5. Post-Gricean developments
   后格赖斯时期的发展

常考考点：

语用学的定义；语义学与语用学的区别；语境与意义；言语行为理论(发话行为、行事行为和取效行为)；合作原则。实例分析言语行为、合作原则的违反和会话含义。“话语意义”和“句子意义”的区别。

本章内容索引：

Ⅰ. Pragmatics

1. Definition
2. Difference between pragmatics and semantics

Ⅱ. Speech Act Theory

1. Performatives and Constatives
   (1) Definition
   (2) Felicity Conditions
2. A Theory of the Illocutionary Act
3. Searle's Classification of Speech Acts
   (1) Representatives
   (2) Directives
   (3) Commissives
   (4) Expressives
   (5) Declarations

Ⅲ. Cooperative Principle (CP)

1. Cooperative Principle and Its Maxims
2. Violation of the Maxims

Ⅳ. **Conversational Implicature**

1. Definition
2. Characteristics of Conversational Implicature
   (1) Calculability
   (2) Cancellability
   (3) Non-detachability
   (4) Non-conventionality

Ⅴ. **Politeness Principle (PP)**

Ⅵ. **Post-Gricean Developments**

1. Relevance Theory
2. The Q-and R-principles
3. Levinson's Q-, I-and M-principles

▼4. A socio-cognitive approach

I. Pragmatics 【考点：Pragmatics 与 Semantics 的异同】	**I. 语用学**
1. Definition Pragmatics is the study of language in use, focusing on the study of speaker's meaning, utterance meaning or contextual meaning.	**1. 定义** 语用学是研究语言实际运用的学科，集中研究说话人意义、话语意义或语境意义。
2. Difference between pragmatics and semantics Pragmatics and semantics are both linguistic studies of meaning, so they are related to as well as different from each other. Pragmatics takes context into consideration while semantics concentrates on the study of literal meaning without context.	**2. 语用学和语义学的区别** 虽然语用学和语义学都是研究语言意义的学科，但是它们有着很大的差别： 语用学主要研究在特定的语境中说话人所想要表达的意义，而语义学研究的是句子的字面意义，通常不考虑语境。
II. Speech Act Theory The speech act theory was proposed by the Oxford philosopher John Austin in his *How to Do Things with Words*. It is a philosophical explanation of the nature of linguistic communication. It aims to answer the question "What do we do when using language?"	**II. 言语行为理论** 言语行为理论是牛津大学哲学家约翰·奥斯丁在他《如何以言行事》一文中提出的。它从哲学意义上对语言交际的本质进行解释，其目的在于回答"用语言干什么"这个问题。
1. Performatives and Constatives Austin first divided the sentences into two types: performatives and constatives and made a distinction between them.	**1. 施为句和叙事句** 奥斯汀提出自己理论的第一步是把句子分成两类：施为句和叙事句。并对施为句和叙事句作了区分。

(1) Definition **Performatives** are statements which are used to do something, which do not state or describe a fact and are not verifiable. **Constatives** are statements that state or describe a fact and are thus verifiable. 【考点：判断一句子属于施为句还是叙述句】	**(1) 定义** **施为句**是用来做事的，既不陈述事实，也不描述情况，且不能验证其真假；**叙事句**要么用于陈述，要么用于验证，可以验证其真假。
(2) Felicity Conditions Though performatives cannot be valued from the traditional view of truth value, it is still necessary for them to meet certain conditions to be felicitous, which are known as felicity conditions proposed by Austin. The following is the simplified version: ① There must be a relevant conventional procedure, and the relevant participants and circumstances must be appropriate. ② The procedure must be executed correctly and completely. ③ The relevant people must have the requisite thoughts, feelings and intentions, and must follow it up with actions as specified. However, Austin soon discovered that these conditions can only be applied to some cases.	**(2) 合适条件** 虽然施为句不能应用传统的真值判断法，但必须满足一定条件才是合适的。我们把奥斯汀的合适条件简化如下： ① 必须有一个相应的规约程序，并且相关的参与者与环境是合适的。 ②该程序必须正确全面地得到执行。 ③ 有关人必须有相关的思想、感情和意图，而且必须有相关的后续行为。 但是奥斯汀很快就认识到，这些条件只适用于部分情况。
2. A Theory of the Illocutionary Act Later on, Austin gave up his initial distinction between constatives and performatives. He set up another model to explain the way acts were performed by means of language. According to his new model, a speaker might be performing three acts at the same time when speaking. The three acts are locutionary act, illocutionary act, and perlocutionary act. **A locutionary act** is the one of uttering words, phrases, clauses. It is the act of conveying literal meaning by means of syntax, lexicon and phonology. **An illocutionary act** is the act of expressing the speaker's intention. It is the act performed in saying something. **A perlocutionary act** is the act performed by or as a result of saying something. It is the consequence of, or the change brought about by the utterance; it is the act performed by saying something. 【考点：分析三种言语行为的区别；指出一对话中包含的言语行为】	**2. 行事行为理论** 后来，奥斯汀放弃了他最初对叙事句和施为句所做的区分。他建立了另一种模式来解释如何通过语言实施行为。根据这种新的模式，说话人说话时可以完成三种行为：发话行为，行事行为和取效行为。 **发话行为**是说出词、短语、分句的行为，是通过句法、词汇和音位手段表达字面意义的行为。 **行事行为**是表达说话人意图的行为，是在说话过程中所完成的行为。 **取效行为**是通过说话完成或通过说话所产生的行为，是由话语所带来的结果和变化。

Of the three speech acts, linguists are most interested in the illocutionary act for this kind of speech act is in agreement with the speaker's intention. And in their study of language communication, linguists are most attracted by how a speaker expresses his intentions and also how his intention is recognized by the hearer.	在上述三种言语行为中，语言学家最感兴趣的是行事行为，因为这种言语行为与说话人的意图一致。在研究语言交际时，语言学家最感兴趣的是说话人如何表达他的意图和听话人如何识别说话人的意图。
3. Searle's Classification of Speech Acts	**3. 言语行为的分类**
The American philosopher-linguist John Searle has made great contribution to the development of the speech act theory, especially his classification of illocutionary acts. According to Searle, speech acts are divided into five general categories. That is, five general types of things we do with language. Each type has a common, general purpose. 【考点：指出一句包含的行事行为类型；区分五种行事行为并举例】	美国的哲学语言学家约翰·舍尔对言语行为理论的发展做出了巨大的贡献，尤其是他对行事行为的分类。根据舍尔的理论，言语分为五种基本类型，即我们运用语言所做的事情有五种基本类型，每种类型都有一个共同的基本目的。
(1) Representatives	**(1) 阐述类**
Stating or describing, saying what the speaker believes to be true. Stating, believing, swearing, hypothesizing are among the most typical of the representatives.	说话人进行陈述或描写，说自己相信是真的话。陈述、相信、发誓、假设都是最典型的阐述类。
(2) Directives	**(2) 指令类**
Trying to get the hearer to do something. Inviting, suggesting, requesting, advising, warning, threatening, ordering are all specific instances of this class.	说话人试图让听话人做某一件事。邀请、建议、请求、警告、威胁、命令都是最典型的指令类。
(3) Commissives	**(3) 承诺类**
Committing the speaker himself to some future course of action. Promising, undertaking, vowing are the most typical cases.	说话人使自己对某一未来的行为做出许诺。允诺、承担、许愿都是最典型的承诺类。
(4) Expressives	**(4) 表达类**
Expressing feelings or attitude towards an existing state, e. g. apologizing, thanking, congratulating.	说话人对现存事态表明自己的感受或态度，例如道歉、致谢、祝贺等。
(5) Declarations	**(5) 宣告类**
Bringing about immediate changes by saying something.	说话人通过说话使现有的事态马上发生变化。
Ⅲ. Cooperative Principle (CP)	**Ⅲ. 合作原则**
1. Cooperative Principle and Its Maxims	**1. 合作原则及其准则**
Quite often a speaker can mean much more than what is said and the hearer can understand the speaker's meaning. Oxford philosopher H. P. Grice believes that there must be some mechanisms governing the production and comprehension of these utterances. He argues that there is a set of assumptions guiding the conduct of conversation. This is what he calls the Cooperative Principle. He formulates the principle and its maxims as follows:	说话人经常在话语中传达着比话语表层更多的信息，听话人也能够明白说话人所要表达的意思。格赖斯认为一定存在一些管理这些话语产生和理解的机制。他把这种机制称为合作原则，并做出了如下阐述：

"Make your conversational contribution such as is required, at the stage at which it occurs, by the accepted purpose or direction of the talk exchange in which you are engaged."	"使你所说的话，在其所发生的阶段，符合你所参与的交谈的公认目标或方向。"
【考点：简答——合作原则及其准则的主要内容】	
There are four maxims under this general principle: the maxim of quantity, quality, relation and manner.	在这个大原则下有四条准则，它们分别为数量、质量、关系和方式准则。
Quantity	**数量准则：**
1. Make your contribution as informative as is required (for the current purposes of the exchange).	1. 使你的话语如(交谈的当前目的)所要求的那样信息充分。
2. Do not make your contribution more informative than is required.	2. 不要使你的话语比要求的信息更充分。
Quality	**质量准则：**
Try to make your contribution one that is true.	设法使你的话语真实。
1. Do not say what you believe to be false.	1. 不要讲明知是虚假的话。
2. Do not say that for which you lack adequate evidence.	2. 不要说没证据的话。
Relation	**关系准则：**
Be relevant.	所谈内容要密切相关。
Manner	**方式准则：**
Be perspicuous.	要清晰。
1. Avoid obscurity of expression.	1. 避免含糊不清。
2. Avoid ambiguity.	2. 避免歧义。
3. Be brief (avoid prolixity).	3. 要简练(避免冗长)。
4. Be orderly.	4. 要有序。
2. Violation of the Maxims	**2. Violation of the Maxims**
【考点：指出给定话语违反了合作原则的哪条准则】	
The use of "principle" and "maxim" does not mean that everybody will follow the CP and its maxims all the time. People do violate the maxims and tell lies, which gives rise to the Conversational Implicature. The following provides different circumstances of the violation of cooperative principle and its maxims.	使用原则和准则这两个术语，并不是说每个人一直遵守合作原则及其四条准则。人们会违反准则，会撒谎。也因为如此而产生了会话含义。以下是违反合作原则具体准则的几种情况。
① Violation of the Maxim of Quantity;	①违反数量准则;
—When is Susan's birthday party? —Sometime next week. [Not enough information is given.] —We'll all miss Bill and Jane, won't we? —Well, we'll all miss Bill. [We didn't miss Jane.] Tautology 同义反复句 e. g. War is war. [War is cruel.]	

② **Violation of the Maxim of Quality;** (tell lies; rhetoric device) e. g. He is made of iron. (Metaphor) [He has some properties similar to those of iron.] She is the cream in my coffee.	②违反质量准则;
③ **Violation of the Maxim of Relation;** —How do you like my painting? —I'm afraid I don't have an eye for beauty. [I don't like it at all.] —What do you think of the party? —I thought the party we had was too big. [The party was dull or boring.]	③违反关系准则;
④ **Violation of the Maxim of Manner.** —Where is your mother? —She's either in her room or at the market. [I don't know exactly where she is.]	④违反方式准则。
Ⅳ. Conversational Implicature **1. Definition** According to Grice, it refers to the extra meaning not contained in the utterance, but understandable to the listener only when he shares the speaker's knowledge or he knows why and how he violates intentionally one of the four maxims of CP.	**Ⅳ. 会话含义** **1. 会话含义** 根据格赖斯的理论，会话含义指不包含在话语之内的额外意义。这种额外意义只有当听话者和说话者具有共同知识，或听话者知道说话者为什么和如何有意违背会话合作原则中的某一准则时，才是可以理解的。
2. Characteristics of Conversational Implicature **(1) Calculability** The fact that hearers are able to understand the conversational implicature speakers try to convey indicates that implicatures are calculable. They can be deduced from some previous information.	**2. 会话含义的特征** **(1) 可推导性** 说话人试图传递他的会话含义，而听话人也能够理解这些会话含义，这一事实说明，会话含义是可以推导的。它们可以根据已知信息被推导出来。
(2) Cancellability Cancellability is also referred to as defeasibility. The presence of a conversational implicature count on a number of factors including the conventional meaning of words used, the CP, the linguistic and situational contexts, etc. Therefore, if any of the factors changes, the implicature will correspondingly change.	**(2) 可取消性** 也被称为可废除性。会话含义的存在依赖于一些因素：所用词的规约意义，合作原则，语言和情景语境等。所以，如果其中一个因素变了，含义也会相应地发生变化。

(3) **Non-detachability**

Non-detachability means that a conversational implicature is attached to the semantic content of the utterance rather than the linguistic form. Therefore, use of a synonym may still keep the implicature intact. That is to say, even if the specific words are changed, an implicature will not be detached, or separated from what is said as a whole.

(4) **Non-conventionality**

Conversational implicature is different from the conventional meaning of words. It is indeterminate and it changes with context.

V. Politeness Principle (PP)

The Cooperative Principle alone cannot fully explain how people talk. It describes how conversational implicature is given rise to but it does not tell us why people do not say directly what they mean. The reason has something to do with another principle which applies to conversation in addition to the CP—the Politeness Principle (PP). Leech puts forward the Politeness Principle to "rescue the Cooperative Principle" in the sense that politeness can satisfactorily explain exceptions to and apparent deviations from the CP. Therefore, his Politeness Principle is not only an addition to Grice's CP, but a necessary complement needed for case where CP fails to offer a reasonable explanation.

Following Grice's presentation of the CP, Leech puts forward six maxims of the Politeness Principle which runs as follows:

Minimize (other things being equal) the expression of impolite beliefs and maximize (other things being equal) the expression of polite beliefs.

(1) Tact Maxim: Minimize cost to hearer; maximize benefit to hearer.

(2) Generosity Maxim: Minimize benefit to speaker; maximize cost to speaker.

(3) Approbation Maxim: Minimize dispraise of hearer; maximize praise of hearer.

(4) Modesty Maxim: Minimize praise of speaker; maximize dispraise of speaker.

(3) **不可分离性**

不可分离性是说，会话含义是依附于话语的语义内容，而不是语言形式。因此，我们能够用同义成分来替换话语的某一部分，而不改变原来的含义。换言之，即使改变话语的具体词语，会话含义也不会从整个话语中分离出去。

(4) **非传统性**

会话含义与词语的常规意义显然不同。会话含义是不确定的，它会随着语境的变化而变化。

V. 礼貌原则

单就合作原则而言，它并不能完全解释人们交流谈话的方式。合作原则描述了会话含义是如何产生的，但并没有给出关于人们间接地表达他们的意思的原因。其实，原因是跟会话的另一个原则相关——礼貌原则。为了"挽救"合作原则，Leech提出了礼貌原则，因为礼貌原则成功地解释了一些合作原则无法解释的现象。因此，礼貌原则绝不仅仅是对合作原则的增加，而是一个必不可少的补充，尤其是在合作原则无法做出合理解释的地方。

基于格赖斯对合作原则的描述，Leech也提出了礼貌原则的如下六条准则：

如果其他情况相同，尽量少表达不礼貌的信念，尽量多表达有礼貌的信念。

(1) 得体准则(tact maxim)：使他人受损最小；使他人受惠最大。

(2) 慷慨准则(generosity maxim)：使自身受惠最小；使自身受损最大。

(3) 赞誉准则(approbation maxim)：尽量少贬低别人；尽量多赞誉别人。

(4) 谦虚准则(modesty maxim)：尽量少赞誉自己；尽量多贬低自己。

(5) Agreement Maxim: Minimize disagreement between speaker and hearer; maximize agreement between speaker and hearer.	(5) 一致准则(agreement maxim): 尽量减少双方的分歧; 尽量增加双方的一致。
(6) Sympathy Maxim: Minimize antipathy between speaker and hearer; maximize sympathy between speaker and hearer.	(6) 同情准则(sympathy maxim): 尽量减少对别人的反感, 尽量增大双方的同情。
【考点: 名词解释; 分析一段话中包含的礼貌原则准则】	
Ⅵ. Post-Gricean Developments 【考点: 指出后格赖斯时期的理论发展及各理论的作者】	**Ⅵ. 后格赖斯时期的发展**
1. Relevance Theory	**1. 关联原则**
Dan Sperber and Deirdre Wilson formally propose this theory in their book *Relevance: Communication and Cognition* in 1986. They believe that all Gricean maxims, including the CP, should be reduced to a single principle of relevance, which can be defined as: Every act of ostensive communication communicates the presumption of its own optimal relevance.	1986 年, 斯波伯(Sperber)与威尔逊(Wilson)在他们的《关联性——交际与认知》一书中正式提出了这一理论。他们认为格赖斯准则, 包括合作原则本身, 都可以简化成为一条关联原则。关联原则是这样定义的: 每一个明示交际活动, 都传递一种假定: 该行动本身具备最佳关联性。
"Ostensive communication" or "inferential communication", stands for "ostensive-inferential communication". It means that communication is not simply a matter of encoding and decoding, but also involves inference on the part of the hearer and ostension (making clear of one's intention to express something) on the part of the speaker.	"明示交际"或"推理交际", 是"明示—推理交际"的简称。换言之, 交际不只是简单的编码和解码的过程, 它也涉及听话人的推理和说话人的明示(一种表明说话人自身意图的行为)。
Extent-condition format for relevance:	关联性的程度条件:
(1) Extent-condition 1: an assumption is relevant in a context if its contextual effects in this context are large.	(1) 程度条件 1: 如果一个设想在一个语境的语境效应大, 那么这个设想在这个语境中就具有关联性;
(2) Extent-condition 2: an assumption is relevant in a context if the effort required to process it in this context is small.	(2) 程度条件 2: 如果一个设想在一个语境中所需的处理努力小, 那么这个设想在这个语境中就具有关联性。
2. The Q-and R-principles	**2. Q 原则和 R 原则**
Laurence Horn proposed and developed the less reductionist, bipartite model. The Q-principle is from the first maxim of Grice's Quantity, and the R-principle the Relation maxim, but they are more extensive than the previous Gricean maxims.	这是个简化的二元模式, 由霍恩提出并发展。Q 原则源于格赖斯数量准则的第一条次则, R 原则源于关系准则。但二者比格赖斯的准则内容更宽泛。

(1) The Q-principle (Hearer-based)

Make your conversation sufficient (cf. $Quantity_1$).

Say as much as you can (given R).

(2) The R-principle (Speaker-based)

Make your contribution necessary (cf. Relation, $Quantity_2$, Manner).

Say no more than you must (given Q).

3. Levinson's Q-, I-and M-principles

This tripartite model was proposed by Stephen Levinson in his 1987 paper. Levinson believes that the Q-, I-, and M-principles, in essence, is a reinterpretation of Grice's two maxims of Quantity and a maxim of Manner . The maxims of Quality are kept unchanged as in the case in Horn's theory. Levinson disagree with Sperber & Wilson's and Horn's accounts in which the second maxim of Quantity is subsumed under the principle of relevance. Thus he renames the second maxim of Quantity the Principle of Informativeness, I-Principle for short; and the first maxim of Quantity the Principle of Quantity, Q-Principle for short. As for the M-principle, he combines his own ideas with the criticism of Horn's principles.

▼4. A socio-cognitive approach

Socio-cognitive approach to pragmatics is one of the recent attempts to integrate the different schools of pragmatics, such as relevance theorists, neo-Griceans, and even European Continentals.

This socio-cognitive approach was represented by Istvan Kecskes who proposed that "communication is characterized by the interplay of two sets of traits that are inseparable, mutually supportive, and interactive". These two traits are individual traits and social traits respectively as follows: prior context vs. actual situational context; salience vs. relevance; egocentrism vs. cooperation and attention vs. intention.

(1) Q原则(基于听话人)

你的话语要充分(参照数量准则第一条次则)。

说的尽可能多(在符合R原则的前提下)。

(2) R原则(基于说话人)

你的话语应是必须的(参照关系准则、数量准则第二条次则和方式准则)。

只说必须的(在符合Q原则的前提下)。

3. 数量原则、信息量原则和方式原则

这个三分模式是莱文森在他1987年的一篇论文中提出的。莱文森说，实质上，数量原则、信息量原则和方式原则是对格赖斯数量原则的两条次则和方式原则的重新解释。质量准则就像在霍恩的理论中一样，原封不动地保留了下来。莱文森不同意斯波伯和威尔逊的做法，把数量准则第二条次则归属于关联原则或R原则。他把数量准则第二条次则重新命名为“信息量原则”，简写为I原则；数量准则第一条次则命名为“数量原则”，简写为Q原则。讲到方式原则时，莱文森把对霍恩原则的批评和表达自己的观点结合在一起。

4. 社会认知法

近年来，将各种不同的语用学流派如关联理论家、新格赖斯派乃至欧洲大陆派整合到一起研究语用学成为一种新的研究动态，社会认知法就是其中的一种。

社会认知法由Kecskes提出，他认为交流过程的主要特点是两个不可分离，相互支持的互动特性集合的互相影响和互相作用。这两个特性集合如下：之前的语境和实际的情景语境；显著性和相关性；自我中心主义和合作意识；注意和意图。

Therefore, any analysis of communication should consider both individual traits and social traits at the same time, which is the central argument of the socio-cognitive approach. In addition, the social cognitive approach to pragmatics emphasizes that emotional and cultural factors should also be taken into account in the analysis of language communication.	因此根据这一方法，任何交流过程的分析都要同时考虑这两个特性集合，这也是社会认知途径的中心。此外，语用学研究的社会认知法也强调在分析语言交流时需要考虑情感和文化因素。

8.2 考研真题与典型题详解

Ⅰ. Fill in the blanks.

1. There has been a maxim in ________ which claims that "You are what you say".（中山大学 2008 研）
2. The theory of conversational implicature was proposed by ________.（中山大学 2008 研）
3. ________ were sentences that did not state a fact or describe a state, and were not verifiable.
4. In making conversation, the general principle that all participants are expected to observe is called the ________ principle proposed by J. Grice.
5. In Austin's *How to Do Things with word*, he first distinguishes performatives and ________, later on Austin made a flesh start to distinguish ________, ________ and perlocutionary act.

Ⅱ. Multiple Choice

1. The speech act theory was developed by ________.（对外经贸 2006 研）
   A. John Searle　　B. John Austin
   C. Levinson　　D. G. Leech
2. ________ is using a sentence to perform a function.（西安外国语学院 2006 研）
   A. Perlocutionary act　　B. An illocutionary act
   C. A locutionary act　　D. Speech act
3. By saying "You have left the door wide open", a speaker might be performing the three acts: locutionary, illocutionary and perlocutionary ________.（西安交通大学 2008 研）
   A. at the same time　　B. one after another
   C. two first and then the other　　D. one first and then the other two
4. The Illocutionary Act was developed by ________.（西安交通大学 2008 研）
   A. John Austin　　B. Levinson　　C. John Lyons　　D. John Searle
5. According to the conversation maxim of ________ suggested by Grice, one should speak truthfully.（西安外国语学院 2006 研）
   A. quantity　　B. quality　　C. relevance　　D. manner
6. Which of the following is NOT one of the four maxims of the Cooperative Principle?（对外经济贸易大学 2006 研）
   A. the maxim of quantity　　B. the maxim of quality
   C. the maxim of manner　　D. the maxim of strength
7. Four categories of Maxims in Grice's Cooperative Principle include all the following except

__________.（大连外国语学院 2008 研）

A. Manner B. Relation C. Qualification

Ⅲ. Explain the following terms.

1. Locutionary Act, Illocutionary Act and Perlocutionary Act（北航 2010 研；中国海洋大学 2021 研）
2. Performatives（中山大学 2008 研）
3. Conversational implicature（川大 2010 研；武汉大学 2004 研；北京交通大学 2007 研）
4. Cooperative principle（北二外 2010 研；北京师范大学 2003 研）
5. Violation of maxims（北交大 2006 研）
6. Applied linguistics（中山大学 2011 研）

Ⅳ. Short answer questions

1. What are the major concerns of pragmatics?（人大 2006 研）
2. How would you describe this short exchange in terms of the ardors performed by the speakers?

   Motorist：My car needs new exhaust system.

   Mechanic：I'll be busy with this other car all day.（浙江大学 2005 研）
3. What are the four maxims of the co-operative principle? Which maxim does this speaker seem to be particularly careful about："Well, to be quite honest, I don't think she is ill today."（北二外 2010 研；上海交大 2006 研）
4. Conversational implicature is comparable to illocutionary force in speech act theory in that they are both concerned with the contextual side of meaning, or 言外之意 in Chinese.（中山大学 2005 研）
5. Decide which maxim of the cooperative principle has been flouted in the following utterances and what implicature can be drawn.（厦门大学 2006 研）

   （1）A：Can you tell me the secret?

   B：But John is there.

   （2）A：Let's go to the movies.

   B：I'll bring the Kleenex.

   （3）A：Would you drive a Mercedes?

   B：I wouldn't drive ANY expensive car.
6. What's conversational implicature?（西安交大 2008 研）
7. Analyze the following dialogue with reference to Grice's Cooperative Principle：（北二外 2007 研）

   A：Where is X?

   B：He's gone to the market. He said so where he left.
8. In what ways do people cooperate in their conversations?（人大 2006 研）
9. What is your understanding of Relevance Theory?（南开大学 2009 研）
10. Do you think B is cooperative in the following dialogue? Support your argument with Cooperative Principle.（南开大学 2004 研）

    A：When is the bus coming?

    B：There has been an accident further up the road.

V. Essay questions

1. When a teacher says "It's so hot in here." during a class, what does she probably mean? Refer to the theory of pragmatics when you analyze the situation.（人大 2002 研）
2. A speech act consists of three related acts according to J. L. Austin's Speech Act theory. What are they? Analyze the following conversation in the light of Speech Act theory.（北航 2008 研）
   Customer：Waiter! There's a fly in my soup.
   Waiter：Don't worry, there's no extra charge.
3. Imagine you were at a bus stop and two people approached you one after the other. The first said：
   "哎，几点了?"
   and the second said：
   "不好意思，打搅一下，请问您戴表了吗?"
   What assumptions would you make if you were addressed in these two ways and why would you make them?（北外 2007 研）
4. Discuss the following advertisement extensively："你不理财，财不理你".（浙江大学 2007 研）
5. What kind of linguistic phenomenon can you identify in the following dialogue? Define, analyze and explain the phenomenon.（北外 2010 研）
   甲：上车请买票。
   乙：三张天安门。
   甲：您拿好。
6. What is the relationship between speech event and speech act?（Explain with an example）.（南开大学 2005 研）
7. What are the characteristics of Grice's "conversational implicature"?（中山大学 2011 研）
8. What is communicative competence?

参考答案及解析

Ⅰ. Fill in the blanks

1. sociolinguistics
   （社会语言学家莱考夫认为："言为身份"（You are what you say），（Lakoff, 1991）是指语言可以反映出说话者的相关社会信息。）
2. Grice
   （格赖斯认为一定存在一些管理话语产生和理解的机制。他把这种机制称为合作原则，在这个大原则下有四条准则，它们分别为数量、质量、关系和方式准则。）
3. Performatives
   （施为句是用来做事的，既不陈述事实，也不描述情况，且不能验证其真假。）
4. Cooperative
   （通常在对话中，所有的参与者都被希望能够遵守由格赖斯提出的合作原则，这样就不会有会话含义的产生。）
5. constatives, locutionary act, illocutionary act

（约翰·奥斯丁在他《如何以言行事》一文中，首先区分了施为句和叙事句，之后他又建立了另一种模式来解释如何通过语言实施行为。根据这种新的模式，说话人说话时可以完成三种行为：发话行为，行事行为和取效行为。）

Ⅱ. Multiple Choice

1. A （言语行为理论是哲学家约翰·奥斯丁在他《如何以言行事》一文中提出的。它从哲学意义上对语言交际的本质进行解释，其目的在于回答“用语言干什么”这个问题。塞尔在奥斯丁的基础上对言语行为理论作了进一步发展。）
2. D （约翰·奥斯丁在他《如何以言行事》一文中提出言语行为理论，此理论对语言交际的本质进行解释，即指出言语行为是指用一句话来发挥作用去完成某些事情。）
3. A （奥斯汀认为说话人说话时可以完成三种行为：发话行为，行事行为和取效行为。）
4. D （美国的哲学语言学家约翰·舍尔对言语行为理论的发展做出了巨大的贡献，尤其是他对行事行为的分类。）
5. B （格赖斯的合作原则有四条准则，它们分别为数量、质量、关系和方式准则。其中质量准则指设法使你的话语真实。1. 不要讲明知是虚假的话；2. 不要说没证据的话。）
6. D （格赖斯的合作原则有四条准则，它们分别为数量、质量、关系和方式准则。）
7. C （参见第6题解析。）

Ⅲ. Explain the following terms

1. According to Austin, a speaker might be performing three acts simultaneously when speaking.

   A locutionary act is the uttering of words, phrases, and clauses, which conveys meaning by giving out meaningful sounds. Therefore, when somebody says “Morning”, we can ask a question like “What did he do?”, and the answer could be “He offered a greeting.”

   An illocutionary act is the act of expressing the speaker’s intention; it is the act performed in saying something. Therefore, for the same example, we can say “He meant it as a greeting”.

   A perlocutionary act is the effect of the utterance. Thus, by saying “Morning!” the speaker has made it clear that he wants to keep friendly relations with the hearer.
2. Performatives are sentences that do not state a fact or describe a state. They cannot be said to be true or false. The uttering of these sentences is, or is part of, the doing an action. The judge’s imprisonment sentence, the president’s war or independence declaration, etc., are performatives.
3. Conversational implicature refers to a type of implied meaning, which is deduced on the basis of the conventional meaning of words together with the context, under the guidance of the CP and its maxims. For example, the implicature of “He is a tiger” could probably be he has some characteristics of a tiger.
4. Cooperative principle was proposed and formulated by Grice. It expresses that in making a conversation, the participants must first of all be willing to cooperate; otherwise, it would not be possible for them to carry on the talk. It goes like this: “make your conversational contribution such as is required, at the stage at which it occurs, by the accepted purpose or direction of the talk exchange in which you are engaged”. This principle can be further specified as the four following maxims: Quantity, Quality, Relation; Manner.
5. There are circumstances where speakers may not follow the maxims of the cooperative principle.

For example, in conversation, a speaker may violate the maxim expectations by using an expression like "No comment" in response to a question. Although it is typically not "as informative as is required" in the context, it is naturally interpreted as communicating more than is said (i. e. the speaker knows the answer).

This typical reaction to any apparent violation of the maxims is actually the key to the notion of conversational implicature. When we violate any of these maxims, our language becomes indirect. In this way, we can convey more than is literally said. For example, there is violation of the first maxim of Quantity, and sometimes the first Quantity maxim can be in conflict with the Quality maxim.

6. Applied linguistics: It is a branch of linguistics which studies the application of linguistics in reality. For example, there are studies on multilingualism, language acquisition, first and second language teaching and learning.

Ⅳ. Short answer questions

1. Pragmatics is the study of the language in use. It is mainly about how speakers use language appropriately and effectively in accordance with a given context. It is concerned with the study of meaning as communicated by a speaker (or writer) and interpreted by a listener (or reader). It has more to do with participants of communication and context in which communication takes place. Hence the study of speaker meaning, that of contextual meaning, of what is unsaid but communicated.
2. In the motorist's utterance, there are two types of speech acts performed, namely representative and directive, and as to the latter one, it is recognized as an indirect speech act, which is performed through the performance of the former one. Thus, by stating that his car needs new exhaust system, the motorist has in fact asked the mechanic to equip a new exhaust system for him.

   Similarly, in the mechanic's utterance, there are two types of speech acts performed; one is representative, the other commissive. The commissive speech act in fact is an indirect one since it is recognized through the performance of representative action. That is to say, by stating that he will be busy with another car all day, the mechanic has in fact told the motorist that he could not repair his car right away.
3. The four maxims of the co-operative principle are as follows:

   Quantity. (1) Make your contribution as informative as is required (for the current purposes of the exchange). (2) Do not make your contribution more informative than is required.

   Quality. Try to make your contribution one that is true. (1) Do not say what you believe to be false. (2) Do not say that for which you lack adequate evidence.

   Relation. Be relevant.

   Manner. Be perspicuous. (1) Avoid obscurity of expression. (2) Avoid ambiguity. (3) Be brief. (4) Be orderly.

   In the utterance given, it is probable that the speaker is particularly careful about the maxim of Quality, which rules that do not say that for which you lack adequate evidence.
4. We may summarize conversational implicature as a type of implied meaning. It could be inferred only by the dependence on the context of the utterance and shared knowledge between the speak-

er and listener. Illocutionary force, on the other hand, refers to speaker's meaning, contextual meaning, or extra meaning, that is, the meaning the speaker wants to convey in a specific context. By an illocutionary force, we can say "What does he mean by saying that?" In this sense, implicature is comparable to illocutionary force in speech act theory in that they are both concerned with the contextual side of meaning, or 言外之意 in Chinese.

5. In the exchanges, the maxim of relation has been flouted. As to instance (1), A will assume that if B is cooperative his reply must be relevant in a different sense: I will not talk about my secret now because I do not want to let John know. In (2), the answer of B seems irrelevant to A's utterance. By doing so, A will likely derive the implicature that B has accepted his suggestion, and is going to get prepared. In (3), by violating the maxim of relation, B intends to implicate that Mercedes is an expensive car and he would not drive a Mercedes.
6. The conversational implicature is a message that is not found in the plain sense of the sentence. The speaker implies it. The hearer is able to infer (work out, read between the lines) this message in the utterance, by appealing to the rules governing successful conversational interaction. Grice proposed that implicatures like the second sentence can be calculated from the first, by understanding three things: 1) the usual linguistic meaning of what is said; 2) contextual information (shared or general knowledge); 3) the assumption that the speaker is obeying what Grice calls the cooperative principle.
7. In this dialogue, the second maxim of Quantity is violated, which requires one's utterance not to be over informative. The first part of B's answer is enough for A's question, but by adding the second part, the speaker may implicate that he is not sure whether X has really gone to the library.
8. In daily conversations people do not usually say things directly but tend to imply them, and according to Grice, they seem to observe willingly or unwillingly certain principle, which is called "Cooperative Principle": "Make your conversational contribution such as is required, at the stage at which it occurs, by the accepted purpose or direction of the talk exchange in which you are engaged". Under this principle, there are four maxims, namely, Quantity, Quality, Relation, and Manner.
9. Relevance theory is a proposal (by Dan Sperber and Deidre Wilson) that seeks to explain the second method of communication: implicit inference. It argues that the human mind will instinctively react to an encoded message by considering information that it conceives to be relevant to the message. By "relevance" it is meant whatever allows the most new information to be transmitted in that context on the basis of the least amount of effort required to convey it.

   Relevance Theory's central insights are formalized in the following two-part principle, the Presumption of Optimal Relevance:

   The ostensive stimulus is relevant enough for it to be worth the addressee's effort to process it. The ostensive stimulus is the most relevant one compatible with the communicator's abilities and preferences.
10. On the face of it, B violated the maxim of relation since he did not provide a direct answer to A's question. But A would assume that B is cooperative in the conversation, and would try to explore the link between the seemingly irrelevant response to something relevant. Thus, A

would interpret B's utterance in such a way that because there had been as accident further up the road, it was quite possible that the road was blocked; in a consequence, the bus would not be able to come.

V. Essay questions

1. This utterance would be semantically ambiguous if it was seen isolated without any context of situation. Its interpretation has to rely on the context in which it was uttered.

   There could be generally two types of situation in which this utterance could happen. One may be that it is summer; the teacher just came into the class and was sweating heavily. The other may be that in class the students are quite active towards the questions or problems the teacher has posed, for example, discussing in group, or debating in a large scale.

   According to the cooperative principle, in our conversation, in order to be cooperative, that is, to make his intentions to be known by the hearer, the speaker will try to make his conversational contribution such as is require, at the stage at which it occurs.

   Therefore, according to the third maxim of cooperative principle, RELATION, which says "be relevant", the utterance could be interpreted differently as follows:

   In the first situation, when the students hear the teacher saying "it's so hot in here", they would probably assume that the teacher is obeying the Cooperative Principle, and what he says is relevant to the context, which is that the teacher is sweating, and maybe accompanied by fanning himself with his hand. Therefore, what the teacher means is probably that the temperature is high. What's more, if the windows in the classroom are closed, this utterance will go further to be an implication of an request for opening the windows.

   In the second situation, the students would assume that the teacher should have observed the maxim of relation, since it is under normal circumstances. Given the context in which the students are discussing or debating about certain questions furiously, the hearer would tend to interpret the teacher's utterance as: "You are discussing (or debating) so actively.", which implies a praise for the active participation of the students in class activity.

2. A speech act consists of three related acts according to J. L. Austin's Speech Act theory, namely, locutionary act, illocutionary act and perlocutionary act. The locutionary act is the ordinary act we perform when we speak. It is the act of saying. The illocutionary act is the act performed in the performing of a locutionary act, that may said to be the extra meaning of the utterance; while perlocutionary act concerns the consequential effects of a locution upon the hearer, depending on specific circumstances. Austin suggests that the three kinds of acts are performed simultaneously when a speaker saying something.

   In this conversation, by saying "Waiter! There's a fly in my soup", the locutionary act of this utterance is that the customer produces a number of sounds with its literal meaning that there is a fly in his/her soup. The illocutionary act is that the customer intends not to just review the information to the waiter, but might express his feelings and expect the waiter to do something. It might be a complaint, a warn, a criticism, or a threaten, but whatever it might be, it is no doubt a force, making the waiter to change soup or give some compensation. The perlocutionary act of the utterance here is the waiter's doing nothing but giving a strange respond.

As to the waiter's responding, by saying that he not only produces a number of sounds to state that there is no extra charge, but also shows his possible misinterpretation or his sense of humor or his indirect refusal.

3. As to the first one, an immediate assumption coming to our mind would be the person is asking for the time. The assumption that the hearer gets arises out of the conventional meaning of the expression. The conventional meaning is related to the existing knowledge of the world, and is the meaning that is achieved by the conventions, and is generally accepted by the society. It can be accessed to when we turn to the knowledge towards the world that we have. The expression "几点了" is such a conventional meaning that when it is spoken out, everyone will unexceptionally accept it as a way of asking for the time.

   As to the explanation of the second one, Levinson's M-principle could come into use. Considering the context, which is in the bus stop, what it expresses is no longer a conventional one, but rather a conversational implicature. According to M-principle, the speaker normally will not use a prolix, obscure sentence. It is the ability not only to apply the grammatical rules of a language in order to form grammatically correct sentences but also to know when and where to use these sentences and to whom.

4. This advertisement is an interesting one, for its witty use of pun words. There are two places of punning. First, "理财" could be interpreted in two different ways: one is "to manage one's money", the other is "not to ignore money". Second, in the second part of the sentence, "财" is punned through homophony: it could be interpreted as "财", therefore, the whole part "财不理你" could mean "fortune will ignore you", or rather, "fortune will pass you away". This character could also interpreted as "才", therefore, the whole part "财不理你" could mean "I will ignore you", or rather, "I will show you my cold shoulder" (Here "I" refers to the company which put out this advertisement).

   Therefore, this utterance could be possibly interpreted in the following ways. 1) If you do not handle your money in a proper way, then money will pass you by. 2) If you do not handle your money properly, then I won't take care of any of your business. 3) If you ignore money, and do not pay any attention to it, then money will pass you by. 4) If you ignore money, then I will ignore you, too, and I won't take care of any of your business. In these four interpretations, it is clear to see that in 1 and 4, the advertiser conveyed the messages to the readers as if he was having a face-to-face talk to a friend. This has in some way made the piece of ad interesting to read.

   It is known the punning is by nature ambiguous. Therefore, according to Grice, the advertisement has violated the principle of avoiding ambiguity under Manner Maxim. By such a violation, the advertiser has possibly intended to make the potential consumers pay more attention to it, and spend more time on it, since it is known that ambiguity will increase the time for processing the sentence; and by interpreting it in additional ways, the readers are also expected to get another interesting message from this ad. All of these could eventually come to a higher memorability of the advertisement.

5. This conversation consists of the linguistic phenomenon which is called the "Cooperative Principle", proposed and formulated by P. Grice, based on such a pragmatic hypothesis that the par-

ticipants must first of all be willing to cooperate; otherwise, it would not be possible to carry on talk. It goes as follows:

Make your conversational contribution such as required at the stage at which it occurs by the accepted purpose or direction of the talk exchange in which you are engaged. To be more specific, there are four maxims under this general principle:

The maxim of quantity

a) Make your contribution as informative as is required (for the current purpose of the exchange).

b) Do not make your contribution more informative than is required.

The maxim of quality

a) Do not say what you believe to be false.

b) Do not say that for which you lack adequate evidence.

The maxim of relation

Be relevant.

The maxim of manner

a) Avoid obscurity of expression.

b) Avoid ambiguity.

c) Be brief (avoid unnecessary prolixity).

d) Be orderly.

There are circumstances where speakers may not follow the maxims of the cooperative principle. For example, in this conversation, the speaker may violate the maxim expectations by using an expression like "三张天安门" in response to a question. Although it is typically "more informative than is required" in the context, it is naturally interpreted as communicating more than is said (i. e. the speaker knows the answer). This typical reaction (i. e. there must be something "special" here) of listeners to any apparent violation of the maxims is actually the key to the notion of conversational implicature. When we violate any of these maxims, our language becomes indirect. In this way, we can convey more than is literally said.

6. Speech act refers to an utterance as a functional unit in communication. There are many kinds of speech acts, such as requests, orders, commands, complaints, and promises. A speech act that is performed indirectly is sometimes known as an indirect speech act. Speech event refers to a particular instance when people exchange speech, e. g. an exchange of greetings, an enquiry, a conversation. Speech events are governed by the rules and norms for the use of speech, which may be different in different communities. The structure of speech events varies considerably according to the genre they belong to.

Both speech act and speech event are concerned about the actual utterance of sentences. But speech act deals with a particular utteranceh that has locutionary act, illocutionary act and perlocutionary act. Speech event is related to certain speech situations that are composed of many utterances, though may be not speech act.

For example, when you ask for the time at a bus stop with the sentence, "What time is it?" your meaning is that you want to know the time. This speech act takes place within a speech event, which could be called asking for the time. Such an event is very brief and usually has three speech acts: asking the time, giving the time, and thinking.

Speech events usually take place within the larger context of speech situations. Based on the differences between speech act and speech event, the former is usually studied in pragmatics while the latter is the focus of socio-linguistics.

7. Conversational implicature as a type of implied meaning, which is deduced on the basis of the conventional meaning of words together with the context, under the guidance of the CP and its maxims. In this sense, implicature is comparable to illocutionary force in speech act theory in that they are both concerned with the contextual side of meaning, or 言外之意 in Chinese.

Toward the end of his "Logic and Conversation", Grice mentioned briefly some characteristics of conversational implicature.

(1) Calculability

The fact that speakers try to convey conversational implicatures and hearers are able to understand them suggests that implicatures ate calculable. They can be worked out on the basis of some previous information.

(2) Cancellability

Cancellability is also known as defeasibility. We said that the presence of a conversational mplicature relies on a number of factors: the conventional meaning of words used, the CP, the linguistic and situational contexts, etc. So if any of them changes, the implicature will also change. For example, once Premier Zhu began his talk with a reference to MIT, saying that when he was in Tsinghua, which was known as China's MIT, he wished he could have a chance to study and get a degree at MIT some day. Now he went on, "但是，校长先生请不要误会，我绝对不是要个荣誉学位。"

(3) Non-detachability

By non-detachability is meant that a conversational implicature is attached to the semantic content of what is said, not to the linguistic form. Therefore it is possible to use a synonym and keep the implicature intact. In other words, an implicature will not be detached, separated form the utterance as a whole, even though the specific words may be changed. For example, with "John's an enormous intellect." we can also say "John's a genius."

(4) Non-conventionality

Conversational implicature is by definition different from the conventional meaning of words. To show the differences more clearly, we can have a look at some examples of entailment, e. g. I saw a boy. I saw a child.

（此题考查格赖斯会话含义的特点，共四点分别举例说明。）

8. Communicative competence includes:

(1) Knowledge of the grammar and vocabulary of the language;

(2) knowledge of rules of speaking (e. g. knowing how to begin and end conversations, knowing what topics may be talked about in different types of speech events, knowing which address forms should be used with different persons one speaks to and in different situations);

(3) knowing how to use and respond to different types of speech acts, such as requests, apologies, thanks, and invitations;

(4) knowing how to use language appropriately.

When someone wishes to communicate with others, they must recognize the social setting, their relationship to the other person(s), and the types of language that can be used for a particular occasion. They must also be able to interpret written or spoken sentences within the total context in which they are used, or marked expression without reason; on the hearer's side, if the speaker used a prolix or marked expression, he did not mean the same as he would have had he used the unmarked expression. That is to say, in the normal situation, in a bus stop as the example above has shown, the intention of that the speaker asks others whether they wear the watch or not is not merely to care about the recipient has a watch or not, but has some other reason, because it would be bizarre to ask a stranger in the bus stop about such a personal staff.

Therefore, the hearer has to assume that the expression is related to the situation, and this expression is not what it literally means. Following this, the hearer reaches a connection between the bus stop and the watch, which is the time. As a consequence, he knows what the speaker intends is the inquiring of the time.

第 9 章　语言与文学

9.1　复习笔记

本章要点：

1. Foregrounding; literal language and figurative language
   前景化；字面语言和比喻语言
2. The language in poetry, fiction and drama
   诗歌、小说和戏剧中的语言
3. The cognitive approach to literature
   从认知角度研究文学

常考考点：

文体学概念；前景化；原语言和比喻语言；言语和思维的表达；了解诗歌、小说和戏剧语言的分析方法；掌握押韵和音步的概念以及正确辨别和不同的视角在小说作品中的运用

本章内容索引：

Ⅰ. Stylistics

1. Definition
2. Literary Stylistics
   (1) Foregrounding
   (2) Literal language and Figurative Language

Ⅱ. The Language in Poetry

1. Sound patterning
2. Different forms of sound patterning
3. Metrical patterning
4. Conventional forms of meter and sound
5. The poetic functions of sound and meter
6. How to analyze poetry

Ⅲ. The Language in Fiction

1. Fiction prose and points of view
   (1) I-narrators
   (2) Third-person narrators
   (3) Schema-oriented language
   (4) Given vs. New information
   (5) Deixis
2. Speech and thought presentation
   (1) Speech presentation
   (2) Thought presentation

(3) Stream of consciousness writing

3. Prose style

(1) Authorial style

(2) Text style

4. How to analyze the language of fiction

Ⅳ. The Language in Drama

1. How to analyze drama

2. Analyzing dramatic language

Ⅴ. The Cognitive Approach to Literature

1. Figure and Ground

2. Image Schemata

3. Cognitive Metaphor

Ⅰ. Stylistics **1. Definition** It is a branch of linguistics that studies the features of situationally distinctive uses (varieties) of language, and tries to establish principles capable of accounting for the particular choices made by individual and social groups in their use of language.	**Ⅰ. 文体学** **1. 定义** 文体学作为语言学的分支，主要研究特殊语境中语言的特征(即语言的多样性)，并试图建立一些规则，以解释个体和社团在语言使用过程中的特殊选择。
2. Literary Stylistics Literary stylistics is a branch of linguistics that studies the relationship between language and literature, which focuses on the linguistic features associated with literary style.	**2. 文学文体学** 文学文体学是研究语言与文学关系的学科，其研究焦点是与文学文体相关联的语言特征。
(1) Foregrounding Foregrounding, a popular term in stylistics, originates from visual arts, which corresponds to backgrounding. Russian formalist linguists, Prague school scholars and modern stylisticians have all applied this term in stylistic studies. It is defined as "artistically motivated deviation". This deviation, or unconventional usage, involves all aspects of language: vocabulary, sound, syntax, meaning, graphology, etc.	**(1) 前景化** 前景化的概念来源于视觉艺术，与"背景"一词相对应，已经成为文体学的常用术语。俄国形式主义语言学家、布拉格学派学者和现代文体学家都曾在文体研究中使用这一术语。它被定义为"以艺术手法为动机的偏离"。这种偏离，或非常规用法，覆盖了语言的所有层面；词汇、语音、句法、语义，笔迹等。
(2) Literal language and Figurative Language Literal meaning is the first meaning of a word provided by a dictionary definition. The figurative use of language is a word or phrase that departs from everyday literal language for the sake of comparison, emphasis, clarity or freshness.	**(2) 字面语言和比喻语言** 词典定义中所提供的一个词的第一个意义通常是它的字面意义。比喻语言是为了达到对比、强调、明确或标新的目的而使用的不同于日常常规语言的词句。

Trope is another word for the figurative use of language. It refers to language used in a figurative way for rhetorical purposes. Tropes occur frequently in the use of language and take many different forms.

【考点：指出句中包含的修辞方法】

Simile: A simile is a way to compare one thing with another and to explain what one thing is like by showing how it is similar to another thing. The words *as* or *like* are clear marks that explicitly signal a simile in a text.

Metaphor: Like a simile, a metaphor also makes a comparison between two elements that are not similar, which is, however, implied rather than stated.

Metonymy: It is a figure of speech in which one word is substituted for another on the basis of some material, causal or conceptual relation.

Synecdoche: It refers to representing an object by the use of the name of part of it, and vice versa.

语言中表示比喻用法的另一个词是 Trope（修辞、比喻）。它是指为了修辞目的而通过比喻途径来使用的语言。比喻在语言运用中频繁出现，并且采用许多不同形式。

明喻：明喻是把一种事物和另一种事物作比较，并通过展现一种事物如何与另一事物相似来解释这种事物是什么样子的方法。它用 as 或 like 等词在文本中作为明确标志。

暗喻：像明喻一样，暗喻也是对两个并不相像的要素作出对比，这种对比是隐含的而不是直接表达的。

转喻：一种一个词或词组被另一个与之有紧密联系的词或词组替换的修辞方法。

提喻：提喻是用事物的一部分名称来指代整个事物，反之亦然。

II. The Language in Poetry

II. 诗歌语言

1. Sound patterning

1. 语音模式

【考点：指出两词的押韵模式】

Rhyme

End rhyme (**cVC**): rhyme at the end of lines.

押韵

尾韵：每行结尾的押韵。

2. Different forms of sound patterning

2. 不同形式的语音模式

Alliteration (**Cvc**): the initial consonants that are identical.

Assonance (**cVc**): describes syllables with a common vowel.

Consonance (**cvC**): syllables ending with the same consonants.

Reverse rhyme (**CVc**): syllables sharing the vowel and initial consonants, unlike the vowel and the final consonant as is the case in rhyme.

Pararhyme (**CvC**): two syllables with the same initial and final consonants, but different vowels.

Repetition: the repetition of syllables.

头韵：在头韵里，句首的辅音是一致的。

准押韵：准押韵通过一个共同的元音来描述音节。

辅音韵：以相同辅音结尾的音节

反韵：指音节拥有共同的元音和首辅音，而不是元音和末辅音押韵。

押副韵：当两个音节具有相同的首辅音和尾辅音。

反复：音节的重复。

3. Metrical patterning

When stress is organized into regular rhythm, meter is formed. An iamb is an example of a unit of meter. Feet is used to describe units of meter. Pentameter, thus, refers to the number of feet in the line.

4. Conventional forms of meter and sound

(1) Couplets: two lines of verse, usually connected by a rhyme.

(2) Quatrains: four-line stanzas, quite common in English poetry.

(3) Blank verse: It is made up of lines in iambic pentameters that do not rhyme.

(4) Sonnet, free verse, limericks, etc.

5. The poetic functions of sound and meter

(1) For aesthetic pleasure;

(2) To adapt to a poetic fashion, such as convention/style/poetical form;

(3) To express or create new poetic forms;

(4) To show technical skills and seek for intellectual pleasure;

(5) To emphasize or contrast;

(6) Onomatopoeia.

6. How to analyze poetry

(1) Information about the poem: the title, the poet, the period when it was written, the genre it belongs to, e. g. lyric, dramatic, epic sonnet, or satire, etc.

(2) How the poem is structured: the layout, number of lines, length of lines, regular meter, end rhymes, other forms of sound patterning.

Ⅲ. The Language in Fiction

1. Fiction prose and points of view

【考点：第一人称叙述者与第三人称叙述者的区别】

(1) I-narrators

The person who tells the story after the event may also be a character in the fictional world of the story. The story-teller is called a first-person narrator or I-narrator by the critics because he or she refers to himself or herself in the story with the first person pronoun *I*.

3. 韵律模式

当重读被组织成有规律的节奏时，就形成了韵律。抑扬格是韵律单位的一种。韵律单位叫做音步。pentameter（五音步诗行）是指诗句里有五个音步。

4. 传统的韵律模式与语音模式

（1）对句：对句为两行诗句，一般由押韵联系在一起。

（2）四行诗：即四行为一节的诗，是英语诗歌中很常见的形式。

（3）无韵诗：无韵诗是由不押韵的抑扬格五音步诗组成的。

（4）十四行诗、自由体诗、打油诗等。

5. 语音和韵律在诗歌中的功能

（1）追求审美趣味；

（2）适应传统/风格/诗歌形式；

（3）表情达意或者革新一种形式；

（4）展示专业技巧，寻求精神满足感；

（5）突出强调或对照；

（6）拟声现象。

6. 如何分析诗歌

（1）有关诗歌的信息：诗的题目，诗人姓名，诗歌创作时期，诗歌所属类型，例如抒情诗、戏剧诗、叙事性十四行诗、讽刺诗等。

（2）诗歌构建的方式：布局、诗的行数、诗行的长度、规则的韵律、尾韵、语音模式的其他形式。

Ⅲ. 小说中的语言

1. 小说与视角

（1）第一人称叙述者

讲故事的人也可能成为故事虚构世界中的一个角色，在事件发生后讲述故事。在这种情形下，评论家们称叙述者为“第一人称叙述者”或“I 叙述者”，因为叙述者在故事里提到他或她自己的时候，总是用第一人称代词“我(I)”。

(2) Third-person narrators If the narrator is not a character in the fictional world, he or she is usually referred to as a third-person narrator because when all the characters are mentioned in the fictional world of the story, the third-person pronouns, *it*, *she*, *he* or *they* are used. It is arguably the dominant narrator type.	**(2) 第三人称叙述者** 如果叙述者不是虚拟世界中的角色，他或她常常被称为"第三人称叙述者"，因为故事虚构世界中的所有人物被提及时，用的都是第三人称代词"他，她，它或他们"。
(3) Schema-oriented language Viewpoint is influenced by schema. Different participants who are in the same situation may have different schema, leading to their different viewpoints.	**(3) 图示语言** 叙述视角也受图式的影响。处于相同情形中的不同参与者会有不同的图式，这和他们的不同视角有关系。
(4) Given v. s. New information Given information is the information that the addresser believes is known to the addressee, whereas new information refers to the information that the addresser believes is not known to the addressee.	**(4) 旧信息与新信息** 旧信息是说话人认为听话人已经知道的信息，而新信息则是说话人认为听话人所不知道的信息。
(5) Deixis Deixis is related to speaker and it can easily be applied to show the particular and changing viewpoint. It is collective and orientational features of human languages, which refer to points in time, space, and the speaking event between interlocutors. Its meaning is relative to the situation. 【考点：指出一段话中所包含的指称词—时间、地点、人物指称】	**(5) 指称** 指称与说话者相关，所以很容易用于表明特定的变化中的视角。指称用来指语言中这样一些特征，它们直接指示一个话段说出时的情景在人称、时间或处所方面的特点，其意义因而相对那个情景而言。
2. Speech and thought presentation **(1) Speech presentation** Direct speech (**DS**): Direct speech is what the character said in its fullest form and with quotation marks. Indirect speech (**IS**): The propositional content of what the speaker said is presented, but it is not stated in the original words. Narrator's representation of speech acts (**NRSA**): It is the speech act of the speaker that is presented rather than what he is actually said. It can be regarded as a summary of a longer piece of discourse and gives more background information. Narrator's representation of speech (**NRS**): It is a sentence merely telling us that speech occurred, which does not even point out the speech act involved.	**2. 言语和思维表达** **(1) 言语表达** 直接引语：在直接引语中，人物所说的话是以最全面的形式出现的并且带有引号。 间接引语：我们能够知道说话者表达的命题含意，但并不是说话者的原话。 叙述者对言语行为的表达：我们不知道说话者说话的内容，我们只知道他用言语行为来做事。这种叙述可以被看作是对较长语篇的概括，比起间接言语，它提供了更多的背景信息。 叙述者对言语的表达：仅仅是一个告诉我们某人说话了的句子，甚至连具体是什么言语行为都没说。

【考点：言语表达的几种形式及区别；指出一句使用了哪种言语表达形式】

(2) Thought presentation

The categories used by novelists to represent the thoughts of their characters are exactly the same as those used to represent a speech.

Direct thought (DT): It is used to present conscious and deliberative thought.

Free indirect thought (FIT): It refers to a kind of thought presentation between DT and IT, which is certainly not DT, but takes on some features of the thoughts in the character's mind.

(3) Stream of consciousness writing

It is used for describing the free association of ideas and impressions in the characters' mind, which features a highly elliptical sentence structure.

3. Prose style

(1) Authorial style

It is the "world view" kind of writing style, which belongs to a particular writer and can be identified. This way of writing distinguishes the work of one author from that of others.

(2) Text style

Text style pays close attention to how language choice helps to construct the meaning of the text.

4. How to analyze the language of fiction

(1) Patterns of lexis (vocabulary);

(2) Patterns of grammatical organization;

(3) Patterns of textual organization;

(4) Foregrounded features, including figures of speech;

(5) Whether any patterns of style variation can be detected;

(6) Various discoursal patterning, like turn-taking or patterns of inferencing;

(7) Patterns of viewpoint manipulation, including speech and thought presentation.

(2) 思维表达

小说家们在表达人物思维时所采用的区分类别，与用来表达言语时采用的类别完全相同。

直接思维：直接思维倾向于被用来表达有意识的、缜密的思维。

自由间接思维：这种思维方式介于直接思维和间接思维之间，有一些思维的特征。

(3) 意识流写作

意识流写作被用来描述思维中印象和观念的自由联系。句子结构高度省略。

3. 散文风格

(1) 作者风格

人们谈及风格时，通常是指作者的风格，即"世界观"式的作者风格。换言之，是指一种写作方式：属于特定作者，可以识别。这种写作方式使一个作者的作品区别于其他作者的作品。

(2) 文本风格

文本风格紧密关注的是，语言选择如何帮助建构文本意义。

4. 如何分析小说的语言

(1) 词汇模式（词汇量）；

(2) 语法组织模式；

(3) 文本组织模式；

(4) 前景化特征，包括修辞手法；

(5) 是否能观察到任何风格变化的模式；

(6) 各种类型的话语模式，如话轮模式和推论模式；

(7) 视角处理的模式，包括言语和思维的表达。

Ⅳ. The Language in Drama

1. How to analyze drama

(1) Drama as poetry: it might be appropriate to analyze everything to do with meter, sound patterning, syntax and figurative language, for sound and meter are as meaningful in many dramatic texts as in poetry.

(2) Drama as fiction: The play can be analyzed more or less like fiction.

(3) Drama as conversation: A crucial aspect distinguishing drama from poetry and fiction lies in its emphasis on verbal interaction, and the way relationships between people are established and developed through their conversation.

2. Analyzing dramatic language

(1) Turn quantity and length.

How much a character speaks can reflect either their relative importance in the play, or their self-evaluation of their importance. Generally, the speech of the central character is longer and appears more frequently than that of the minor characters.

(2) Exchange sequence: The patterns of exchange of a dramatic dialogue.

(3) Production errors: Deliberately used forms such as hesitation.

(4) The cooperative principle.

(5) Status marked through language: Many of the features of language can be indicative of the relative status and changes in status of characters. Particularly, language can be used for marking to what degree the relationship between the speaker and listener is determined by a social power difference, and to what extent it is based on solidarity.

(6) Register: It is used to describe the relationship between a particular language style and its context of use.

(7) Speech and silence: It is concerned with the language features of female characters in plays. There is evidence showing that men tend to speak more than women in mixed sex conversations.

Ⅳ. 戏剧语言

1. 如何分析戏剧

(1) 像分析诗歌一样分析戏剧：既然语音和韵律在剧本里与在诗歌里一样，都具有价值，那么所有处理韵律、语音模式、句法和比喻性语言的方法都同样适用于戏剧分析。

(2) 像分析小说一样分析戏剧：可以分析戏剧中的角色和情节，把戏剧大体上看作小说。

(3) 像分析会话一样分析戏剧：戏剧不同于诗歌和小说的一个关键方面在于：它强调语言的交流，以及通过会话来建立和发展人们之间相互关系的方式。

2. 分析戏剧性语言

(1) 话轮数量和长度。

在戏剧中，一个角色讲话内容的多少，能够体现出该角色的相对重要性，或体现角色对自身重要性的理解。一般来说，中心角色比次要角色的言语更长，出现频率更高。

(2) 交际序列：戏剧对话的交流方式。

(3) 产生性错误：故意使用一些形式，比如犹豫的状态。

(4) 合作原则。

(5) 通过语言标记地位：上面讨论的许多语言的特性，都可以用来标记人物的相对地位，以及人物地位的变化。尤其是，语言也可以用来标记说话者和受话人之间的关系在多大程度上基于社会地位的差异，以及在多大程度上基于社会地位的一致性。

(6) 语域：语域是语言学里用来描述一种特定的语言风格及语境之间关系的术语。

(7) 言语和沉默：剧中女性人物的语言特征。有证据表明，在男女混合的交谈中，男人比女人往往谈得更多。

V. The Cognitive Approach to Literature **1. Figure and Ground** The figures are the foregrounded literary elements, which are also known as "attractors" or "attention" in cognitive linguistics. The feature opposite to the figure is the ground that is known as "neglect". **2. Image Schemata** Image schemata can be roughly described as the recurring patterns of our daily perceptual communication and physical experiences. **3. Cognitive Metaphor** A way of mapping specific characteristics, usually specific and physical, of a source domain onto a target domain to better understand abstract concepts.	**V. 从认知角度分析文学** **1. 图形和背景** 前景化的文学成分，如图形，在认知语言学中被称为“关注点”或者“抢眼点”。与图形相反的特征，即“背景”，则被称为“忽略”。 **2. 意象图式** 意向图式大致可描述为我们日常的感知交往和身体经验的反复呈现模式。 **3. 认知隐喻** 把源域的特征投射到目标域上。

9.2 考研真题与典型题详解

I. Fill in the blanks.

1. The part of linguistics that studies the language of literature is called ________. It focuses on the study of linguistic features related to literary style. (人大 2006 研)
2. "The world is like a stage" is an example of ________, and "All the world is a stage" is an example of ________. They are often used in analyzing features of literary language. (人大 2006 研)
3. At different times, different patterns of metre and sound have developed and become accepted as ways of structuring poems. Among them, ________ consists of lines in iambic pentameter which does not rhyme. (中山大学 2008 研)
4. A ________ foot contains two syllables. A stressed syllable comes first, following by an unstressed syllable. (中山大学 2005 研)
5. The term ________ was originally coined by the philosopher William James in his principle of Psychology (1890) to describe the free association of ides and impression in mind. It was later applied to the writing of William Faulkner, James Joyce and Virginia Woolf. (中山大学 2005 研)
6. Euphemism, which serves as a polite substitute for ________, is a mild, indirect or less offensive word or expression substituted when the speaker or writer fears that more direct, wording might be harsh or offensive.

II. Multiple Choice

1. "Formal" and "informal" are features of ________. (对外经贸 2005 研)
   A. slang　B. lingua franca　C. style　D. jargon
2. ________ is a figurative use of language which implies a comparison between two unlike elements. (西安外国语学院 2006 研)

A. Simile B. Metaphor C. Metonymy D. Synecdoche

3. The cognitive approach to literature does not include __________

A. Figure and Ground B. Image Schemata

C. Cognitive Metaphor D. Judgment and comparison

Ⅲ. True or False

1. Metonymy is a kind of figurative language which is usually classed as a type of synecdoche. It refers to using the name of part of an object to talk about the whole thing, and vice versa, as the use of "hands" in "We are short of hands".（大连外国语学院 2008 研）
2. Blank verse consists of lines in iambic pentameters which do not rhyme.（南开大学 2004 研）
3. The initial consonants are identical in alliteration.（南开大学 2004 研）
4. The term Stream of consciousness writing was originally coined by the philosopher William James in his *Principle of Psychology* to describe the free association of ideas and impressions in the mind.（南开大学 2004 研）
5. Authorial style looks closely at how linguistic choices help to construct textual meaning. When we examine it, we will need to examine linguistic choices which are intrinsically connected with meaning and effect on the reader.（大连外国语学院 2008 研）
6. The opinion that a language is primitive reflects the social judgment of the language.（对外经贸 2005 研）

Ⅳ. Explain the following terms.

1. Foregrounding（北交大 2007 研）
2. Speech and thought presentation（中山大学 2006 研）
3. Metonymy（北航 2010 研）
4. Stylistics
5. Third-person narrators

Ⅴ. Short answer questions

1. What are the differences between simile and metaphor?（南开大学 2004 研）
2. How to analyze dramatic language?

Ⅵ. Essay questions

1. What is the relationship between language and literature?（中山大学 2006 研）
2. What is the main difference between literal language and figurative language?（中山大学 2008 研）
3. Read the following sentence and illustrate the ideas behind this statement: "Register is the term used in linguistics to describe the relationship between a particular style of language and its context of use."（中山大学 2006 研）
4. List different types of Speech presentation and Thought presentation.

参考答案及解析

Ⅰ. Fill in the blanks.

1. stylistics

（文体学作为语言学的分支，主要研究文学文体中语言的特征，并试图建立一些规则，以解释个体和社团在语言使用过程中的特殊选择。）

2. simile; metaphor

（明喻是通过展现一种事物如何与另一事物相似来解释这种事物是什么样子的方法，它用 as 或 like 等词在文本中作为明确标志。暗喻也是对两个并不相像的要素作出对比，这种对比是隐含的而不是直接表达的。）

3. blank verse

（不同时代，诗会有不同的韵律模式和语音模式。传统的韵律模式和语音模式包括对句，四行诗，无韵诗等。其中无韵诗是由不押韵的抑扬格五音步诗组成的。）

4. trochee

（扬抑格音步即重轻格或长短格，其由一重读音节后跟一个轻读音节构成。）

5. stream of consciousness

（意识流写作起初是由威廉姆·詹姆斯用来描述思维中印象和观念的自由联系，这种方法的句子结构高度省略。之后许多作家如威廉·福克纳，詹姆斯·乔伊斯，弗吉尼亚·伍尔夫也都在写作中有所用到。）

6. taboo expressions

（凡是表示禁忌或敏感事物的含蓄、迂回或动听的言词，都叫委婉语。特别是发言者或作者怕直接表达会显得没礼貌或太犀利时，可以用委婉语来表达。）

Ⅱ. Multiple Choice

1. C （风格一般有正式与非正式之分。）
2. B （暗喻是对两个并不相像的要素作出对比，这种对比是隐含的而不是直接表达的。）
3. D （从认知角度分析文学有三种方法：图形和背景，意象图式和认知隐喻。）

Ⅲ. True or False

1. F （转喻是一种一个词或词组被另一个与之有紧密联系的词或词组替换的修辞方法。提喻是用事物的一部分名称来指代整个事物，反之亦然。所以上述例子使用了提喻。）
2. T （无韵诗是由不押韵的抑扬格五音步诗组成的。）
3. T （在压头韵里，句首的辅音是一致的。）
4. T （意识流写作是由哲学家威廉·詹姆斯在他的《心理学原理》中用来描述思维中印象和观念的自由联系。）
5. F （作者风格通常是指作者的风格，即“世界观”式的作者风格，是指一种写作方式属于特定作者，可以识别。而文本风格紧密关注的是，语言选择如何帮助建构文本意义。）
6. F （语言并不是简单的，其具有多样性，个体和社团在语言使用过程中会有其特殊的选择。）

Ⅳ. Explain the following terms.

1. Foregrounding: This term is meant for what is unusual, attractive, unconventional, salient. In literature, foregrounding is often achieved through unconventional expressions which attract the readers' attention. The main manifestations of foregrounding are deviation and parallelism.
2. Speech and thought presentation: These two terms are used for the language in fiction, referring to the presenting forms for indicating the narrator's speech or thought. The speech presentation may have the following four possibilities: direct speech, indirect speech, narrator's representation of speech acts, and narrator's representation of speech. The Thought presentation can also be categorized into: narrator's representation of thought, narrator's representation of thought

acts, indirect thought, free indirect thought, and direct thought.

3. Metonymy is a figure of speech used in rhetoric in which a thing or concept is not called by its own name, but by the name of something intimately associated with that thing or concept. For instance, "Washington", as the capital of the United States, can be used as a metonym (an instance of metonymy) for the United States government.
4. Stylistics is a branch of linguistics studies the features of situationally distinctive uses (varieties) of language, and tries to establish principles capable of accounting for the particular choices made by individual and social groups in their use of language.
5. If the narrator is not a character in the fictional world, he or she is usually called a third-person narrator because reference to all the characters in the fictional world of the story will involve the use of the third-person pronouns, *it*, *she*, *he or they*. This second main type of narrator is arguably the dominant narrator type.

V. Short answer questions

1. Simile is a way of comparing one thing with another, of explaining what one thing is like by showing how it is similar to another thing , and it explicitly signals itself in a text, with the words *as* or *like*. For example, the phrase *as cold as ice* is a common simile.

   Although metaphor also makes a comparison between two unlike elements, this comparison is implied rather than stated. That is, it differs from simile in that the words such as *like* or *as* do not appear. For example, "The life is a stage" is a metaphor.
2. (1) Turn quantity and length

   How much a character talks can be indicative either of their relative importance in the play, or of how important they appear to think they are. Generally speaking, central characters have longer and more speeches than minor characters.

   (2) Exchange sequence: The patterns of exchange of a dramatic dialogue which are considered appropriate by speakers of English. For example, the two-part exchanges such as greeting-greeting, question-answer.

   (3) Production errors: Deliberately used forms such as hesitation to convey something about the character

   (4) The cooperative principle: this principle is proposed by Grice. He asserted people used to make sense of their conversation by enabling them to distinguish between sentence meaning and utterance meaning. He also suggested that people actually break these maxims quite often when they talk.

   (5) Status marked through language: Many of the properties of language discussed can be used to signal the relative status and changes in status, of characters. Particularly, language can be used to signal to what extent the relationship between an addresser and addressee is based on a social power difference, and to what extent it is based on solidarity.

   (6) Register: It is the term used in linguistics to describe the relationship between a particular style of language and its context of use. An example of a linguistic register is legal discourse, we recognize a legal document when we see one, but lawyers are the only people who are trained to produce them using appropriate linguistic choices.

(7) Speech and silence: Concerning female characters in plays, there is evidence that men tend to talk more than women in mixed sex conversations.

Ⅵ. Essay questions

1. Literature is closely related to language. Generally speaking, it is marked by careful use of language, such as creative metaphors, elegant syntax, and so on. It reaches to human beings mostly via language. It could be seen as a language in use. The existence of literature owes a lot to language. The language used in literature is quite often different from language used in other fields, such as everyday use.

   In linguistics, the term "genre" is used to refer not only to types of literary works but also to any identifiable type of discourse, whether literary or not. Therefore, literature could be viewed as a particular range of genres or discourse types; that is, as a particular subset of the repertory of genres, existing in a given speech community. For example, written literature is discourse that may be read at a far distance in time a place from its origin. More generally speaking, literary discourse has many other general linguistic characteristics, such as certain kinds of phonological, syntactic, and semantic phenomena, occurring with much greater frequency in literature than in other kinds of discourse.

   What's more, studying the language of literature text as language can enhance our appreciation of the different systems of language organization, because the literary texts often reveal the nature of the language in which they are written.

2. The first meaning for a word that a dictionary definition gives is usually its literal meaning, while figurative language is not intended to be interpreted in a literal sense.

   Appealing to the imagination, figurative language provides new ways of looking at the world. It always makes use of a comparison between different things. Figurative language compares two things that are different in enough ways so that their similarities, when pointed out, are interesting, unique and/or surprising. Figurative language uses "figures of speech" to express something other than the literal meaning of the words, in other words, figurative language cannot be taken literally (or should not be taken literally only). Simile, metaphor, metonymy, synecdoche, personification, apostrophe, are all forms of figurative language.

   For example, the literal meaning of the word "tree" is "a large plant". However, once we start talking about a tree in the context of "a family tree" for example, it is no longer a literal tree we are talking about, but a figurative one. The literal use of the word "tree" refers to an organism which has bark, branches and leaves. A "family tree" shares some of these qualities-graphically, a plan of a family and a representation of a tree can look similar, and in a way they are both a process of organic growth, so we use the same term for both. But when we use the term for a plant it is a literal usage and when we use the term to describe our ancestry, it is a figurative usage.

3. The register is what you are speaking at the time, depending on what you are doing and the nature of the activity in which the language is functioning. A register can be defined as a configuration of meanings that are typically associated with a particular situational configuration of field, mode, and tenor. Therefore, a register must also include the expressions, the lexico-grammatical

and phonological features, which typically accompany or realize these meanings. Text can be seen as an instance of a register.

Register is seen as the linguistic consequence of interacting aspects of context, which Halliday calls "field, tenor, and mode." Field refers to the topics and actions which language is used to express. Tenor denotes the language users, their relationships to each other, and their purposes. Mode refers to the channel through which communication is carried out. These three contextual variables are intended to help the linguist tie linguistic analysis to the relevant contextual variables. By understanding the semiotic properties of a situation (i. e., the values for field, tenor, and mode), language users can predict the meanings that are likely to be exchanged and the language likely to be used. And while people are communicating they make predictions by using the values of field, tenor and mode to understand register and that their assessment facilitates their own participation.

4. (1) Speech presentation:

Direct speech (**DS**): With the direct speech, what the character said is in its fullest form and with quotation marks.

Indirect speech (**IS**): The propositional content of what the speaker said is presented, but it is not stated in the original words.

Narrator's representation of speech acts (**NRSA**): We don't know what the speaker said, and all we know is that he used the speech act of doing something. It can be regarded as a summary of a longer piece of discourse and give more background information than indirect speech.

Narrator's representation of speech (**NRS**): It is a sentence which merely tells us that speech occurred, and which does not even specify the speech act involved.

(2) Thought presentation: The categories used by novelists to represent the thoughts of their characters are exactly the same as those used to represent a speech.

Direct thought (**DT**): DT tends to be used for presenting conscious, deliberative thought.

Free indirect thought (**FIT**): It refers to a kind of thought presentation between DT and IT, which is certainly not DT, but takes on some features of the thoughts in the character's mind.

第 10 章　语言和计算机

10.1　复习笔记

本章要点：

1. Computer-assisted language learning
   计算机辅助语言学习
2. Machine translation
   机器翻译
3. Corpus linguistics
   语料库语言学
4. Computer mediated communication
   计算机中介交际

常考考点：

CALL 的定义；CALL 和 CAI、CAL 的区别；机器翻译的定义；计算机语料库的定义；计算机中介交际的定义及其形式等。

本章内容索引：

Ⅰ. Introduction to Computational Linguistics

1. Computer Literacy
2. Computational Linguistics

Ⅱ. Computer-assisted Language Learning

1. CAI/CAL vs. CALL
2. Stages of CALL Development
3. Technology

▼4. MOOC

Ⅲ. Machine Translation (MT)

1. Definition and Categories
2. History of Development of MT
3. Research Methodology
   (1) The linguistic approach
   (2) The transfer approach
   (3) The interlingual approach
   (4) The knowledge-based approach
4. MT and the Internet
5. Speech Translation
6. MT and Human Translation

Ⅳ. Corpus Linguistics

1. Corpus and Corpus Linguistics
2. Criticisms and Revival
3. Concordance
4. The Roles of Corpus Data

I. Introduction to Computational Linguistics **1. Computer Literacy** It's specifically refers to those who can use a computer and have extensive knowledge and skills in computer software.	**I. 计算机语言学简介** **1. 计算机操作能力** 特指那些能使用计算机并具有大量计算机软件知识和技巧的人。
2. Computational Linguistics **▼(1) Components of computational linguistics** Computational linguistics consists of two parts: theoretical computational linguistics which focuses on issues related to theoretical linguistics and cognitive science and applied computational linguistics which applied linguistics focuses on the actual products of human language use.	**2. 计算机语言学** **(1)计算机语言学的组成成分** 计算机语言学包含有理论计算机语言学和应用计算机语言学两个成分。理论计算机语言学主要研究理论语言学和认知科学的相关问题，应用语言学主要研究人类语言使用的实际产物。
(2) The applied computational linguistics It can be seen as the branch of applied linguistics that deals with human language through computers. Computational linguistics includes: the analysis of linguistic data to create a sequence through which a language learner can obtain various grammatical laws or the frequency of occurrence of a particular lexical item; the electronic generation of artificial speech and the automatic recognition of human language; it also includes automatic translation and discourse processing between different natural languages; and human-computer communication.	**(2)应用计算机语言学** 可以看作是应用语言学的分支，即通过计算机处理人类语言。计算机语言学包括：对语言数据的分析，建立一个序列，通过它，语言学习者可以获得各种语法规律或某一特定词项的出现频率；人工言语的电子生成和人类语言的自动识别；它也包括不同自然语言之间的自动翻译和语篇处理；人与计算机的交流。
II. Computer-assisted Language Learning **1. CAI/CAL vs. CALL** (1) Computer-assisted instruction (CAI), which is the use of computers in a teaching program. (2) Computer Assisted Learning (CAL), which emphasizes the use of computers in both teaching and learning to help learners achieve instructional goals through students' own reasoning and practice. (3) Computer Assisted Language Learning (CALL): If CAI or CAL deals with teaching and learning in general, CALL is used to deal with language teaching and learning. CALL especially refers to the application of computers to the teaching of a second or foreign language. 【考点：名词解释；CALL 与 CAI/CAL 的区别】	**II. 计算机辅助语言学习** **1. CAI/CAL vs. CALL** (1)计算机辅助教学(CAI)，就是在教学过程中使用计算机。 (2)计算机辅助学习(CAL)，强调在教和学两方面使用计算机，通过学生自己的推理和实践，帮助学习者达到教学目标。 (3)计算机辅助语言学习(CALL)：如果说 CAI 或 CAL 是处理一般的教和学，那么 CALL 则是用来处理语言教学的。CALL 特别是指将计算机运用到第二语言或外语的教学中去。

2. Stages of CALL Development

(1) Stage 1: In this stage, computers were restricted to be used in research institutions with very large mainframes.

(2) Stage 2: Small computers appeared, which were cheaper than the previous ones. This made possible the creation of a new generation of programs.

(3) Stage 3: Computers were used as a stimulus for communication among students. As a result, the computer ceased to be an individual resource for each student and was increasingly seen as the focal point of group learning, which made many activities known as "communicative" activities feasible, such as interactive multi-character games.

(4) Stage 4: Word processing is no longer about writing specific programs for language teaching, but about adapting language teaching to enable students to write in a non-permanent form and to modify their work.

3. Technology

(1) Customizing, template, and authoring programs

The greatest flexibility in using CALL for teaching lies in the area of programming. Teachers are able to use these programs to create simple or elaborate software programs on their own materials. Programming can range from simple modular programs to very complex programming languages. This allows the potential for development of multimedia and makes less complex programming possible.

(2) Computer networks

Apart from individual programs, computers are connected together through networks, expanding access to foreign language teaching. Local area networks are classrooms, laboratories or other buildings where computers that are connected together by fiber optic cables. They provide a novel way for teachers to create new activities, and in the case of students is to create more activities that can provide more time and experience in the target language.

2. CALL 的发展阶段

(1) 阶段1：在这个阶段，计算机限制在研究机构中运用，其主机非常大。

(2) 阶段2：小型计算机出现了，比以前的要便宜。这使得新一代程序的产生变为可能。

(3) 阶段3：计算机被用作学生之间交流的激发点。结果，对每个学生而言，计算机不再是个人资源，它逐渐被视为小组学习的焦点，这就使得许多被称为"交流性"的活动变得可行，例如，交互的多角色游戏。

(4) 阶段4：文字处理不再是为语言教学编写具体的程序，而是适应语言教学，使学生用一种非永久性形式写作并能修改它们的作品。

3. 技术

(1) 定制、模块和编程

使用 CALL 进行教学的最大弹性在于编程的领域。教师们能够就他们自己的材料，运用这些程序来创造简单的或精心制作的软件程序。编程的范围是从简单模块程序到十分复杂的编程语言。这使得多媒体有了发展的潜能，也使不太复杂的编程成为可能。

(2) 计算机网络

除了单独的程序以外，计算机通过网络连在一起，扩大了外语教学的途径。局域网就是指在教室、实验室或其他建筑里，计算机通过光缆连接在一起。它们为教师们提供了一种新颖的方式，来创造新的活动，就学生而言就是创造更多的活动，能提供更多目标语言的时间和经验。

(3) Compact disk technology Compact disk technology is used for many purposes in foreign language education, including information retrieval, interactive audio and interactive multimedia programs. The development of compact discs (CD-ROMs) from compact disks has made it possible to store large amounts of information on a single disk for quick access to information.	**(3) 软盘技术** 软盘技术在外语教育中用处很多，包括信息检索，交互音频和交互式多媒体程序。由软盘发展起来的光盘(CD-ROM)使得大量信息可以储存在一张磁盘上，以便快速获取信息。
(4) Digitized sound Many programs have added a new physical feature, digitized sound. Laser disks utilizing digitized speech provide fast and free access to information and excellent sound quality. With such programs, students can hear the pronunciation of a phrase, word or even a syllable or tone of voice. They can listen to the original pronunciation and their own and compare the two until they feel their pronunciation has grown or has been correct.	**(4) 数字化语音** 许多程序已增添了一个新的物理特性，数字化语音。利用数字化语音的激光盘，提供了快速自由的获取信息和优良的声音质量。有了这种程序，学生们能听到一个短语，单词甚至一个音节或声调的发音。它们可以听原来的发音和自己的发音，并比较二者，直到他们觉得自己的发音已经有了长进或已经正确。
***(5) Universal Serial Bus** There are at most two serial ports in most computers, which in most cases run very slowly. And USB is designed to solve these problems.	**(5) 通用串行总线** 大多数计算机至多有两个串行口，多数情况下运行很慢。USB 就是为了解决这些问题。
◆4. MOOC MOOC (Massive Open Online Course) is an online course designed for unrestricted participation and open access via the Web. In addition to traditional course materials such as video lectures, readings, and problem sets, many MOOCs offer interactive user forums to support community interaction between learners, professors, and teaching assistants. As MOOCs has evolved, a distinction has emerged between CMOOCs, where the C stands for connected or linked, and EMOOCs, a type of catechism that emphasizes a philosophy of connection, peer review, and group work. The material should be aggregated, combinable, transformative and progressive, and this type of MOOCs seeks to connect learners to answer questions or collaborate on group projects. In contrast, the X in X MOOCs stands for extension, and this type of MOOCs has similarities to traditional courses in that its video lectures and self-test questions have a clear outline, the instructor himself is the authoritative knowledge provider, and interaction is limited to seeking help from the instructor and students facilitating each other.	**4. 慕课** 慕课是一种旨在通过网络进行无限制的参与和开放访问的在线课程。除了传统的课程材料，如视频讲座，阅读和问题集，许多慕课还提供互动的用户论坛来支持学习者，教授和助教之间的社区互动。 随着慕课的发展，出现了 C 慕课和 E 慕课之间的区别。C 慕课中的 C 代表连接或联系，该种慕课类型强调联系哲学，同行审查，小组合作。教学材料应该是聚合的，可结合的，可转变用途的并且不断推进的，这种慕课试图将学习者联系起来回答问题或合作完成集体项目。相反地，X 慕课中的 X 代表拓展，该种慕课类型与传统的课程具有相似性，它的视频讲座和自我测试问题具有明确的大纲，指导者本身就是权威的知识提供者，互动也仅限于寻求指导者帮助和学生之间互相促进。

However, it is important to note that the effectiveness of the catechism remains to be studied and that the MOOCs' system itself has some problems.

Ⅲ. Machine Translation (MT)

1. Definition and Categories

Definition: Machine translation refers to using machine, mostly computer, to translate discourses from one natural language to another.

Categories: Machine translation can be divided into two categories: those that do not require help and those that do, to be specific, Unassisted MT and Assisted MT.

Unassisted MT translates the discourse into another language directly after translation without human involvement. Assisted MT awaits processing by human translators after, and sometimes before, the translation to obtain a higher quality translation. Usually, this enhancement process is done by using a dictionary and applicable syntax to qualify the use of words.

2. History of Development of MT

(1) The independent work by MT researchers

In the early 1950s, the objectives of the study had to be moderate due to the limitations of the level of hardware. The research was carried out alone, without the necessary help of linguistic experts. As a result, the first researchers of machine translation had to resort to methods based on unrefined dictionaries, that is to say, mainly word-by-word translation, as well as the use of statistical methods.

(2) Towards good quality output

Around 1960, there is great advance in computer hardware and the original programming languages has appeared.

(3) The development of translation tools

There are three chief lines of research have continued to develop since the 1970s: computer-based tools for translators, operational machine translation systems assisted by human being in a variety of ways, and "pure" theoretical research focuses on improvements in machine translation methods.

然而，需要注意的是慕课的有效性仍有待研究，并且慕课系统本身也存在一定的问题。

Ⅲ. 机器翻译

1. 定义和类别

定义：机器翻译是指使用机器将语篇从一个自然语言翻译至另一个自然语言。

类别：机器翻译可以分为两类：不需要帮助的和需要帮助的。

不需帮助的机器翻译将语篇翻译后，不需人力参与，可直接译成另一语言。需要帮助的机器翻译在翻译后，有时在此之前，有待人力翻译者的加工，以获得较高翻译质量。通常，这个提高过程是通过使用词典和适用的句法来限定词汇的使用。

2. 机器翻译的发展历史

(1) 研究者的独立工作

在50年代初期，由于受到硬件水平的限制，研究的目标必须适中。研究是在没有语言学专家必要的帮助下，独自进行的。结果，最早的机器翻译研究者只好求助于以未加提炼的字典为基础的方法，就是说，主要是逐字翻译，以及运用统计方法。

(2) 瞄准高质量的输出

1960年前后，计算机硬件得到了很大的改进，最早的编程语言出现了。

(3) 翻译工具的发展

从20世纪70年代以来有三条主线持续发展：供翻译者使用的基于计算机的工具，以各种各样的方式涉及人工辅助的操作性机器翻译系统，和针对机器翻译方法改进的"纯粹"理论研究。

3. Research Methodology

Machine translation research methodology can be described from two parts: the application of linguistic theory on the one hand, and what MT researchers actually do on the other, which can be further subdivided into the following stages:

(1) The linguistic approach

Machine translation research has been regarded as a field to experiment with new linguistic theories or new computational techniques. MT has been considered as an experimental basis for linguistic theory, since the quality of translation and translation can be judged by non-experts.

(2) The transfer approach

According to most views of machine translation transfer theory, some kind of transfer component may be in the machine translation system. Such component is specific so that a pair of languages can produce a target sentence. The transfer component has a corresponding lexicon. A great deal of work depends on specific information about the comparison of the two languages.

(3) The interlingual approach

It is based on the understanding below does the interlingua approach been viewed. That is, between each two languages in a group of languages, only each member language is required to be translated into an intermediate language (interlingua), and from the intermediate language into some language.

(4) The knowledge-based approach

There are three types of knowledge needed for improving MT systems.

①Context-independent linguistic knowledge (semantics).

②Context-dependent linguistic knowledge, which sometimes becomes pragmatic knowledge (pragmatics).

③ Common sense/real world knowledge (non-linguistic knowledge).

4. MT Quality

People have to admit that there are errors in all existing practical translations. One can still find some errors that do not occur when human doing translations. For example, pronoun misuse, preposition misuse, syntactic confusion, improper wording, singular becoming plural, tense errors, etc. Translation is not a work that keeps meaning.

3. 研究方法

机器翻译研究方法可以从两个方面来叙述，一方面是语言学理论的应用，另一方面是 MT 研究者们实际所从事的内容。它可以继续细分为以下几个阶段：

(1) 语言学方法

机器翻译研究已经被看作一个试验新的语言理论或新的计算技术的领域。MT 已经被视为语言理论的实验基础，因为翻译和翻译的质量能由非专家来判断。

(2) 转移法

根据机器翻译转移理论的多数观点，在机器翻译系统中有某种转移成分。这种成分是特定的，从而一对语言可产生一个目标句子。转移成分有一个相应的词库。大量的工作取决于具体的对两种语言比较的信息。

(3) 语际法

语际法基于这样的理解：在一批语言的每两种语言之间，只要求将每一个成员语言翻译成中间语言(interlingua)，并从中间语言翻译成某种语言。

(4) 基于知识的方法

需要三种知识来改进机器翻译系统。

① 不依赖语境的语言学知识(语义学)；

② 依赖语境的语言学知识，有时成为语用知识(语用学)；

③ 常识/真实世界的知识(非语言学知识)。

4. 机器翻译的质量

人们不得不承认在所有现有的实际翻译中都会有错误。人们仍然能发现，有些错误是人工翻译不会出现的。例如，代词误用、介词误用、句法混乱、措辞不当、单数成了复数、时态错误等。翻译不是一项保留意义的工作。

5. MT and the Internet

Naturally, the rapid growth of real-time online translation on the Internet itself has been witnessed. The consensus is that the impact of the Internet will be even more profound in the future. In the future, there will be fewer and fewer "pure" machine translation systems while computer-based tools applications are getting more, and of which automatic translation is merely one part.

6. Speech Translation

It is considered as low possibility in practical use by almost everyone at the time late 1980s and early 1990s, when research projects about Language Translation were carried out initially. However, it is may be of higher possibility that a large number of Speech Translation systems will be used for small-scale natural language communication, such as database queries, business negotiation interactions, intra-company communication, etc.

7. MT and Human Translation

【考点：机器翻译育人工翻译的关系】

It's obviously that, at the beginning of the new era, machine translation and human translation can and will coexist relatively harmoniously. We still need the contributions of human translators. When translations have to focus on the "publishable" quality, both human translation and machine translation have their own values. For texts translation, machine translation is often an ideal solution where the quality requirement of the output is not high. But for the one-to-one exchange of information, human translators may always be useful. As for oral translation, it will definitely be a market for human translators.

Ⅳ. Corpus Linguistics

1. Corpus and Corpus Linguistics

Corpus(plural form as corpora): a collection of linguistic data, which can be composed of written texts or transliterations of recorded speech. The chief target of a corpus is to identify hypotheses about language, such as, making sure how the use of a particular phonetic, word, or syntactic structure changes.

Corpus Linguistics: Discuss about the principles and practice when using corpora in language research. A computer corpus is a significant section of machine-readable texts.

5. 机器翻译与互联网

自然而然地，我们已经看到互联网本身实时在线的翻译正快速成长。人们一致赞同，互联网的影响在未来将更加深远。在未来，"纯粹"的机器翻译系统将越来越少，基于计算机的工具和应用将越来越多，而自动翻译仅仅是其中的一个部分。

6. 口语翻译

当言语翻译的研究项目在20世纪80年代末90年代初开始时，人人都知道实际应用不太可能。但更有可能的是为数众多的口语翻译系统被应用于小范围的自然语言交流，例如数据库的询问，商业谈判的交往，公司内部的交流等等。

7. 机器翻译和人工翻译

在新世纪之初，很明显，机器翻译和人工翻译能够且将会相对协调地同时存在。我们仍旧需要那些人工翻译者所作出的贡献。当翻译不得不讲究"可发行"质量时，人工翻译和机器翻译都具有各自的作用。对语篇翻译来说，在对输出的质量要求不高的地方，机器翻译常常是一种理想的解决方法。对信息的一对一交换而言，人工翻译家可能总是会有作用的。至于口语翻译，一定会是人工翻译者的市场。

Ⅳ. 语料库语言学

1. 语料库与语料库语言学

语料库(corpus 复数形式 corpora)：一个语言数据的集合，可以由书面文本构成，也可以由录音言语的转写本构成。语料库的主要目的是鉴定关于语言的假说——例如，确定一个特定的语音、单词，或句法结构的使用是如何变化的。

语料库语言学：论述语言研究中使用语料的原理和实践。一个计算机语料库是机器可读文本的重要躯干。

2. Criticisms and Revival Although corpus linguistics has contributed to the development of American structuralism in linguistics, Chomsky changed the direction of linguistics in a relatively short period of time, making it turn from empiricism to rationalism. For this reason, it obviously invalidates the corpus as a source of evidence in linguistic investigation. Chomsky proposed that corpora is no longer a useful tool for linguists, because linguists must seek to generalize language competence rather than language performance. Although Chomsky's criticism made corpus linguistics lose its authority, there were still some corpus-based work continuing.	**2. 语料库语言学受到的批判及其复兴** 尽管语料库语言学对语言学上的美国结构主义的发展做出了贡献，但 Chomsky 在相当短暂的时间内，改变了语言学的方向，使其远离了实证主义，而朝向理性主义。为此，它显然使语料库作为一种在语言调查中的证据资源而失效。Chomsky 提出，语料库对语言学家而言，不再是有用的工具，因为语言学家必须寻求概括语言能力而不是语言的使用。虽然 Chomsky 的批判使语料库语言学失去了权威性，但他们并没有停止所有基于语料库的工作。
3. Concordance Computers are able to search for a specific word, a string of words, or even a certain section of an article, which can also retrieve all instances of a word. Moreover, it can count the number of occurrences of a word, thereby collecting information about the frequency of the word as well. Then we can classify the data in certain way, such as, by the alphabetical order of the words that are next to the search term, which is often referred to as concordance.	**3. 共现索引** 计算机有能力搜索一个特定的词，词串，甚至一个语篇里的某一言语部分。计算机也能检索一个词所有的实例。它还能计算一个词出现的次数，从而收集到有关这个词的频率信息。然后我们可以以某种方式对数据分类——例如，按紧接被检索词词语的字母顺序进行分类。这通常被称为共现索引。
4. The Roles of Corpus Data The significance of corpora to language learning equals to empirical evidence to language learning. Linguists are able to make objective statements, not subjective descriptions, and not based on the inherent personal perception of language by empirical data. In terms of this, the corpus surely plays an important role in different areas of language learning.	**4. 语料库数据的作用** 语料库对语言学习的重要性与经验证据对语言学习的重要性一样。实证数据使语言学家做出客观的描述，而不是主观的描述，也不是基于个人固有的对语言的感知。从这点出发，语料库对语言学习的不同领域起着重要的作用。

10.2 考研真题与典型题详解

Ⅰ. Fill in the blanks.

1. Corpus linguistics deals with the principles and practice of using ________ in language study.（中山大学 2005 研）
2. In the Phases Ⅳ of CALL Development, instead of writing specific programs for language teaching, ________ has adapted to language teaching by enabling students to compose and try out

their own writings in a non-permanent form.

3. MT can be divided into two types: __________ and __________.
4. __________ a collection of linguistic data, either compiled as written texts or as a transcription of recorded speech.
5. __________ refers to the use of machine (usually computers) to translate texts from one natural language to another.
6. Computational linguistics has __________ and __________ components, where the former component takes up issues in theoretical linguistics and cognitive science, and the latter component focuses on the practical outcome of modeling human language use.
7. __________ is an online course aimed at unlimited participation and open access via the web.

Ⅱ. True or false

1. MT may commit those errors that no human translators would commit, such as wrong pronouns, wrong prepositions, garbled syntax, incorrect choice of terms, plurals instead of singulars.
2. Around 1960, computer software is greatly improved and the first programming languages appeared.
3. CAL especially refers to the use of a computer in the teaching or learning of a second or foreign language.
4. Three types of knowledge are needed so that MT systems can be improved: semantics, pragmatics and common sense.
5. Computational linguistics focuses on the practical outcome of modeling human language use and can be regarded as a branch of applied linguistics, thus it only has applied components.
6. Computational linguistics is an interdisciplinary field concerned with the statistical or rule-based modeling of natural language from a computational perspective.

Ⅲ. Explain the following terms.

1. CAL (大连外国语学院 2008 研)
2. CAI and CAL (武汉大学 2008 研)
3. CALL (人大 2006 研)
4. corpus linguistics (南开大学 2004 研)
5. Concordance (北航 2010 研)
6. Corpus
7. MOOC

Ⅳ. Essay questions

1. Read the following quote from Chomsky. What do you think about Chomsky's criticism and the revival of corpus linguistics? (中山大学 2005 研)

It seems clear that the description which is of greatest psychological relevance is the account of competence, not that of performance, for anyone concerned with intellectual processes, or any question that goes beyond mere data arranging, it is the question of competence that is fundamental. ...

These rather obvious comments apply directly to study of language, child or adult. This it is absurd to attempt to construct a grammar that describes observed linguistic behaviour directly, ... a direct record—an actual corpus—is almost useless as it stands, for linguistic analysis of any but the most superficial kind. . . .

2. In what way are language and computer related, and how has their relationship affected language learning?（北外 2010 研）
3. What is the relationship between MT and Human Translation?

参考答案及解析

Ⅰ. Fill in the blanks.

1. corpora
（语料库语言学指论述语言研究中使用语料的原理和实践。）
2. word processing
（计算机运用到第二语言教学中的第四个阶段，文字处理不再是为语言教学编写具体的程序，而是适应语言教学，使学生用一种非永久性形式写作并能修改它们的作品。）
3. unassisted MT, assisted MT
（机器翻译可以分为两类：不需要帮助的和需要帮助的。）
4. Corpus
（语料库是一个语言数据的集合，可以由书面文本构成，也可以由录音言语的转写本构成。）
5. Machine translation
（机器翻译是指使用机器将语篇从一个自然语言翻译至另一个自然语言。）
6. theoretical; applied
（计算机语言学包含有理论计算机语言学和应用计算机语言学两个成分。理论计算机语言学主要研究理论语言学和认知科学的相关问题，应用语言学主要研究人类语言使用的实际产物。）
7. MOOC
（慕课是一种旨在通过网络进行无限制的参与和开放访问的在线课程。）

Ⅱ. True or false

1. T （人们仍然能发现，有些错误是人工翻译不会出现的。例如，代词误用、介词误用、句法混乱、措辞不当、单数用成复数、时态错误等。）
2. F （1960 年前后，计算机硬件而不是软件得到了很大的改进，最早的编程语言出现了。）
3. F （CALL 特别是指将计算机运用到第二语言或外语的教学中去，不是 CAL。）
4. T （需要三种知识来改进机器翻译系统：① 不依赖语境的语言学知识，即语义学；② 依赖语境的语言学知识，有时称为语用知识，即语用学；③ 常识/真实世界的知识，即非语言学知识。）
5. F （计算机语言学包含有理论计算机语言学和应用计算机语言学两个成分。理论计算机语言学主要研究理论语言学和认知科学的相关问题，应用语言学主要研究人类语言使用的实际产物。）
6. T （计算语言学是一个跨学科的领域，它涉及从计算的角度对自然语言进行统计或基于规则的建模。）

Ⅲ. Explain the following terms.

1. CAL is short for Computer-assistant Learning. It emphasizes the use of a computer in both teaching and learning in order to help the learners to achieve educational objectives through their own reasoning and practice, a reflection of newly advocated autonomous learning. The first kind of CAL programs which were developed reflected principles similar to programmed instruction the computer leads the student through learning task step-by-step, asking questions to check comprehension. Depending on the student's response, the computer gives the student further practice or progresses to new material.
2. Computer-assisted instruction (CAI) means the use of a computer in a teaching program. This includes:
   a. A teaching program which is presented by a computer in a sequence. The student responds on the computer, and the computer indicates whether the responses are correct or incorrect.
   b. The use of computers to monitor student progress, to direct students into appropriate lessons, material, etc. This is also called computer-managed instruction.

   Parallel to CAI, there is CAL (Computer-Assistant Learning). The former aims at seeing educational problems on the part of the teacher, whereas the latter emphasizes the use of a computer in both teaching and learning in order to help the learner achieve educational objectives. The first kind of CAL programs which were developed reflected principles similar to programmed instruction. The computer leads the student through learning task step-by-step, asking questions to check comprehension. Depending on the student's response, the computer gives the student further practice or progresses to new material (see branching). In more recent CAL courseware students are able to interact with the computer and perform higher-level tasks while exploring a subject or problem.
3. CALL: It is the abbreviation of computer-assisted language learning, which refers to the use of a computer in the teaching or learning of a second or foreign language. In this kind of CALL programs, the computer leads the student through a learning task step-by-step, asking question to check comprehension. Depending on the student's response, the computer gives the student further practice or progresses to new material.
4. Corpus linguistics: an approach to investigating language structure and use through the analysis of large databases to real language examples stored on computer. Issues amenable to corpus linguistics include the meanings of words across registers, the distribution and function of grammatical forms and categories, the investigation of lexicon-grammatical associations, and issues in language acquisition and development.
5. Concordance: The computer has the ability to search for a particular word, sequence of words, or perhaps even a part of speech in a text. The computer can also retrieve all examples of a particular word. It can also calculate the number of occurrences of a certain word so that information on the frequency of the word may be gathered. We may also be interested in sorting the data in some way—for example, alphabetically on words occurring in the immediate context of the word. This is usually referred to as concordance.
6. Corpus is a collection of linguistic data, either compiled as written texts or as a transcription of

recorded speech. The main purpose of a corpus is to verify a hypothesis about language—for example, to determine how the application of a particular sound, word, or syntactic construction varies.

7. MOOC (Massive Open Online Course) is an online course aimed at unlimited participation and open access via the web. In addition to traditional course materials such as filmed lectures, readings, and problem sets, many MOOCs provide interactive user forums to support community interactions among students, professors and teaching assistants.

Ⅳ. Essay questions

1. Regarding linguistics as a branch of psychology, Chomsky insisted that what should be studied is linguistic competence, not performance. As he has claimed, the description of language performance only tells what is there, and is very inadequate in telling why language performs in the way as it does, or rather, how the intellectual processes affects it.

   What's more, language performance is more than often degenerated; there are false statements, hesitations, and so on. Therefore, the corpus linguistics which is based on the language performance is somewhat distorted from the goal of linguistics. Because, according to Chomsky, what linguistics is aimed for, should be the discovering of the constants, the general principle which all languages are constructed and operated as systems of communication in societies in which they are used.

   Therefore, he suggested the construction of universal grammar, which is the ideal knowledge of language, is what linguists should be concerned with, and the postulation of grammar based on the observed behavior is also a distortion.

2. With the development of the computer technology and internet system, more and more people touched upon the computer field. Computer has been used in the classroom for foreign language teaching and learning. CAI stands for computer-assisted instruction, which means the use of a computer in a teaching program. CAL stands for computer-assisted learning, which means the use of computer in both teaching and learning. Following CAI and CAL, CALL, acronym for Computer Assisted Language Learning, refers to the use of a computer in the teaching or learning of a second or foreign language. If CAI or CAL deals with teaching and learning in general, then CALL deals with language teaching and learning in particular. CALL provided a beneficial and convenient approach for language learners to improve their ability. For example, students can gain a quick access to any materials on the internet. The computer is not an individual resource for each student any more, instead, it is a trigger for interaction between the students and it is the focus for group work which allows some activities, such as the activity role-play interaction. The use of multimedia technology enables different information types to be simultaneously available on the computer, as a result, spoken language and moving video are produced other than mere presentation of written sentences.

3. At the beginning of the new century, it is already apparent that MT and human translation can and will co-exist in harmony. When translation has to be of "publishable" quality, both human translation and MT have their roles.

   For the translation of texts where the quality of output is much less important, machine translation is often an ideal solution. It is undeniable that there are still faults in all present actual translations produced. One can still find those errors that no human translators would ever commit, such as wrong pronouns, wrong prepositions, garbled syntax, incorrect choice of terms, plurals instead of singulars, etc. Translation is not an operation that preserves meaning. Three types of knowledge are needed so that MT systems can be improved: (1) Linguistic knowledge independent of context (semantics); (2) Linguistic knowledge that relates to context, sometimes called pragmatic knowledge (pragmatics); (3) Common sense/real world knowledge (non-linguistic).

For the one-to-one interchange of information probably always need a human translator. As for spoken language translation, there must surely always be a market for the human translator.

第 11 章　第二语言和外语教学

11.1　复习笔记

本章要点：

1. The relation between linguistics and language teaching
   语言学与语言教学之间的关系
2. Grammar, input and language learning
   语法、输入与语言学习
3. Interlanguage in language teaching
   语言教学中的中介语
4. Linguistics and syllabus design
   语言学与教学大纲设计
5. Contrastive analysis and error analysis
   对比分析与错误分析
6. Corpus linguistics and language teaching
   语料库语言学与语言教学

常考考点：

语言学与语言教学的关系；语言学与语言学习；语言学与教学大纲设计；二语学习者的主要障碍；对比分析与错误分析；中介语；语料库语言学与语言教学等。

本章内容索引：

Ⅰ. Definition of Applied Linguistics

Ⅱ. The Relation between Linguistics and Language Teaching

Ⅲ. Linguistics and Language Learning

1. Grammar and Language Learning
2. Input and Language Learning
3. Interlanguage in Language Learning

Ⅳ. Linguistics and Language Teaching

1. The discourse-based view of language teaching
2. The universal grammar (UG) and language teaching

Ⅴ. Syllabus Design

1. Syllabus and curriculum
2. Theoretical views behind syllabus design
3. Types of syllabus
   (1) The structural syllabus
   (2) The situational syllabus
   (3) The communicative syllabus

(4) The task-based syllabus

4. Current trends in syllabus design

(1) The co-existence of the old and the new

(2) The emphasis on the learning process

(3) The inclusion of non-linguistic objectives in syllabus

(4) The emergency of the multi-syllabus

Ⅵ. Contrastive Analysis (CA) and Error Analysis (EA)

1. Contrastive Analysis (CA)

2. Error Analysis (EA)

(1) Error vs. mistake

(2) Different types of errors

3. The procedure of error analysis

(1) Recognition

(2) Description

(3) Explanation

Ⅶ. Corpus Linguistics and Language Teaching

1. Types of corpora

(1) General corpora

(2) Specialized corpora

(3) Sample corpora

(4) Monitor corpora

2. Information provided by corpora

(1) Frequency information

(2) Context and co-text information

(3) Grammatical information

(4) Collocation and phraseology information

(5) Pragmatics information

▼Ⅷ. Foreign Language Education Policy

Ⅰ. Definition of Applied Linguistics	**Ⅰ. 应用语言学的定义**
Broadly speaking, applied linguistics refers to the study of language and linguistics in relation to language-related problems, such as lexicography, translation, etc. Applied linguistics uses information from linguistics with the aim to develop its own theoretical models of areas, such as syllabus design, speech therapy, language planning, stylistics etc. Narrowly speaking, applied linguistics refers to the study of second and foreign language learning and teaching, i. e. the study of language and linguistics in relation to language learning and teaching.	从广义上讲，应用语言学是对语言、语言学与语言相关的问题的研究，例如词典编纂学，翻译等。应用语言学运用来自语言学的信息来发展它自身理论模块部分，例如教学大纲设计，言语治疗，语言规划，文体学等。从狭义上讲，应用语言学是指对第二语言和语言教学的研究，例如研究语言和语言学与语言教学的关系。

Ⅱ. The Relation between Linguistics and Language Teaching

Language teaching is a section of applied linguistics and applied linguistics is a branch of linguistics. Some knowledge of linguistics will not only help language teachers to better understand the nature of language, but also give them a better understanding of language teaching. Linguistic theories explicitly or implicitly influence the approaches and methods of language teaching.

【考点：语言学与语言教学对于语言的不同看法】

Ⅲ. Linguistics and Language Learning

Many language learning theories are proposed based on certain linguistic theories. Actually, the knowledge of linguistics make us better understand what language learners can learn, how they learn and what they learn ultimately. Therefore, linguistics has always played a significant part in the studies of language acquisition and learning.

1. Grammar and Language Learning

(1) Many traditional language teachers adopted discrete-point grammar instruction in classroom teaching, which has been widely criticized for its focus on forms and ignorance of meanings. A recent movement called "focus on form" seems to be the outcome of the compromise between the "purely form-focused approaches" and the "purely meaning-focused approaches". It has a more balanced view on the role of grammar in language teaching.

(2) The relevance of Universal Grammar (UG) and complexity language structures are the two variables concerning the amenability of language elements to focus on form. The advocates of focus on form claim that if an L2 structure is part of UG, the amenability is high; otherwise, the amenability is low. In focus on form teaching, different measures will be taken according to whether the amenability of a structure is high or low.

▼(3) One of the existing grammar models that have been widely applied in language teaching is the functional grammar. Based on Halliday's work, Lock's functional description of

Ⅱ. 语言学与语言教学的关系

语言教学是应用语言学的一个部分，而应用语言学又是语言学的一个分支。掌握一些语言学的知识不仅有助于这些读者进一步认识语言本质，也有助于他们更加深入地理解如何教好语言。语言学理论直接地或间接地影响着语言教学的途径和方法。

Ⅲ. 语言学与语言学习

许多语言学习理论都是基于某种语言学理论提出的。事实上，语言学知识能够使我们真正理解学习者能够学习什么样的语言，怎样学习语言以及最终能够学到什么。因此，语言学在语言习得研究和语言学习研究中一直起着十分重要的作用。

1. 语法与语言学习

(1)很多传统的语言教师将语法割裂为孤立的语法知识点来分别讲解，这种做法已经受到广泛的批评，因为它仅仅关注语言形式而忽略了语言的意义。作为"完全以语言形式为中心"和"完全以语言意义为中心"的折中途径，近年来出现的"关注语言形式"(focus on form)对语言教学中语法的作用采取了一种折中的态度。

(2)主要有两个变量影响语言成分在"关注语言形式"中的顺从性，即普遍语法(UG)的相关度和语言结构的复杂度。"关注语言形式"的支持者们认为，如果二语中的某个结构是普遍语法的一部分，它的顺从性就高；否则，顺从性则低。在"关注语言形式"的教学中，我们会根据语言结构顺从性的高与低来采取不同的措施。

(3) 在现今语言教学中广泛运用的一种语法模型是功能语法。基于韩礼德的著作，洛克对英语进行

the English language aims to help English teachers understand the relationship between different elements of grammar and how these elements affect the creation of meanings in specific contexts. Lock analyses the key grammatical categories and components in English and explains typical problems that second language learners may encounter in grammar learning.

了功能描述，旨在帮助英语教师理解语法不同成分和这些成分是如何影响具体语境中意义创建之间的关系。洛克分析了英语中的关键语法范畴和成分，并解释了二语学习者在学习语法过程中遇到的典型问题。

2. Input and Language Learning

Evidently, language learning occurs naturally when the learner has sufficient access to target language input. This input can be either in written or spoken form. In terms of spoken input, it may occur in the interactive activities (i. e. the conversations between learners and native speakers, teachers, or another learners) or in non-interactive context (for example, listening to the music or watching movies).

2. 输入和语言学习

当学习者接受了足够的目的语输入时，语言学习自然而然就会发生。输入可以是口头语言，也可以是书面语言。口头语言输入可能发生在交互活动中(即如学习者与母语者、教师或者是其他学习者的对话)，或者出现一个没有交互的语境中(例如听音乐或者看电影)。

(1) Authentic Input

Proponents of meaning-oriented language instruction tend to insist on authentic input. That is to say, the input should relate to real life, and it usually neglects the grammar.

(1) 真实性输入

那些更强调意义的语言教学者主张提供真实性输入。即输入要与现实生活紧密相连，这种输入通常忽略语法。

(2) Comprehensible Input

According to Krashen's INPUT HYPOTHESIS (1985), learners acquire language as a result of understanding the input. Krashen proposed the concept of "i + 1" principle: the language learners are exposed to should be just far enough beyond their current competence, so that they can understand most of it but still be challenging to make progress. Input should be neither too difficult nor too easy for the language learners.

【考点：名词解释——Input Hypothesis】

(2) 可理解的输入

克拉申的语言输入假说认为，学习者掌握语言是理解了输入的结果。他提出了"i + 1"的概念：学习者所接触到的语言应该和学习者的水平保持一定的距离，大部分的内容可以理解但仍然有一些对他们来说是具有挑战性的。输入对学习者来说，既不应该太难也不应该太容易。

3. Interlanguage in Language Learning

The language constructed by second or foreign language learners in the process of learning is often regarded as the interlanguage. Interlanguage is usually understood as a language system between the target language and the learner's native language. Compared with the target language, the interlanguage is not perfect, but it is not mere translation of the learner's native language. However, interlanguage should not be considered as a bridging language or a simple mixture of the target language and native language. Interlanguage is a dynamic language system, which develops from elementary level to native level.

3. 中介语和语言学习

正处于学习过程的二语或外语学习者构建的语言通常被称为中介语。中介语通常被理解为介于目的语和学习者母语之间的语言。与目的语相比，中介语还不够完善，但它也不只是学习者母语的简单翻译。我们也不能把中介语看成是母语和目标语的过渡阶段或者是二者的简单混合。中介语是一个动态的语言系统，它不断地从初级水平向地道的母语水平发展。

Ⅳ. Linguistics and Language Teaching

It can be said that all aspects of language teaching can be inspired by linguistics. From the macro perspective, linguistic theories influence the overall development of approaches to language teaching. From the micro perspective, linguistic knowledge helps teachers better explain the specific language items they teach.

1. The discourse-based view of language teaching

(1) According to the discourse-based view of language, linguistic patterns exist across stretches of text. The discourse-based view of language is concerned with complete texts, both spoken and written, and the social and cultural contexts in which these discourses occur.

(2) The discourse-based language teaching emphasizes the development of learners' discourse competence, which is close to the well-known concept of communicative competence. Communicative competence refers to the learner's ability to communicate effectively and appropriately in specific contexts. Communicative competence involves knowledge of the grammar and vocabulary, knowledge of rules of speaking, knowledge of how to use and respond to different types of speech acts and social conventions, and knowledge of how to use language appropriately.

(3) The discourse-based method of language teaching is criticized for some drawbacks. It overemphasizes the external factors in the process of language acquisition and pays little attention to the internal factors. It is in common with the behavioristic understanding of language acquisition because environmental factors and input are the core of language acquisition. It gives too much importance to the role of learning competence and language functions in language acquisition, thus fails to notice universal principles that guide language acquisition.

【考点：基于语篇的语言教学的利弊】

2. The universal grammar (UG) and language teaching

(1) UG aims to explain why L1 acquisition can be so quick with very limited exposure to external input. The view supports the idea that the external input in itself may not account for language acquisition.

Ⅳ. 语言学与语言教学

可以说语言教学的方方面面都可以从语言学中获得启示。从宏观上看，语言学理论影响着教学法的总体发展方向。从微观上看，语言学知识能帮助教师更好的解释他们所教语言知识的细节。

1. 基于语篇的语言教学

(1) 以语篇为基础的语言观认为，语言范式存在于语篇之中。以语篇为基础的语言观关注的是口头和书面的完整语篇以及这些语篇所在的社会和文化背景。

(2) 基于语篇的语言教学强调培养学习者的语篇能力，这是与众所周知的交际能力很相近的一种能力。交际能力是指学习者在具体的语境中恰当并且有效的运用语言进行交际的能力。交际能力包括语法词汇知识、会话规则以及怎样运用和回答不同类型的言语行为和社会习俗，以及怎样恰当得体地运用语言。

(3) 基于语篇的语言教学观还有很多不足之处，因此受到人们的批评。它过分强调了语言习得过程中的外部因素，而没有对内部因素给予足够的重视。它与行为主义语言习得观有一个共同之处，即把环境因素和语言输入视为语言习得的核心。它过于关注语言习得中学习能力和语言功能的作用，却没有注意到指导语言习得的一些普遍规律。

2. 普遍语法与语言教学

(1)普遍语法要回答的一个主要问题是为什么第一语言习得可以基于很少的外界输入而能快速获得成功。普遍语法认为语言习得本质上并不依靠外在的语言输入。

(2) Chomsky argues that a native speaker possesses a kind of linguistic competence. Children are born with some universal knowledge of language. In the process of acquiring their native language, they constantly compare their innate language system with that of their mother tongue and modify their grammar. Hence, language learning is not a simple process of habit formation, but a process of constantly building and testing hypothesis.

(2)根据乔姆斯基的观点，每一个母语者都具有一种语言能力。孩子出生时就具有一些带有普遍性的语言知识。在母语习得过程中，人们不断把先天这种内在的语言体系与母语相比较，从而调整自己的语法结构。因此，语言学习不是一个简单的习惯形成过程，而是一个不断地建立和验证假设的过程。

(3) There are also some criticisms towards the language teaching theories based on universal grammar. It can be said that UG is developed specifically to explain how language works. However, UG supporters have to study the process of language acquisition to account for the language itself. The acquisition part is thus of secondary importance in UG. A second drawback is that UG only focuses on the core grammar and general rules of syntax. Thirdly, the most important function of language is communication, but it is ignored in UG.

(3)基于普遍语法的语言教学理论也受到了人们的批评。普遍语法是专门为了解释语言的运作方式而提出来的。然而，为了解释语言本身，普遍语法支持者也必须研究语言习得的过程。但有关语言习得的论述在普遍语法理论中只是次要的。普遍语法的第二个不足在于它只关注英语句法的核心语法和通用的规则。第三，语言最重要的功能在于交际，但是这一点被普遍语法忽略掉了。

(4) UG has made great contributions in explaining the development of interlanguage and the influence of the first language. Also, it has offered invaluable information on how L2 teachers (or educational linguists) should teach vocabulary items and grammar. But there is no hard evidence to support the existence of UG.

(4)普遍语法在解释中介语的发展和母语的影响等方面做出了重要的贡献。在语言教师(或教育语言学家)如何开展进行词汇教学和语法教学这个问题上，普遍语法提供了重要的信息。然而另一方面，还没有确凿的证据来支持普遍语法的存在。

V. Syllabus Design

V. 教学大纲设计

Syllabus design is the fundamental part in language teaching. In some sense, syllabus design is a bridge between language teaching theory and language teaching practice. The syllabus applies teaching theory to teaching practice and establishes an operational framework for practice. The most important part of syllabus design is selecting and sequencing language items.

教学大纲的设计在语言教学中有着举足轻重的地位。从某种意义上说，大纲设计是联系教学理论和教学实践的桥梁。教学大纲把教学理论应用到教学实践之中并且为实践建立了一个可操作的框架。设计教学大纲最重要的部分是选择和安排教学内容。

1. Syllabus and curriculum

1. 教学大纲和课程计划

(1) A syllabus refers to the specific activities that will happen in the classroom, which usually includes the aims and contents of teaching and sometimes includes suggestions of

(1) 教学大纲用来指教室中具体发生的活动，通常包括教学的目标和内容，有时也指教学方法。而课程计划所提供的原则是：对语言

methodology. Curriculum however, offers (i) general statements about the rationale about language, language learning and language teaching, (ii) detailed specification of aims, objectives and targets, and (iii) implementation of a program. In some sense, a syllabus is part of a curriculum.

【考点：Syllabus 和 Curriculum 的区别】

(2) Another difference is that syllabus is often used to refer to concepts that are similar to a language teaching approach, while curriculum is a specific document designed for the language program of a particular country or region.

理念，语言学习和语言教学的基本原理的概括；对教学目的和目标的具体说明；教学计划的具体实施。从某种意义上说，教学大纲是实施课程计划的一部分。

（2）另一点是大纲经常用来指称和语言教学途径非常相似的概念，而课程计划则指为某国家或地区的语言课程所设计的具体文件。

2. Theoretical views behind syllabus design

The process of syllabus design in foreign language teaching mainly includes selecting and grading what is to be taught. Selection contains two sub-processes:

(1) to confine the language to a particular dialect and register;

(2) to select within the register of the items that are to be taught based on certain criteria such as frequency of occurrence, learnability and classroom needs. The whole process of selection should be applied at all levels of language, such as phonology, grammar, lexis, contexts (semantic and cultural).

2. 教学大纲设计的理论背景

外语教学中大纲设计过程主要包括选择和排列教学内容。选择的过程包括两个步骤：

首先，把语言限定在某个特定的方言和语域内。

第二，根据一定的标准，例如出现的频率、难易度或者课堂需求等，从所选语境中进一步选择要学习的语言。整个的过程应该在语言的所有层次上进行，例如语音、语法、词汇、语境（语义或文化的）。

3. Types of syllabus

(1) The structural syllabus

The structural syllabus is oriented syllabus based on a selection of language items and structures. The underlying assumption is that language is a system which consists of a set of grammatical rules; learning language is about learning these rules and then applying them to practical language use.

The main drawback of such a syllabus is that it focuses only on the grammatical forms and the meaning of individual words, whereas the meaning of the whole sentence is considered to be self-evident, whatever its context may be. It doesn't teach students how to use these sentences in real context. Therefore, students who have been trained by a structural syllabus usually prove to be communicatively incompetent.

【考点：结构教学大纲的特点及弊端】

3. 教学大纲类型

（1）结构教学大纲

结构主义大纲主要以语法教学为导向，以语言结构为基础。语法大纲潜在的理念是把语言看作一系列由语法规则组成的体系；学习语言就是要学习这些规则并且把这些规则应用到实际语言运用中。

结构教学大纲的主要缺点在于它注重语法形式和单个词语的意思，认为不论是在什么语境下整句话的意思都是显而易见的。它没有教授学生们如何在真实的语境下使用这些句子。因此，经过结构教学大纲训练出来的学生通常是缺乏实际交际能力的。

(2) The situational syllabus The situational syllabus has no strong linguistic basis, yet it can be argued that the situationalists see language as a communicative tool. The purpose of the situational syllabus is distinguishing the situations in which the target language is applied. The selection and organization of language items are according to situations. In contrast, the situational syllabus has certain advantages over the structural syllabus because it begins to focus on the learner's direct communicative needs. However, since the situational syllabus relies on whatever linguistic description is available, such a syllabus is grammatically-oriented in nature. In addition, the arrangement of the situations is not systematic. 【考点：与结构大纲相比，情景教学大纲的特点及利弊】	**(2) 情景教学大纲** 情景教学大纲没有坚实的语言学理论基础。我们可以认为情景教学大纲的编写者们视语言为一种交际工具。编写情景大纲的目的是要具体区分目的语使用的不同场景。语言的选择和组织都是以情景为线索的。 相比之下，情景教学大纲比结构教学大纲更具有优势，因为它开始关注了学习者直接的交流需要。然而，情景式大纲要依附于已有的语言观，而现在这个语言观仍然是结构主义的，因此从本质上看，情景式大纲仍然是以语法为主线的。另外，这些情景的组织安排也没有什么系统性可寻。
(3) The communicative syllabus Communicative syllabus focus on the learner's communicative competence. Based on a notional-functional syllabus, it teaches the language needed to express and understand different functions of language, and emphasizes the process of communication.	**(3) 交际教学大纲** 交际教学大纲的目的是培养学生的交际能力。它以功能—意念大纲为基础，它教授表达和理解不同语言功能时所需要的语言，并且强调交际的过程。
(4) The task-based syllabus Task-based syllabuses focus more on the classroom learning process that motivates learning, rather than the language knowledge and skills that students need to master. These syllabuses consist of a list of tasks and activities undertaken by learners in class in the target language.	**(4) 任务型教学大纲** 任务型教学大纲更加关注激发学习的课堂学习过程，而不是学生所要掌握的语言知识和技能。这些教学大纲对于课堂上学习者所进行的任务和活动列出了说明。
4. Current trends in syllabus design **(1) The co-existence of the old and the new** Although many different types of syllabuses have been proposed over the past three decades, currently, the traditional syllabuses (e.g. the grammatical syllabus and lexical syllabus) have not been completely abandoned, and the later models (e.g. the content syllabus and the task-based syllabus) have not been universally accepted.	**4. 教学大纲设计的现行趋势** **(1) 新旧并存** 虽然过去三十年里提出了许多不同类型的教学大纲，但是目前传统的教学大纲(如语法教学大纲和词汇教学大纲)还没有完全被摒弃，较新的模式(如内容教学大纲和任务型教学大纲)还没有被普遍接受。

(2) The emphasis on the learning process

Compared with the traditional syllabuses, the new models (e. g. the content syllabus, the procedural syllabus and the task-based syllabus) focus more on the process of language learning rather than the product of language learning.

(3) The inclusion of non-linguistic objectives in syllabus

Compared with traditional syllabuses, the new models usually include a set of non-linguistic objectives, such as learning strategies development and affective cultivation.

(4) The emergency of the multi-syllabus

The integrated syllabus is also called the multi-syllabus. Designing a multi-syllabus is not simply combining elements from different types of syllabuses. Rather, it is a matter of selection of priority.

Ⅵ. Contrastive Analysis (CA) and Error Analysis (EA)

The study of the roles that the native language plays is called the research of language transfer, by which is meant the psychological process whereby prior learning is carried over into a new learning situation, or "the influence as a result of the similarities and differences between the target language and any other language that has been previously (and perhaps imperfectly) acquired".

1. Contrastive Analysis (CA)

Contrastive Analysis aims to compare languages (e. g. , L1 and L2) in order to determine potential errors for the ultimate purpose of isolating what needs to be learned and what does not need to be learned in a second language learning situation. The goal of contrastive analysis is to predict what areas will be easy to learn and what areas will be hard to learn. Contrastive Analysis was associated in its early days with behaviorism and structuralism.

2. Error Analysis (EA)

The fact that not all errors can be explained by CA resulted in a disillusionment with contrastive analysis. Gradually CA was replaced by the error analysis movement; a main claim is that many errors made by L2 learners result from factors other than L1 interference.

(2) 强调学习过程

与传统的教学大纲相比，较新的模式(如内容教学大纲、程序教学大纲和任务型教学大纲)更关注语言学习的过程，而不是语言学习的结果。

(3) 大纲中包含非语言目标

与传统的教学大纲相比，新的大纲通常包括一系列非语言目标，例如学习策略和情感态度的培养。

(4) 多元大纲的出现

综合性的教学大纲也称作多元教学大纲。设计多元教学大纲并不是简单地把不同类型大纲中的要素拼凑在一起，而是优先考虑哪些内容。

Ⅵ. 对比分析和错误分析

对母语作用的研究通常被称作语言迁移研究，语言迁移指先前学习的心理过程转移至新的学习环境，或者指“由于目的语与先前(可能不完全)习得的其他任一门语言之间的异同所导致的影响”。

1. 对比分析

对比分析是通过对比不同语言(如第一语言和第二语言)来确定潜在错误的方法，从而把第二语言学习环境下必须学习的和不必学习的东西最终区分开来。对比分析的目的是预测哪些领域容易学得，哪些领域不易学得。早期的对比分析与行为主义和结构主义相关。

2. 错误分析

并非所有的错误都可以由对比分析进行解释，这使得人们对对比分析不再抱有过大的希望。对比分析逐渐被错误分析所取代，除了第一语言的影响外，还有其他因素的影响。

(1) error vs. mistake

In the literature of error analysis, it is often necessary to distinguish between the concepts of error and mistake. Errors are usually due to the learner's lack of knowledge. In other words, errors occur when the learners do not know the correct form or do not use the language correctly. Mistakes often occur when learners fail to perform their competence. That is to say, learners have learned certain knowledge or skills, but fail to use the language correctly due to lack of attention or the influence of other factors.

(2) different types of errors

① interlingual errors and intralingual errors

According to the source of errors, errors can be divided into interlingual errors and intralingual errors. Interlingual errors (or transfer errors) occur when the learners misuse language items that have the same characteristics as their mother tongue. Intralingual errors (or developmental errors) are errors made within the target language itself. For example, the overgeneralization of a rule by extending it beyond its use.

② omissions, additions, double markings, misformations and misorderings

In terms of the nature of errors, errors often fall into five types: omissions, additions, double markings, misformations and misorderings.

3. The procedure of error analysis

(1) Recognition

If the sentence produced by the language learner is grammatically incorrect, then error exists. If the sentence is grammatically correct but inappropriate in the communicative context, then mistake exists.

(2) Description

We can find out errors and mistakes by comparing the sentence produced by the learners with the correct one produced by the native speakers.

(3) Explanation

When an error is recognized and described, we then try to explain why the error happened. That is to say, we make hypothesis about the mental processes that lead the learner to make such a mistake.

(1) 错误与失误

错误分析的文献中经常要区分错误(error)和失误(mistake)这两个概念。错误通常是由于学习者知识不足所致。换言之，由于学习者不知道正确的形式或者不能正确地使用语言而出现的错误。失误则是由于学习者没能发挥出自己的能力而出现差错。也就是说，学习者学会了某种知识或技能，但是由于不注意或者其他因素的影响而没能正确地使用语言。

(2) 不同类型的错误

① 语际错误与语内错误

根据错误来源，错误经常分为语际错误和语内错误。学习者由于误用与母语有共同特征的语言项目而产生的错误叫语际错误(或迁移错误)。语内错误是在目的语内部所犯的错误(也称为发展性错误)。例如，将某一规则扩展到超出其使用的范围而造成的过度概括。

② 省略、添加、双重标记、形式错误和顺序错误

根据错误性质，错误经常可以被划分为五种类型：省略、添加、双重标记、形式错误和顺序错误。

3. 错误分析的步骤

(1) 识别错误

如果语言学习者所使用的句子不合乎语法，那就会产生错误。如果句子语法正确但在交际情景下使用不恰当，那就会产生失误。

(2) 描述错误

可以通过把错误与操母语者造出的句子相比较来发现错误。

(3) 解释错误

当错误被发现并被描写出来，我们应该尝试去解释为什么会产生错误。换句话说，我们要作一个关于致使学习者犯下这样错误的心理过程的假设。

Ⅶ. Corpus Linguistics and Language Teaching

A corpus is a collection of texts input into a computer. Language corpus provides the possibility for materials developers to choose authentic, natural and typical languages. Two of the most important factors in a corpus are the size and types of texts selected. Generally speaking, the use of a corpus determines the number and type of materials in the corpus.

1. Types of corpora

(1) General corpora

This kind of corpus is not a collection of material from different specialist areas—technical, dialectal, juvenile, etc. It is a collection of material which is broadly homogeneous, but the source is different. Unless the researcher isolates a particular corpora, the individuality of each corpus is vague. General corpora are useful for the study of language.

(2) Specialized corpora

This kind of corpus serves the specific purposes of language. If we need to use the language in a certain profession, then we choose texts from that domain.

(3) Sample corpora

Sample corpora is based on genre, which is a collection of a large number of short extracts randomly selected from various genres.

(4) Monitor corpora

Monitoring corpus is a kind of dynamic storage of corpus. It has the capacity to hold "a state of the language" for research purposes.

2. Information provided by corpora

(1) Frequency information

Corpora can tell us how often certain language items or structures are used. This kind of information is useful when we try to choose what to teach, choose what to focus on, and decide what senses to focus on in the language classroom.

(2) Context and co-text information

Context refers to the environment in which a language is used. Co-texts are the linguistic environments. Sometimes it is very difficult to tell the differences between two words or phrases that have a similar meaning. However, if we look at contextual and co-textual information, there are significant differences between them.

Ⅶ. 语料库语言学与语言教学

语料库是输入到计算机中一大批语料的集结。语料库为教材编写人员选择真实、自然、典型的语言提供了可能。语料库中两个最重要的因素是所选材料的长度和类型。一般来说，对语料库的使用决定了语料库中材料的数量和类型。

1. 语料库的分类

(1)通用语料库

通用语料库不是一个收集了不同专业领域，如技术、方言、少年等材料的集结。构成通用语料库的语料在大体上是同质的，但这些语料的来源不同。除非研究人员分离出一个特定的语料，否则每个语料的个体性都比较模糊。通用语料库对语言的整体研究是有用的。

(2)专用语料库

专用语料库服务于语言的特定目的。如果我们需要在某个领域中使用什么语言，那么我们就从该领域中选择语料。

(3)样本语料库

样本语料库基于体裁，它是从各种体裁中随机抽取的大量短篇摘要的集结。

(4)监控语料库

监控语料库比较庞杂，它是对语料的一种动态存储。出于研究目的，它能时刻把握“语言的状态”。

2. 语料库提供的信息

(1)频率信息

语料库可以告诉我们某些语言项目或语言结构的使用频率。当我们试图选择要教什么，选择要关注什么，并决定在语言课堂上关注哪些意义时，语料库是很有用的。

(2)语境与共文信息

语境是指语言的使用环境。共文是指语言环境。有时很难区分两个意思相似的单词或短语之间的区别。然而，如果我们看关注一下语境和共文信息，就会发现它们之间存在的显著差异。

(3) Grammatical information We usually get grammar information by consulting grammar books. However, what the corpora show is far more complicated than what grammar books tell about grammar. For example, information from corpora has shown that conditionals in English are far more than 3 (first, second and third conditionals). **(4) Collocation and phraseology information** It is often not easy for second and foreign language learners to learn which words are frequently used together, e. g. should we say *make effort or take effort*? The answer can be found in corpus. **(5) Pragmatics information** Information from corpora can tell us how language is actually used in communication. For example, students are often told that if someone says "How do you do", students should say "How do you do?". Data from corpora suggest that in this case there is more than one way to response. For example, we can also say "Nice to meet you." **▼Ⅷ. Foreign Language Education Policy** A main reason why foreign language education has been criticized in China is that for most students learning foreign languages is mainly because it is a required subject in the high-stakes exams. The fact that most students have no genuine incentive to learn a foreign language and those who have already learned a foreign language but rarely have chance to use it in life arise the slogan of "no need to learn". However, the truth is that language is not only a tool for daily communication; it is also a tool for thinking, a tool for us to understand the world, a tool that mediates social relations. On the other hand, with the rapid development of China's economy, tourism, foreign trade and internationalization of education, the societal and individual needs to learn and use foreign languages have increased to an unparalleled level in the past few decades. What's more, though English or other foreign languages are not widely used in China, learning English and other foreign languages can make millions of Chinese receive education abroad. Therefore, we have enough to say why Chinese need to learn foreign languages.	**(3)语法信息** 我们通常通过查阅语法书来获取语法信息。然而，语料库所展示的内容远比语法书籍所讲述的语法要复杂得多。例如，来自语料库的信息显示，英语中的条件句远远多于三个(第一、第二和第三条件句)。 **(4)搭配与短语信息** 对于第二语言学习者和外语学习者来说，想要知道哪些单词经常一起使用通常是困难的。例如，我们应该说"make effort"还是"take effort"呢？这一问题在语料库中一搜索就可以知道答案了。 **(5)语用信息** 语料库中的信息可以告诉我们语言是如何在交际中使用的。例如，学生经常被告知，如果有人对你说了"How do you do"，那么应该回应"How do you do?"。而来自语料库的数据显示，在这种情况下，有不止一种的回应方式。例如，我们也可以说"Nice to meet you."。 **Ⅷ. 外语教育政策** 外语教育在中国饱受批评的一个重要原因是对于大多数学生来说，学习外语主要是因为外语是一些重要考试中的必修科目。因此很多学生没有学习外语的内在真正动力以及很多人学了外语但在生活中很少有使用机会的现实导致了"外语无用论"这一极端观点的出现。 然而，外语本身不仅仅是日常交流的工具，也是思考的工具，是我们认识和理解世界的工具，是调解社会关系的工具。另一方面，随着中国经济，旅游，对外贸易以及教育国际化的发展，学习和使用外语的需要也日渐凸显。此外，尽管英语和其他外语在中国并没有广泛使用，但通过学习这些外语，很多中国人才有机会去国外求学。因此我们有足够的理由学习外语。

11.2 考研真题与典型题详解

Ⅰ. Fill in the blanks.

1. The type of language constructed by second or foreign language learners who are still in the process of learning a language is often referred to as ________. (中山大学 2008 研)
2. ________ is formed when the leaner attempts to learn a new language, and it has features of both the first language and the second language but is neither. (中山大学 2006 研)
3. Hymes' theory leads to notion/function-based syllables, and a step further, ________ syllabuses. (中山大学 2005 研)
4. Error is the grammatically incorrect form; ________ appears when the language is correct grammatically but improper in a communicational context. (中山大学 2008 研)
5. As a compromise between the "purely form-focused approaches" and the "purely meaning-focused" approaches, a recent movement called ________ seems to take a more balanced view on the role of grammar in language learning. (中山大学 2011 研)

Ⅱ. Multiple Choice

1. In Krashen's monitor theory, "i" in "i + 1" hypothesis of second language acquisition refers to ________. (对外经贸 2006 研)

   A. interaction B. interference C. input D. intake

2. The ________ is a syllabus in which the language content is arranged in terms of speech acts together with the language items needed for them. (西安外国语学院 2006 研)

   A. structural syllabus B. situational syllabus

   C. notional syllabus D. functional syllabus

3. Negative transfer in learning a second language is known as ________.

   A. interference B. interlanguage C. fossilization D. acculturation

4. ________ sees errors as the result of the intrusion of L1 habits over which the learner had no control.

   A. error analysis B. performance analysis

   C. contrastive analysis D. discourse analysis

Ⅲ. Explain the following terms.

1. Applied linguistics (武汉大学 2006 研)
2. Interlanguage (北外 2010 研; 北航 2010 研; 上海交大 2005 研)
3. Contrastive analysis (北航 2010 研; 浙江大学 2004 研)
4. face validity (南开大学 2011 研)
5. Error Analysis(中山大学 2011 研)

Ⅳ. Short answer questions

1. How do you understand interlanguage? (西安交通大学 2008 研)
2. What are the four obvious barriers to adult *L2* acquisition? (浙江大学 2003 研)
3. Linguists have taken an internal and/or external focus to the study of language acquisition. What is the difference between the two? (北外 2011 研)
4. What is the difference between mistakes and errors?

5. What are the distinctions between interlingual and intralingual errors?
6. What are the different views of input hypothesis and interaction hypothesis on discourse's contribution to language acquisition?
7. What does the existing functional grammar model suggest about language teaching according to Lock?
8. What do you think of the inclusion of standards as a central component of curricula in recent education reform in China?

V. Essay questions

1. Krashen's Input Hypothesis and Language Learning. (北交大 2006 研)
2. Explain one of the teaching approaches that you're familiar with and discuss its advantages and disadvantages. (浙江大学 2004 研)
3. What do you think are the similarities and dissimilarities between learning a first and a second language? (北外 2003 研)
4. What is communicative competence? How should we develop it in our foreign lauguage learning? (四川大学 2009 研)
5. Read the following paragraphs and then answer four questions. (北外 2011 研)

The idea behind the experiential vision of learning is that the use of the target language for communicative purposes is not only the goal of learning, but also a means of learning in its own right. This may clearly involve students using language which they may not have fully mastered, and contrasts with other more 'traditional' approaches which emphasize part practice (i. e., isolating parts of the whole for explicit study and learning) leading up in a more or less controlled manner to integrated language use for communicative purposes. An experiential approach to learning may therefore involve a degree of what Johnson (1982) refers to as an 'in at the deep end strategy'. Simply throwing learners into wholly uncontrolled and undirected language use is, of course, as dubious a strategy with respect to language learning as doing the same with someone who is learning to swim. For this reason, considerable effort has been devoted by methodologists, material writers, and teachers in recent decades to the way in which two sets of factors can be combined. One is the basic insight that language use can serve a significant role in promoting learning, and the other is the acknowledgement that use of the language needs to be structured in a coherent and pedagogically manageable way. The experiential vision of learning has evolved in a variety of ways since the 1960s and is now encountered in a number of differing forms. Nevertheless, most experiential approaches to learning rest on five main principles which were developed in the earlier days of the communicative movement, even if certain receive more attention in one variant than in another. These principles are the following: message focus, holistic practice, the use of authentic materials, the use of communication strategies, and the use of collaborative modes of learning. (Tudor 2001: 79)

An analytical view of learning posits that according explicit attention to the regularities of language and language use can play a positive role in learning. Each language manifests a number of structural regularities in areas such as grammar, lexis and phonology, and also with respect to the ways in which these elements are combined to communicate messages. The question, therefore, is not whether languages have structural regularities or not, but whether and in which way explicit attention to such regularities can facilitate the learning of the language. An analytical approach to learning rests on a more or less marked degree of part practice, i. e. , isolating parts of the whole for explicit study and learning, even if its ultimate goal remains the development of learners' ability to put these parts together for integrated, holistic use. At least, two main considerations lend support to an analytical approach to learning. First, in terms of learning in general, the isolation and practice of sub-parts of a target skill is a fairly common phenomenon. ... Second, explicit identification of regularities in a language has advantages which Johnson (1996: 83) refers to as 'generativity' and 'economy'. Mastering a regularity in a language gives learners access to the generative potential of this regularity in new circumstances. ... Explicit presentation or discovery of the structural regularities of a language can therefore represent a short-cut to mastery of this language and support learners' ability to manipulate these regularities for communicative purposes. (Tudor 2001: 86 -7)

1. What are the differences between experiential and analytical modes of language learning?
2. What serves as the theoretical foundation for the experiential mode of language learning and what are its advantages and disadvantages?
3. What serves as the theoretical foundation for the analytical mode of language learning and what are its advantages and disadvantages?
4. How would you balance the two modes of learning in your teaching or learning of a foreign language?

6. How many types of data analysis have been employed in language acquisition research? How are these types of data analysis significant in SLA research?
7. How do you understand the claim that "there is no use learning foreign languages since we rarely use them in life"? Do you agree or not?

参考答案及解析

I. Fill in the blanks.

1. interlanguage
(正处于学习过程中的二语或外语学习者构建的语言通常被称为中介语。中介语通常被理解为介于目的语和学习者母语之间的语言。)
2. Interlanguage
(当学习者学习一种新语言时，就产生了中介语。中介语具有第一语言和第二语言的特征，但中介语是一个动态的语言系统，我们不能把中介语看成是母语和二语的过渡阶段或者是二者的简单混合。)
3. communicative
(海姆斯提出的交际教学大纲以功能—意念大纲为基础，它教授表达和理解不同语言功能时所需要的语言，并且强调交际的过程。)
4. mistake
(错误通常指由于学习者不知道正确的形式或者不能正确地使用语言而出现的错误。失误则是学习者学会了某种知识或技能，但是由于不注意或者其他因素的影响而没能正确地使用语言。）

5. focus on form

（比较了单纯注重形式的方法和单纯注重意义的方法后，注重形式在关于语言学习中语法的地位方面有更平衡的观点。）

Ⅱ. Multiple Choice

1. C （克拉申的“监控理论”中有一种二语习得输入假说，他用 i 表示学习者现有水平，用 1 表示略高于的水平，这就是克拉申的“i + 1”输入假说。）
2. B （在情景教学大纲中，语言内容是根据言语行为和所需的语言来进行组织的，其目的是要具体区分目的语使用的不同场景，语言的选择和组织都是以情景为线索的。）
3. A （语言学习者在学习第二语言时，难免受到母语的种种影响。其中有正面的影响，称作正迁移，也有负面的影响，称作负迁移或者干扰。）
4. C （对比分析是通过对比不同语言来确定潜在错误的方法，它将错误看作是受母语习惯的结果，并认为这是学习者无法控制的。）

Ⅲ. Explain the following terms.

1. Applied linguistics: It is a branch of linguistics which studies the application of linguistics in reality. For example, there are studies on multilingualism, language acquisition, first and second language teaching and learning.
2. It refers to the type of language constructed by second or foreign language learners who are still in the process of learning a language. It's a language system between the target language and the learner's native language, and imperfect compared with the target language, but not mere translation from the learner's native language. For example, when the Chinese student is learning English, he may make errors like “to touch the society”.
3. Contrastive analysis is an approach to analysis of second language acquisition, based on a belief that a more effective teaching pedagogy would come out when the similarities and differences between native language and target language are taken into consideration. By such an analysis, it is supposed that some learning difficulties could be predicted in terms of language transfer.
4. Face validity: Unlike the other three forms of validity, face validity is based on the subjective judgment of an observer. If the test appears to be measuring what it intends to measure, the test is considered to have face validity.
5. Errors are significant in telling the teacher what needs to be taught, in telling the researcher how learning proceeds and those errors are a means whereby learners test their hypotheses about the language to be learnt. They are worth further probing Error Analysis involves, first independently or objectively, describing the learners' interlanguage (that is, their version of the target language and the target language itself), then a comparison of the two is followed to locate mismatches. Different from contrastive analysis, Error Analysis, EA for short, gives less consideration to learners' native language. The procedure of Error Analysis consists of the following steps:

   (1) Recognition

   (2) Description.

(3) Explanation.

For example, explanation: the absence of an item that must appear in a well-formed utterance: e. g. She sleeping. Type of error: Omissions.

IV. Short answer questions

1. The type of language constructed by second or foreign language learners who are still in the process of learning a language is often referred to as interlanguage. Interlanguage is often understood as a language system between the target language and the learner's native language. It is imperfect compared with the target language, but it is not mere translation from the learner's native language. However, interlanguage should not really be seen as a bridging language between the target language and native language. Interlanguage is a dynamic language system, which is constantly moving from the departure level to the native-like level. Therefore, "inter" actually means between the beginning stage and the final stage. There are many examples of interlanguage, such as *I no have a book. I like read books.*
2. A variety of explanations have been put forward for the apparent decline in adults: physical factors such as the loss of "plasticity" in the brain and "lateralization" of the brain; social factors such as the different situations and relationships that children encounter compared to adults; cognitive factors such as the interference with natural language learning by the adult's more abstract mode of thinking; and input factors that adults spend only a few hours each week of school time, rather than via the constant interaction experienced by a child, with a lot of other occupations.
3. The difference between internal and/or external focus to the study of language acquisition.

   (1) The internal focus seeks to account for speakers' internalized, underlying knowledge of language. The external focus emphasizes language use, including the functions of language which are realized in learners' production at different stages of development.

   (2) According to the above difference, the linguist Noam Chomsky claims that human beings are biologically programmed for language and that the language develops in the child just as other biological functions such as walking. Originally Chomsky referred to this innate ability as Language Acquisition Device, also known as LAD. Later Chomsky prefers this innate endowment as Universal Grammar (UG) and holds that if children are pre-equipped with UG, then what they have to learn is the ways in which their own language makes use of these principles and the variations on those principles which may exist in the particular language they are learning.

   The interaetionist view holds that language develops as a result of the complex interplay between the human characteristics of the child and the environment in which the child develops. Integrated with the innatist view, the interactionist further claims that the modified language which is suitable for the child's capability is crucial in his language acquisition.
4. Errors are defined as unintentionally deviant from the target language and not self-corrigible by the learner and suggest failure in competence, while mistakes as either intentionally or unintentionally deviant forms and self-corrigible suggest failure in performance.
5. Interlingua errors mainly result from cross-linguistic interference at different levels such as phonological, lexical, grammatical or discoursal etc. The intralingual errors mainly result from faulty or partial learning of the target language, independent of the native language. There are learning

strategies-based errors, communication strategies-based errors, induced errors and some compound and ambiguous errors among which overgeneralization or cross-association have been well exploited.

6. Input hypothesis proposed by Krashen, holds that language acquisition takes place when a learner understands input that contains grammatical forms that are at "i + 1" (i. e. are a little more advanced than the current state of the learner's interlanguage). In other words, language acquisition depends on comprehensible input. Interaction hypothesis by Michael Long, also emphasizes the importance of comprehensible input but claims that it is most effective when it is modified through the negotiation of meaning.
7. One of the existing grammar models that has been widely applied in language teaching is the functional grammar. Based on Halliday's work, Lock provides a functional description of the English language, which aims at helping language teachers to understand the relationship between different elements of grammar and how these elements interact to create meanings in context. Lock analyses the key grammatical categories and components in English and explains typical problems that second language learners have in acquiring various aspects of grammar.
8. One of the important recent trends in educational reform in China is the inclusion of standards as a central component of curricula. In language curricula, standards are statements of what language knowledge and language skills each student is supposed to learn. The release of the standards is often followed by discussions on their rationality, innovativeness, feasibility or drawbacks, which is unavoidable for all the standards and has received much attention on what the English curriculum standard should be based on. That is, how do curriculum designers decide what the students should learn at certain stage? To answer this question, it seems crucial to resort to theories, among which linguistic theories are fundamental, for setting up these language teaching standards.

V. Essay questions

1. Input hypothesis claims that "Human acquire language in only one way—by understanding messages or by receiving comprehensible input". According to Krashen, input that is useful for L2 acquisition must be neither too difficult nor too easy to understand and ought to be tuned just right to learner's current level, represented as i. In the course of acquiring the L2, learners progress from one level to another. The next level is called "i +1". For i +1 to occur, the input has to be slightly beyond the level at which learners are well proficient. The gap between i and i +1 is bridged by comprehensible input, which is the information drawn from the context and previous experience. Comprehensible input is considered both necessary and sufficient for L2 acquisition to occur and output plays little role. In other words, L2 learning takes place because the data to which learners are exposed contain comprehensible input.

   According to Krashen's acquisition-learning hypothesis, there are two ways to approach language learning: acquisition and learning. Acquisition helps us produce natural, rapid, and fluent speech. Learning, which is a conscious study of form, helps us edit this speech. In other words, when we learn something it won't help us produce fluent communication, but it will help us monitor our communication and correct minor errors.

It can only occur if three conditions are fulfilled: The performer has to have enough time; the performer has to be thinking about correctness and the performer has to know the rule. Learners will be most likely to use the Monitor in formal exam situations, where their attention has been drawn to linguistic form, and where they have enough time. If all these conditions are fulfilled, the Monitor may be used, but may be used inaccurately.

2. The functional language teaching, which emerged during the 70s, is a reaction against both the structurally and situationally based approaches to language teaching. Its main feature is that we should teach people what functions the various linguistic forms fulfill. We should teach people not only what the language is but what the language does. Linguistic forms should not be presented as abstract structures but should always be presented as fulfilling a particular language function. For example, if the simple present tense is to be taught, it should not just be a matter of learning to accurately repeat the structure, but also a matter of knowing what the structure is actually used for.

   Organizing language teaching functionally emphasizes what we can do with language. The basic units of language are seen as short exchanges. Linguistic forms are presented and learned in close relation to their function. Such teaching encourages appropriateness of language in terms of the respective roles of speaker and hearer and also in terms of the topic of conversation. Fluency is stressed and developed.

   The teaching of language functions also presents problems. For example, what is exactly a language function? How many functions are there? In what order should they be taught?

   While functions are a very significant aspect of language use, too great an emphasis on them may ignore other aspects of language, not least its structure. There is also no rigid correspondence between function and form, so some people object that we lose too much control over grammatical complexity if the syllabus is entirely organized on the basis of functions. What's more, some argue that fluency and appropriate use of language may be encouraged but this should not be achieved at the cost of formal accuracy.

3. Similarities between first and second language acquisition:

   (1) Both L1 and L2 are constructed from prior conceptual knowledge. Language emerges as a procedural acquisition to deal with events that the child already understands conceptually and to achieve communicative objectives that the child can realize by the other means.

   (2) Second language learners seem to use similar strategies to those learning their first language.

   (3) Overgeneralization and transfer are used by both L1 and L2 learner as the result of a necessity to reduce language to the simplest possible system, as an effort to lessen the cognitive burden involved in trying to master something as complex as language.

   (4) The L2 learner, like the first, attempts to "regularize, analogize, and simplify" in an effort to communicate.

   (5) Speech addressed to children (motherese) and speech addressed to foreigners (foreign talk) present similarities: shorter sentences, high-frequency vocabulary, "here and now" times, indirect correction, frequent gesture, lack of overt attention to form.

(6) A reasonable hypothesis is that the brain and nervous system are biologically programmed to acquire language (L1 and L2) in a particular sequence and in a particular mode (silent period).

(7) Both groups are probably using the same learning process. For example, the L2 sequence for English grammatical morphemes was similar, though not identical, to that found in L1 acquisition. Other similar sequences of syntactic acquisition have been found in L1 and L2 learning. L2 learners such as L2 learners, like L1 children, at first put negative elements at the beginning of the sentence "No the sun shining" and then progress to negation within the sentence "That's no ready."

Differences between L1 and L2 acquisition:

(1) L2 learners are usually older when learning their L2. Therefore, they are more developed cognitively. They have a greater knowledge of the world in general; they have more control over the input they receive; they are able to learn and apply rules that may aid in facilitating the acquisition process; they have one or more cultures that give them advanced information about expectations, discourse in general, and how to get things done with language.

(2) Older learners may have increased inhibition and anxiety and may find themselves afraid to make errors (poor attitudes and lack of motivation); there might be interference form the L1, particularly for items that are similar, either structurally or semantically.

(3) L1 acquisition is completely successful, but L2 learning is not. The evidence for this deficiency is held to be the lack of completeness of L2 grammars or the fossilization in L2 learning where the learner cannot progress beyond some particular stages, both familiar 'facts' in some sense.

(4) The variation in situation and other factors also produces many differences between L1 acquisition and L2 learning. L1 children mostly acquire language in different settings with different exposure to language than L2 learners and they are at different stages of mental and social maturity.

In all, the differences exist in levels of cognitive development and affect and the similarities exist in the process of acquisition itself.

4. Communicative competence is what a learner knows about how a language is used in particular situations for effective and appropriate communication. Communicative competence includes knowledge of the grammar and vocabulary, knowledge of rules of speaking, knowledge of how to use and respond to different types of speech acts and social conventions, and knowledge of how to use language appropriately.

In order to develop communicative competence in our foreign lauguage learning, language learners are encouraged to deal with accomplishing actions, which are believed to help them acquire the target language. Two types of tasks are usually required to be performed by the learners: real-world tasks and pedagogical tasks. For example, students may be asked to work or discuss in groups.

Besides, teachers can adopt the communicative syllabus which aims at the learner's communicative competence. It teaches the language needed to express and understand different kinds of functions, and emphasizes the process of communication.

5. (1) The experiential mode is totally different from the analytical mode of learning. An experiential approach to learning may involve a degree of what Johnson (1982) refers to as an 'in at the deep end strategy'. Simply throwing learners into wholly uncontrolled and undirected language use is, of course, as dubious a strategy with respect to language learning as doing the same with someone who is learning to swim. For this reason, considerable effort has been devoted by methodologists, material writers, and teachers.

   An analytical approach to learning rests on a more or less marked degree of part practice, i. e., isolating parts of the whole for explicit study and learning, even if its ultimate goal remains the development of learners' ability to put these parts together for integrated, holistic use.

   (2) The experiential mode provides a holistic model of the learning process and a multilinear model of adult development, both of which are consistent with what we know about how people learn, grow, and develop. The theory is to emphasize the central role that experience plays in the learning process, an emphasis that distinguishes experiential mode of language learning from other learning theories. The term "experiential" is used therefore to differentiate experiential mode of language learning both from cognitive learning theories, which tend to emphasize cognition over affect, and behavioral learning theories that deny any role for subjective experience in the learning process.

   However, simply throwing learners into wholly uncontrolled and undirected language use is, of course, as dubious a strategy with respect to language learning as doing the same with someone who is learning to swim. Therefore, this mode of language learning requires the methodologists, material writers, and teachers to combine two sets of factors. One is the basic insight that language use can serve a significant role in promoting learning, and the other is the acknowledgement that use of the language needs to be structured in a coherent and pedagogically manageable way.

   (3) An analytical approach to learning emphasizes the explicit study of the language learning a linguistic and communicative system. It is characteristic of the grammar-translation method, found in the cognitive code approach, in various CALL exercises, and in form-focus learning activities. It is also present in certain types of learner training or awareness raising activities involving the explicit analysis by learners of aspects of the languages teaching and learning or of their own language production.

   Each language manifests a number of structural regularities in areas such as grammar, lexis and phonology, and also with respect to the ways in which these elements are combined to communicate messages. The question, therefore, is not whether languages have structural regularities or not, but whether and in which way explicit attention to such regularities can facilitate the learning of the language.

   The main criticism of analytical learning is that declarative knowledge does not necessarily feed through to the ability to use a language for communicative purposes. In other words, someone may have a good knowledge of structural regularities of a language without being able to make use of the language with the spontaneity and fluency which are required in normal communicative situations.

(4)I would combine the two approaches together to learn a foreign language. First, following the analytical mode of language learning, the basic grammatical knowledge could be captured. Second, with the basic knowledge of structural regularities of a language, the experiential mode of language learning should be followed.

For example, when I learn how to greet in English, the first thing I should know about is how to pronounce "Hello!" or "How are you?" and the meaning of the expression. Then the next, I should learn in the relevant situations. Native speakers may respond to the phatic greeting in a variety of ways depending on the context and on how well they know about the interlocutor; e. g. "Fine. And you?", "Can't complain. ", "You know me!" are just a few instances from the wide repertoire of native speakers of English. Through that process, the knowledge of the language which is gained by the analytical approach could improve the ability to use the language in reality, which can be developed by the experiential approach.

(此题为开放性题目，从如何运用两种语言学习方法来学外语的角度谈即可。)

6. Four types of data analysis have been employed. They are contrastive analysis, error analysis, performance analysis, and discourse analysis.

Contrastive analysis (CA) systematically compares native languages and target languages to find the interference of native language when acquiring target languages. It has a close relationship with behaviourism. Although contrastive analysis was faced with a downfall as behaviorism was challenged, as a methodological option it was not abandoned.

Error analysis (EA) studies and analyzes the errors made by L2 learners and suggests that many learner errors are not due to the learner's mother tongue interference but reflect universal learning strategies such as overgeneralization and simplification of rules. Error analysis also fell into disfavor for (1) its narrowness-focusing on errors only and having difficulty in identifying the unitary source of an error, and (2) its failure to account for all the areas of the SL in which learners have difficulty. Nevertheless error analysis was not doomed to death rather incorporated into performance analysis.

Performance analysis (PA) is an analysis of the learners' interlanguage performance. It is superior to error analysis in that it is not limited to analyzing the errors learners commit. Also like its predecessors, however, performance analysis was found to be too limiting; it did not take the input to the learner into consideration. And this limitation led to the emergence of discourse analysis.

Discourse analysis (DA) recognizes the need to examine not only the learner's performance but also the input to the learner. Another quality of discourse analysis applied to SLA is that researchers are concerned not only with how IL forms evolve, but how learners learn how to use the forms appropriately for a particular discourse function as well.

7. (1) This claim is a little extreme and it ignores some changes in the recent years in China, thus as far as I'm concerned, I do not agree with it. (2) In fact, a major reason that why foreign language education has repeatedly come under criticism is that for most students a foreign language is learned only because it is a required subject in the high-stakes exams. The fact that most

students have no genuine incentive to learn a foreign language and those who have already learned a foreign language but rarely have chance to use it in life arise the slogan of "no need to learn". (3) However, the truth is that language is not only a tool for daily communication; it is also a tool for thinking, a tool for us to understand the world, a tool that mediates social relations. On the other hand, with the rapid development of China's economy, tourism, foreign trade and internationalization of education, the societal and individual needs to learn and use foreign languages have increased to an unparalleled level in the past few decades. What's more, though English or other foreign languages are not widely used in China, learning English and other foreign languages has enabled millions of Chinese to pursue education abroad. Thus we have enough to say why Chinese need to learn foreign languages.

第 12 章 现代语言学理论与流派

12.1 复习笔记

本章要点:

1. The Prague School and Functional Sentence Perspective (FSP)
   布拉格学派与功能句子观
2. The London School and context of situation
   伦敦学派与语境观
3. Halliday and Systemic-Functional Grammar
   韩礼德与系统—功能语法

▼4. Appliable linguistics
   适用语言学

5. Bloomfield and American Structuralism
   布隆菲尔德与美国结构主义
6. Chomsky and Transformational-Generative Grammar
   乔姆斯基与转换—生成语法

常考考点:

各流派的代表人物、理论基础、特点、主要观点、重要概念;语言普遍性和人类行为关系等。

本章内容索引:

Ⅰ. Saussure and modern linguistics

Ⅱ. The Prague School

1. Main points and contribution
2. Functional Sentence Perspective (FSP)
3. Communicative Dynamism (CD)

Ⅲ. The London School

1. Introduction
2. Malinowski's theories
3. Firth's theories
4. Halliday and Systemic-Functional Grammar
5. Systemic grammar and Functional grammar
   (1) Systemic grammar
   (2) Functional grammar

▼Ⅳ. Appliable Linguistics

1. Introduction
2. Principles

Ⅴ. American Structuralism

1. Introduction
2. Three stages of the development

Ⅵ. Transformational-Generative Grammar

1. Introduction
2. The Innateness Hypothesis
3. Generative Grammar
4. Stage of development of TG Grammar
5. Main features of TG Grammar

Ⅶ. Chomsky's Fundamental Contribution

Ⅷ. Revisionists or Rebels

1. Case Grammar
2. Generative Semantics

Ⅰ. Saussure and modern linguistics

Modern linguistics has started from the Swiss linguist Ferdinand de Saussure (1857 – 1913), who is often described as "father of modern linguistics" and "a master of a discipline which he made modern".

According to Saussure, language is a system of signs which uses sounds to express and exchange ideas. The sign is the union of a form and an idea, i. e. the signifier and the signified. The sign is the central fact of language, and therefore the study of language must start from the nature of the sign itself.

Saussure identifies several groups of important concepts: signifier and signified, langue and parole, synchronic and diachronic research, etc.

Ⅱ. The Prague School

【考点：简答——布拉格学派的主要观点及代表人物】

The Prague School can be traced back to its first meeting under the leadership of V. Mathesius.

1. Main points and contribution

The Prague School has three points of special importance:

(1) It stresses that the synchronic study of language is fully justified as it can draw on complete and controllable material for investigation.

Ⅰ. 索绪尔和现代语言学

现代语言学始于瑞士语言学家索绪尔，他被称为“现代语言学之父”和一位“使语言学走向现代的大师”。

索绪尔认为，语言是用声音表达交流思想的符号系统。符号是形式和意义的联合，是表示者和被表示者的结合。符号是语言事实的核心，研究语言必须从符号本身的特性入手。

索绪尔区分了几组重要的概念：能指和所指，语言和言语，共时研究和历时研究等。

Ⅱ. 布拉格学派

布拉格学派的形成可以追溯到马泰休斯领导召开的该学派的第一次会议。

1. 主要观点及贡献

布拉格学派的研究有三大重点：

(1) 强调共时研究的合理性，因为它可以提供完整且易掌控的研究材料。

(2) It emphasizes the systemic character of language, arguing that no element of any language can be satisfactorily analyzed or evaluated if viewed in isolation. In other words, elements are held to be in functional contrast or opposition.

(3) It sees language as a tool performing a range of essential functions or tasks for the community using it.

2. Functional Sentence Perspective (FSP)

Functional Sentence Perspective (FSP) is a theory of linguistic analysis, which refers to an analysis of utterances (or texts) according to the information they contain. The basic principle is that the role of each part of a sentence depends on its contribution to the meaning of the whole sentence.

Some Czech linguists attempted to analyze sentences from a functional perspective. They believe that a sentence contains both the point of departure and the goal of the utterance. The point of departure is equally present to the speaker and to the hearer—it is the ground on which they meet and is regarded as the theme. The goal of discourse is the message that the speaker wants to convey to the hearer, and is called the rheme. The movement from the theme to the rheme reveals the movement of the mind itself.

【考点：指出给定句子的主位和述位】

FSP aims to study the effect of the distribution of known (or given) information and new information in discourse. The known information refers to information that is not new to the reader or hearer. The new information is the message that will be delivered to the reader or hearer. The Subject-Predicate distinction is not always consistent with the Theme-Rheme contrast.

3. Communicative Dynamism (CD)

CD is another version of the same analysis, which was proposed by Firbas. By CD, Firbas means the extent to which the sentence elements contribute to the development of the communication.

Firbas interpreted FSP as the distribution of different degrees of CD. In his view, the initial elements of a sequence carry the lowest degree of CD and with each step forward, the degree of CD gradually increases till the element that carries the highest.

(2) 强调语言的系统性，指出任何语言单位都不能在孤立的情况下得到令人满意的分析及评估。换句话说，语言单位处于功能对比、对立之中。

(3) 它将语言看作是在所属语言群体中发挥一系列功能的工具。

2. 功能句子观

功能句子观是一套语言学分析理论，它是指用所含信息来分析话语或文本。其基本原则就是一句话中各部分起的作用取决于它对全句意义的贡献。

一些捷克语言学家尝试从功能的角度来分析句子。他们相信一个句子包含话语的出发点和话语的目的。话语的出发点叫做主位，它是说话人和听话人都知道的信息；话语的目的是说话人要向听话人传递的信息，叫做述位。从主位到述位的运动揭示了大脑本身的运动。

功能句子观旨在研究话语中新（未知）、旧（已知）信息的分布问题。已知信息指那些对于听话人不再是新信息的部分；新信息是即将向听话人传达的信息。句子中主语－谓语的分布不总是与主位－述位的分布一致。

3. 交际能力

另一种版本的分析法叫做交际能力，由费尔巴斯提出。他用交际动力表示句子成分对交际发展所起的作用。

费尔巴斯把功能句子观解释为不同程度的交际力的分布。他认为，句子前面部分承载的交际力最低，然后逐步增加，直到交际力最大的成分。

Ⅲ. The London School

【考点：简答—伦敦学派的主要观点及代表人物】

1. Introduction

The London School refers to the linguistic scholarship in England. J. R. Firth turned linguistics proper into a recognized distinct academic subject in Britain. Firth, under the influence of the anthropologist B. Malinowski, influenced his student M. A. K. Halliday. They all emphasized the importance of context of situation and the system aspect of language. Therefore, London School is also called systemic linguistics and functional linguistics.

2. Malinowski's theories

(1) Language is a mode of action, rather than a counterpart of thought.

(2) The meaning of an utterance does not come from the ideas of the words that make up the utterance but from its relation to the situational context in which the utterance occurs. His assertion is based on two kinds of observations.

① In primitive communities there is no writing, and language has only one type of use.

In all societies, children learn their languages in this way.

② The meaning of spoken utterances could always be determined by the context of situation. Malinowski distinguished three types of context of situation.

a. situations in which speech interrelates with bodily activity;

b. narrative situations;

c. situations in which speech is used to fill a speech vacuum—phatic communion.

3. Firth's theories

(1) Influenced by Malinowski, Firth saw language as a social process, rather than simply as a set of agreed-upon semiotics and signs. Language is a means of participating in social activities, a means of doing things and of making others do things, a means of acting and living.

(2) In analyzing typical context of situation, one has to carry out the analysis on the following two levels:

①The internal relations of the text:

Ⅲ. 伦敦学派

1. 介绍

伦敦学派专门用来称呼独具英国特色的语言学研究。弗斯使语言学在英国完全成为一门公认的科学。弗斯主要受人类学家马林诺夫斯基影响，而后他又影响了他的学生韩礼德。三人都强调“语言环境”和语言“系统”的重要性。因此，伦敦学派也被称为系统语言学和功能语言学。

2. 马林诺夫斯基的理论

（1）语言是一种行为模式，而不是什么与思想相对应的东西。

（2）话语意义并不来源于构成话语的词的意义，而是来源于话语发生的上下义之间的关系。其断言是根据两大观察结果得出的：

① 在原始社会团体中，书写并不存在，语言只有一种使用方法。

在所有人类社会中，孩子以此种方法习得语言。

② 话语意义经常为语言环境所决定，马林诺夫斯基发现了以下三种语境：

a. 言语与当时身体活动有直接关系的活动；

b. 叙述环境；

c. 言语仅被用来填补言语空白的环境——寒暄交谈。

3. 弗斯的理论

（1）受马林诺夫斯基的影响，弗斯认为语言是种社会过程，而非仅仅一套约定俗成的符号和信号。语言是参与社会生活的工具，是自己做事和使他人做事的手段，是一种行为和生活手段。

（2）在进行典型的语言情境分析时，以下两个层面需要考虑在内：

① 文本本身的内部关系：

a. the syntagmatic relations between the elements in the structure;	a. 结构的成分间的组合关系；
b. the paradigmatic relations between units in the system and find their values.	b. 系统中的单位间的聚合关系。
②The internal relations of the context of situation:	② 语言情景的内部关系：
a. the relations between text and non-linguistic elements, and their general effects;	a. 文本和非语言成分之间的关系，以及总体效果；
b. the analytical relations between "bits" and "pieces" of the text (words, parts of words, phrases) and the special elements within the situation (items, objects, persons, personalities, events).	b. 单词、词的部分以及短语与情景的特殊组成部分直接的分析关系。
4. Halliday and Systemic-Functional Grammar	**4. 韩礼德与系统—功能语法**
(1) M. A. K. Halliday has developed the theories proposed by Firth in the London School. His Systemic-Functional (SF) Grammar is a sociologically oriented functional linguistic approach, which is one of the most influential linguistic theories in the twentieth century.	(1) 韩礼德发展了伦敦学派弗斯提出的理论，他的系统－功能语法是一种具有社会学倾向的功能语言学方法，是二十世纪最具影响力的语言学理论之一。
(2) Systemic-Functional Grammar is based on two facts:	(2) 系统—功能语法的建立基于以下两个事实：
① language users actually choose in a system of systems and strive to achieve different semantic functions in social interactions ;	① 语言的使用者实际是在一组系统中进行选择，并且努力在社会的相互作用中实现不同的语义功能；
② language and human social activities are closely related and inseparable. Therefore, it takes practical uses of language as the object of the research.	② 语言和人类的社会活动紧密联系，不可分离。于是系统—功能语法把语言的实际运用作为研究的对象。
5. Systemic grammar and Functional grammar 【考点：系统语法与功能语法的关系】	**5. 系统语法和功能语法**
(1) Systemic grammar	**(1) 系统语法**
System is a list of choices that are available in the grammar of a language.	系统就是存在于语法中的一系列选择。
Systemic grammar aims to explain the internal relations in language as a system network, or meaning potential, and this network consists of subsystems from which language users make choices.	系统语法的目的是要说明语言作为系统的内部底层关系，它是与意义相关联的可供人们不断选择的若干子系统组成的系统网络。
(2) Functional grammar	**(2) 功能语法**
Functional grammar aims to reveal that language is a means of social interaction, based on the position that language system and the form that make it up are inescapably determined by the use or functions which they serve.	功能语法的目的是要说明语言是社会交往的手段，其基础是：语言系统及其成分不可避免的由它们所提供的作用和功能所决定。

Halliday views children's language development as "the mastery of linguistic functions", and "learning a language is learning how to mean". So he puts forward seven functions in children's model of language, that is, instrumental, regulatory, interactional, personal, heuristic, imaginative and informative function.	韩礼德将儿童的语言发展视为"语言功能的掌握"，并且"学习语言即学习如何表达意思"。因此他提出儿童语言的七大功能：工具、控制、交互、自指性、探索、想象和信息功能。
The adult's language becomes much more complex and it has to serve many more functions, but the original functional range of the child's language is gradually reduced to a set of highly coded and abstract functions, which are **meta-functions**: the ideational, the interpersonal, and the textual functions.	成年人的语言更为复杂，因此应具有更丰富的功能，但儿童的语言功能范围逐渐缩小，简化成为一套高度符号化和抽象化的功能——**元功能**：概念、人际、语篇功能。
【考点：名词解释 & 填空——meta-functions】	
① Ideational function	① 概念功能
The ideational function is applied for conveying new information, to communicate a content that is unknown to the hearer. The ideational function mainly includes "transitivity" and "voice". Transitivity is the grammar of the clause in its ideational aspect. It consists of six different processes: Material, Behavioral, Mental, Verbal, Relational and Existential Process.	概念功能是用来传达新的信息，或是给听话者传递一定的未知内容。它主要包括及物性和语态两部分。及物性就是子句意义中的概念功能，它包括六种不同的过程：物质、行为、心理、言语、关系和存在过程。
② Interpersonal function	②人际功能
The interpersonal function is the full use of language to express social and personal relations. This includes the various ways the speaker enters a speech situation and performs a speech act. Since the clause is not limited to the expression of transitivity, there are non-ideational elements in the adult language system.	人际功能是充分运用语言来表达社会和个人的关系，包括讲话者进入语言情境及言语行为的形成。由于分句不限于表达及物性，因此成人的语言系统中存在非概念的成分。
Interpersonal function is realized by **mood** and **modality**.	人际关系可以通过**语气**和**情态**来实现：
a. Mood indicates the role selected by the speaker in the speech situation and the role assigned to the addressee. Mood is made up of two parts: the "Subject" and the "Finite" element. The subject can be a noun, a noun phrase, or a clause.	a. 语气表明讲话者选择了某种语言角色，同时也赋予了听话者一种言语角色。语气包括"主语"和"限定成分"两部分，主语可以是名词、名词词组或从句。
b. Modality indicates whether the speaker is making a judgment or prediction.	b. 情态说明讲话者是否做出判断或预测。
c. Finite elements include tense morphemes, auxiliary verbs and modal verbs that express tense or modality, and they are part of the verb phrase.	c. 限定成分包括时态语素，助动词和情态动词，它是动词词组的一部分。

d. Residue refers to the rest of the clause. It has three functional elements: the "Predicator", "Complement", and "Adjunct". The usual order in an English clause is "Predicator + Complement + Adjunct". 【考点：划分句子——分别指出语气、情态、限定成分及剩余部分】	d. 剩余部分指除去主语和限定成分的成分。它包括三个功能成分：谓语、补语和附加语。通常情况下的顺序为"谓语 + 补语 + 附加语"。
③ Textual function The textual function refers to the mechanism in language that organizes spoken or written discourse into a coherent and unified text, and at the same time, make a living passage different from a random list of sentences. Two sentences with the same conceptual function and interpersonal function can have different textual functions.	③ 语篇功能 语篇功能是指语言中存在着一种机制将口头或书面的话语组织成连贯统一的语篇，这种机制使实际的言语区别于一系列的随意的句子。概念功能和人际功能完全相同的两个句子可以有不同的语篇功能。
▼Ⅳ. Appliable Linguistics **1. Introduction** Different from "applied" or "applicable" linguistics, Halliday's lecture "Working with Meaning: Towards an Appliable Linguistics" in 2006 marked the emergence of appliable linguistics.	**Ⅳ. 适用语言学** **1. 介绍** 与应用语言学和可应用语言学不同，韩礼德2006年关于"意义的研究：适用语言学"标志着适用语言学的出现。
Based on his view that a theory of language is consumer oriented in nature, he discusses the complementarities between lexis and grammar, "language as system" and "as text", and speaking and writing in his commitment to working towards a coherent account of language which is appliable, so appliable linguistics deals with the development and evaluation of linguistic theories.	基于其关于语言本质的看法即语言本身是使用者导向的，韩礼德讨论了词汇和语法，语言作为系统和语言作为文本，口语和书面语的互补关系，旨在实现在语言的连贯描述和解释，并且使得该解释是适用的，因此适用语言学关注的是语言学理论的发展和对语言学理论的评价。
The notion "appliability" requires that theory and practice should develop according to new situations. Appliable linguistics is not a monopoly of systemic-functional linguists, but a theory for all schools of linguistics. Further, it is not only applicable to the field of linguistics, but also to semiotics and other related disciplines.	适用语言学中"适用性"的含义要求语言学理论和实践要与时俱进，适应新的形势需要。适用语言学不仅仅是系统功能语言学家的理论，而是一个适用于所有语言学流派的理论。进一步说，适用语言学不仅研究语言学，也研究符号学以及其他学科。
2. Principles Appliable linguistics mainly consists of the following four principles. (1) The inseparability of theory and practice; (2) Language as meaning and meaning as choice; (3) social accountability; (4) Multimodal research.	**2. 原则** 适用语言学主要包括以下四个原则：(1)理论和实践的不可分离性；(2)将语言视为意义，而意义是个选择系统；(3)社会责任；(4)多模式研究。

V. American Structuralism 【考点：简答——美国结构主义不同于欧洲语言学风格的特点】	**V. 美国结构主义**
1. Introduction American structuralism is a branch of Synchronic linguistics which emerged independently in the United States at the beginning of the twentieth century. Led by the anthropologist F. Boas, it developed in a very different style from that of Europe. Structuralism is based on the assumption that grammatical categories should be defined not in terms of meaning but in distribution, and that the structure of each language should be described without reference to the alleged universality of such categories as tense, mood and parts of speech.	**1. 简介** 美国结构主义是共时语言学的一个分支，独立地诞生于二十世纪初的美国，在人类语言学家博厄斯的领导下，美国结构主义以不同于欧洲的传统风格发展着。 结构主义基于这样一种猜想：语法范畴应由分布而非意义来定义；同时一语言的结构不应该根据时态、语态及词性等所谓的通用标准来描述。
2. Three stages of the development The development of American Structuralism can be roughly classified into three stages:	**2. 三个发展阶段** 美国结构主义的发展大致可以分为下面三个阶段：
(1) Early period: Boas and Sapir **A. Boas** ① There was no ideal type or form of languages, because there is an infinite variety of human languages. ② Boas first proposed the framework of descriptive linguistics and pointed out its three parts: the sound of languages, the semantic categories of linguistic expression, and the process of grammatical combination in semantic expression.	**(1) 早期：博厄斯与萨丕尔** **A. 博厄斯** ① 不存在理想的语言形式，因为人类语言有着无穷尽的多样性。 ② 博厄斯首次提出描述性语言学的框架，并指出其三大组成部分：语言的语音；语言表达的语法范畴；语义表达中的语法链接过程。
B. Sapir ① Sapir studied the American Indian languages and used native people as his interviewees, which is a novel experience. ② He described the characteristics and development of language from an anthropological perspective, with his main focus on typology. ③ He defines language as "a purely human and non-instinctive method of communicating ideas, emotions and desires by means of a system of voluntarily produced symbols".	**B. 萨丕尔** ① 萨丕尔描写了美洲的印第安语，并用当地土著居民作为受访人，这算是一种新的尝试。 ② 从人类学的角度出发来描写语言的特点及其发展，焦点放在类型学上。 ③ 他将语言定义为：语言是纯粹人为的、非本能的、通过自觉制造出来的符号系统来传达观念、情绪和欲望的方法。

(2) **Bloomfieldian period**

The principal representative of American descriptive linguistics is L. Bloomfield (1887 – 1949). He is a landmark figure in the history of American linguistics. The period between 1933 and 1950 is considered as Bloomfieldian Era. It was during this period that descriptive linguistics formally came into being and reached its prime development.

In Bloomfield's view, linguistics is a branch of psychology, and specifically of the positivistic brand of psychology called behaviourism. Behaviourism refers to a scientific approach based on the theory that people are unable to perceive things they have not experienced. Behaviourism in linguistics holds that children's language learning is achieved through a chain of "STIMULUS-RESPONSE reinforcement", and the adult's use of language can also be considered as a process of stimulus-response. When the behaviourist methodology entered linguistics through Bloomfield's writings, the popular practice in linguistic studies was to take into account what a native speaker says in his language and to discard what he says about it.

Bloomfield put forward the well known formula:

$$S \rightarrow r \cdots\cdots\cdots s \rightarrow R$$

Here S means practical stimulus, r means the substitute reaction of speech, s means the substitute stimulus, and R means external practical reaction.

【考点：布龙菲尔德对于语言学的贡献及其在语言学史上的地位】

(3) **Post-Bloomfieldian period**

① Characterized by a strict empiricism, American linguists such as Harris and Hockett further developed structuralism. With the development of the electronic computer in the 1950s, some linguists began to propose a goal for general linguistics that we should devise explicit discovery procedures that would allow computers to process raw data about any language and form a complete grammar without intervention by the human linguist.

(2) **布龙菲尔德时期**

布龙菲尔德是美国描写语言学的代表。他在美国的语言学史上是一个里程碑似的人物，因此1933至1950年的一个时期被称作“布龙菲尔德时期”。正是在这段时间，美国的描写语言学开始成形，并迎来了它的最初发展阶段。

在布龙菲尔德看来，语言学是心理学的一个分支，确切地说是心理学中带有实证主义特征的分支，通常被称作行为主义。行为主义是一种科学研究方法，其理论基础是：人们无法认识他们未经历的事情。行为主义认为儿童对语言的学习是通过一连串的“刺激—反应强化”来达到的，而成年人对语言的使用也是“刺激—反应”的过程。当行为主义的方法论经由布龙菲尔德的作品进入语言学后，当时比较流行的做法是采纳人们实际对母语的使用，而不是他们对于其母语的看法。

由此，布龙菲尔德提出了一个著名的公式：$S \rightarrow r \cdots\cdots\cdots s \rightarrow R$，该公式中S代表外部刺激，r代表语言的代替反应，s代表语言的代替性刺激，R代表外部的实际反应。

(3) **后布龙菲尔德时期**

①美国语言学家哈里斯，霍凯特进一步发展了结构主义，以严格彻底的经验主义为特点。伴随着20世纪50年代电子计算机技术的发展，一些语言学家开始提出新的目标：发明设计一套新的发现程序，借以用计算机处理原始的语言数据，从而完成一套完整的，不需语言学家参与的语法。

② Pike and Tagmemics According to Pike, a language has its own hierarchical systems independent of meaning. Not only are there hierarchies in language, but everything in the world is hierarchical, including different layers in the system from small to big, from bottom to top, from simple to complex, from part to whole. Therefore, all languages have three interrelated hierarchies: phonological, grammatical, and referential. Each level of these three hierarchical systems has a language unit with four following features: Slot, Class, Role, and Cohesion. These basic units are called grammatical units, or tagmemes.	②派克和法位学 派克认为，语言有独立于意义之外的等级系统，所有的语言有三种相互关联的等级系统：音位、语法和所指等级系统。这三种等级系统中的每一个层次都有具有轨位、类别、作用和接应这四个特点的语言单位。这些基本的单位就叫做语法单位，简称法位。
Ⅵ. Transformational-Generative Grammar (TG Grammar)	**Ⅵ. 转换—生成语法**
1. Introduction The publication of Chomsky's *Syntactic Structures* in 1957 marked the beginning of the TG grammar. Contrary to Bloomfield's data-oriented discovery procedure, Chomsky insists on the hypothesis-deduction method and his research is called evaluation process.	**1. 介绍** 乔姆斯基于1957年出版的《语法结构》标志着转换—生成语法的形成。使用被称作“评价过程”的“假设—演绎”的方法，与布龙菲尔德的发现程序相对。
2. The Innateness Hypothesis 【考点：名词解释——Innateness Hypothesis 和 LAD】 Chomsky believes that language is somewhat innate, and that children are born with what he calls a Language Acquisition Device (LAD). This is a unique kind of knowledge that makes them suitable for language learning. He argues the child comes into the world with specific innate endowment, not only with general tendencies or potentialities, but also with knowledge of the nature of language. From this point of view, it can be seen that children are born with knowledge of the basic grammatical relations and categories, and this knowledge is universal.	**2. 天赋假设** 乔姆斯基认为语言是天生的，儿童与生俱来的拥有一种语言学习的能力，叫做“语言习得机制”。这是一种让他们适合语言学习的独特知识。乔指出儿童天生被赋予一种能力，不仅包括学习语言的趋势和潜能，还包括关于语言性质的知识。从这种观点可看出，儿童天生拥有语法关系及语法范畴的知识，并且这种知识是普遍的。
This approach to language challenged the behaviorism of psychology and the empiricism of philosophy, making linguistics a branch of psychology.	这种处理语言的方法，是对心理学的行为主义和哲学上的经验主义的一种挑战，并使语言学成为了心理学的一个分支。
Chomsky's innate hypothesis was based on his observations of important phenomena that could not be explained by other theories.	乔姆斯基的天赋假设是建立在他对一些重要现象的观察的基础之上的，这些现象无法用其他的理论解释清楚。
(1) Children acquire their mother tongue quickly and with little effort.	(1) 儿童可以高速省力地习得母语；

(2) Children learn their native language in very different environments.

(3) Children master the total grammar of the language in a limited amount of time, through limited exposure to speech.

All these suggest that children are not born knowing a language, but they have a tendency to acquire it, just as they have a tendency to learn to walk.

3. Generative Grammar

【考点：名词解释——Generative Grammar；简答——生成语法的目的】

By a generative grammar, Chomsky simply means "a system of rules that in some explicit and well-defined way assigns structural descriptions to sentences". He argues that every speaker of a language has mastered and internalized a generative grammar that expresses his knowledge of his language.

A generative grammar is not limited to particular languages, but to reveal the unity of particular grammars and universal grammars. It does not stop at describing one language, but as a means to explore the universal rules of language, with a view to ultimately revealing the human cognitive system and human nature.

Chomsky put forward three levels on which to evaluate grammars:

- Observational adequacy level
- Descriptive adequacy level
- Explanatory adequacy level

4. Stage of development of TG Grammar

Chomsky's TG grammar has seen five stages of development:

(1) The Classical Theory

It aims to make linguistics a science.

(2) The Standard Theory

It deals with how semantics should be studied in a linguistic theory.

(3) The Extended Standard Theory

It pays attention to discussion on language universals and universal grammar.

(2) 无论母语习得的环境有多大差异，儿童都可以达到大致相同的水平；

(3) 儿童可以在有限的时间里，通过有限的话语数量掌握完整的语法知识。

以上这些现象表明：儿童虽然没有天生拥有一门语言，但他们拥有语言习得的倾向，正如他们有学习走路的倾向一样。

3. 生成语法

乔姆斯基用"生成语法"这一概念来指"一套用来给句子进行结构描写，定义明确严格的规则系统"。他认为任何一种语言的使用者都掌握并且内化了一种具有生成能力的语法，这种语法可以表达他的语言知识。

生成语法不限于描述个别语法，他旨在揭示个别语法与普遍语法的统一性。他并不止步于描述某一语言，而是作为一种手段用以探索语言的普遍规律，以期最终揭示人类的认知系统及人类本质。

乔姆斯基提出了三个不同的层面来评价语法：

· 观察充分性
· 描写充分性
· 解释充分性

4. 转换—生成语法的发展阶段

乔姆斯基的转换—生成语法经历了五个发展阶段：

(1) 古典理论：旨在把语言学变成一门科学；

(2) 标准理论：研究如何将语义成分加入语法模型；

(3) 扩展的标准理论：讨论语言的普遍性和普遍语法；

(4) The Revised Extended Standard Theory (or GB)

It focuses discussion on government and binding.

(5) The Minimalist program

It is a further revision of the previous theory.

【考点：TG Grammar 发展的五个阶段及每个阶段的主要内容】

(6) After the Minimalist Program

Finally, Chomsky proposes several objectives for further research in this field, such as accounting for: the atoms for computation; the rewiring of the brain; the operations of externalization; whatever else remains in UG; interface operations.

(4) 修正的扩展的标准理论：讨论管辖和约束的问题；

(5) 最简方案：是对前面理论的进一步修正。

(6)最简方案之后：最后，乔姆斯基提出了在这一领域做更深入研究的几个目的，比如：微量计算；大脑的重新布线；操作的外部化；其他任何仍在普遍语法中的东西；界面操作。

5. Main features of TG Grammar

(1) Chomsky defines language as a set of rules or principles.

(2) Chomsky believes that the aim of linguistics is to produce a generative grammar which captures the tacit knowledge of the native speaker of his language. This concerns the question of learning theory and the question of linguistic universals.

(3) Chomsky and his followers are interested in any data that can reveal the native speaker's tacit knowledge. They seldom use what native speakers actually say; they rely on their own intuition.

(4) Chomsky's methodology is hypothesis-deductive, which operates at two levels:

① The linguist formulates a hypothesis about language structure—a general linguistic theory; this is tested by grammars for particular languages;

② Each such grammar is a hypothesis on the general linguistic theory.

(5) Chomsky follows Rationalism in philosophy and Mentalism in psychology.

【考点：简答——TG Grammar 区别于其他研究方法的主要特征】

5. 转换—生成语法的主要特征

(1) 乔姆斯基把语言定义为一套规则或原理；

(2) 乔姆斯基认为语言学家的目标应该是创造一种有生成能力的语法，这个语法能够抓住本族语人所默认的知识。这就与语言习得理论及普遍语法有关；

(3) 乔姆斯基及他的拥护者都对能够揭示本族语人语言知识的语言材料感兴趣。他们很少使用那些本族语人所说的材料；

(4) 乔姆斯基的研究方法是“假设—演绎”，他把这种方法运用于两个层面：

① 语言学家阐明关于语言结构的假设——语言的普遍理论，此理论被个别语言的语法所验证；

② 每一个个别语法又是关于普遍语言的普遍理论的假设。

(5) 乔姆斯基追随了哲学上的理性主义和心理学上的心灵主义。

Ⅶ. Chomsky's Fundamental Contribution

From the 1950s and 1970s, psychological research in the United States shifted from primarily studying behavior to primarily studying cognition. This "cognitive revolutions" was initiated by Chomsky.

Ⅶ. 乔姆斯基的基本贡献

在 20 世纪 50 年代到 70 年代，美国的心理学研究从主要研究行为转变到主要研究认知。这场“认知革命”就是乔姆斯基发起地的。

Ⅷ. Revisionists or Rebels? TG Grammar has been challenged by a number of rebels, among which Case Grammar and Generative Semantics are the representative ones. **1. Case Grammar** Case Grammar is an approach that emphasizes between semantic elements in a sentence. It is a kind of generative grammar explored by C. J. Fillmore in the late 1960s. In this grammar, the verb is considered as the most important part of the sentence, and has a lot to do with various noun phrases. These relationships are called "cases". **2. Generative Semantics** Generative Semantics was proposed in the late 1960s and early 1970s, as a reaction to Chomsky's syntactic-based TG Grammar. The leading figures are J. R. Ross, G. Lakoff, J. D. McCawley, and P. Postal. Generative semantics holds that all sentences are produced by a semantic structure, which is often expressed in the form of propositions that is similar to logical propositions in philosophy.	**Ⅷ. 修正还是反对?** 转换生成语法受到很多反对声音的挑战，其中最有代表的是格语法和生成语义。 **1. 格语法** 格语法是一种强调句子中语义成分之间关系的一种方法，它是一种生成语法。这种语法认为，动词是句子中最重要的部分，并且和各种名词短语有着很多的关系。这些关系就叫着"格"。 **2. 生成语义** 生成语义是20世纪60年代末和70年代初期形成的。生成语义认为所有的句子都是由一个语义结构产生的，这个语义结构经常以命题的形式来表达，类似于哲学中的逻辑命题。

12.2 考研真题与典型题详解

Ⅰ. Fill in the blanks.

1. The structural approach to the analysis of language was started by the Swiss linguist __________ in the beginning of the twentieth century. (中山大学2006研)
2. Functional Sentence Perspective (FSP) is a theory of linguistic analysis which describes how __________ is distributed in sentences. (中山大学2005研)
3. Systemic-Functional Grammar, unlike traditional grammar which takes sentence as the largest unit, takes __________ as the basic unit. (中山大学2008研)
4. In Halliday's Systemic Grammar, a system is a list of things between which it is possible to choose. So they are meanings, which the grammar can distinguish. The items in a system are called __________. (中山大学2008研)
5. The principal representative of American descriptive linguistics is L. Bloomfield, whose book __________ (1933) was once held as the model of scientific methodology. (中山大学2006研)
6. The publication of Syntactic Structures (1957) marked the beginning of the __________. (中山大学2006研)
7. In 1979, Chomsky delivered a series of lectures Pisa, Italy, which were revised later and published under the title of __________. (中山大学2005研)
8. __________ is an approach that stresses the relationships of elements in a sentence. It is a type of generative grammar developed by C. J. Fillmore. (中山大学2006研)

9. __________, born in 1928, is all American linguist, educator, and political activist. He is the founder of transformational-generative grammar, a system that revolutionized modem linguistics.（北京邮电大学 2010 研）

10. The Prague School is best known and remembered for its contribution to phonology and the distinction between __________ and phonology.

11. Chomsky argues that LAD probably consists of three elements, that is a __________, linguistic universal, and an evaluation procedure.

12. Systemic-Functional Grammar takes the actual uses of language as the object of study, while Chomsky's TG Grammar takes the ideal speaker's linguistic __________ as the object of study.

Ⅱ. Multiple Choice

1. According to __________ theory, grammar refers to the initial state of the human language faculty.（西安外国语学院 2006 研）

A. Saussure's　　B. Bloomfield's　　C. Chomsky's　　D. Halliday's

2. __________ rules may change the syntactic representation of a sentence.（西安交通大学 2008 研）

A. Generative　　B. Transformational

C. X-bar　　D. Phrase structure

3. Generally speaking, the __________ specifies whether a certain tagmeme is in the position of the Nucleus or of the Margin in the structure.

A. Slot　　B. Class　　C. Role　　D. Cohesion

4. The most important contribution of the Prague School to linguistics is that it sees language in terms of __________.

A. function　　B. meaning　　C. signs　　D. system

5. Chomsky follows __________ in philosophy and mentalism in psychology.

A. empiricism　　B. behaviourism　　C. rationalism　　D. mentalism

Ⅲ. True or False

1. Functional grammar is an approach to linguistics that goes in through meaning.（对外经贸 2005 研）

2. According to the innateness hypothesis, infants are born able to speak a language.（北二外 2007 研）

3. In the Classical theory, Chomsky's aim is to make linguistics a science. This theory is characterized by three features: (1) emphasis on prescription of language; (2) introduction of transformational rules; and (3) grammatical description regardless of language formation.（南开大学 2004 研）

4. Generative grammar is a system of rules that in some explicit and well-defined way assigns structural descriptions to sentences.（南开大学 2004 研）

5. American Structuralism is a branch of diachronic linguistics that emerged independently in the United States at the beginning of the twentieth century.

6. If two sentences have exactly the same ideational and interpersonal functions, they would be the same in terms of textual coherence.

Ⅳ. Explain the following terms

1. Ferdinand de Saussure（中山大学 2005 研）

2. Textual function（西安外国语学院 2006 研）
3. The London School of Linguistics（中山大学 2005 研）
4. Surface structure（四川大学 2006 研）
5. Transformational-Generative grammar（浙江大学 2003 研）
6. Language Acquisition Device(LAD)（武汉大学 2005 研）
7. Innateness hypothesis

Ⅴ. Short answer questions

1. Why is Saussure hailed as the father of modern linguistics?（四川大学 2006 研）
2. What are the three important points of the Prague School?（北交大学 2005 研）
3. What are the major concerns of the Prague School theory?（北航 2008 研）
4. What is your understanding of Systemic Functional Grammar?（北航 2010 研）
5. What is behaviourism?
6. What is the relationship between linguistics and behaviorism according to Bloomfield?

Ⅵ. Essay questions

1. A discussion on Saussure as the father of modern linguistics.（武汉大学 2008 研）
2. What are the unique features of Halliday's systemic linguistics?（北航 2008 研）
3. How does Halliday relate the functions performed by language to its structures?（北京邮电大学 2010 研；中山大学 2005 研）
4. Chomsky sets up three different targets to aim at：observational adequacy，descriptive adequacy and explanatory adequacy. Define and discuss them.（浙江大学 2007 研）
5. The roles of Transformational-Generative linguistics and Functional linguistics in language teaching and learning.（武汉大学 2007 研）
6. What are the distinctive features of American structuralism?（武汉大学 2011 研）
7. Can you make a brief introduction to Systemic-Functional Grammar?
8. What is characteristic of TG grammar?

参考答案及解析

Ⅰ. Fill in the blanks.

1. Saussure

（对语言的结构性分析方法是在 20 世纪初，由瑞士语言学家索绪尔开启的，他被称为“现代语言学之父”和一位“使语言学走向现代的大师”。）

2. information

（功能句子观是一套语言学分析理论，它是指用所含信息来分析话语或文本。）

3. clause

（与传统语法不同，系统功能语法把句子作为最大单位，把分句作为最小单位。）

4. options

（系统就是存在于语法中的一系列选择。系统语法的目的是要说明语言作为系统的内部底层关系，它是与意义相关联的可供人们不断选择的若干子系统组成的系统网络。）

5. *Language*

（布龙菲尔德是描述语言学的主要代表，他的著作《语言》曾被当做科学方法的典范。）

6. Chomsky Revolution
（1957 年，乔姆斯基写了一本名为《句法结构》的著作，这本书标志着“乔姆斯基改革时代”的到来，从此，乔姆斯基在语言学界的地位变得极为重要。）
7. Lectures on Government and Binding
（1979 年，乔姆斯基开展了一系列的讲座，之后把讲座内容写成一本书，叫做《管辖与约束》，即修正的扩展的标准理论。）
8. Case Grammar
（格语法是美国语言学家菲尔墨在 60 代中期提出来的，它是着重探讨句法结构与语义之间关系的一种语法理论和语义学理论。）
9. Noam Chomsky
（乔姆斯基，生于 1928 年，是美国著名的语言学家，教育家。他是转换生成语法的创始人。）
10. phonetics
（布拉格学派主要的贡献是对音系学的研究和对音系学与语音学的区分。）
11. hypothesis-maker
（乔姆斯基的语言习得机制由 3 个元素组成：对语言的假想，语言的普遍性和评价。）
12. competence
（系统功能语法把实际中的语言现象当做其研究对象，而乔姆斯基的转换生成语法把理想说话者的语言能力作为研究对象。）

Ⅱ. Multiple Choice

1. D （韩礼德认为，人类语言能力的最初形式即是对语法知识的了解。）
2. B （乔姆斯基的转换规则会改变一个句子的句法结构。）
3. A （派克认为，语言的三种等级系统中的每一个层次都具有轨位、类别、作用和接应这四个特点的语言单位。轨位决定了法位在结构中是处于核心还是边缘位置。）
4. A （布拉格学派将语言看作是在所属语言群体中发挥一系列功能的工具，这是其对语言学界的一大贡献。）
5. C （乔姆斯基在他的研究中运用了哲学中的理性主义和心理学中的心灵主义。）

Ⅲ. True or False

1. F （功能语法的基础是语言系统及其成分由它们所提供的作用和功能所决定，而非其意义。）
2. F （乔姆斯基的天赋假设是说，儿童与生俱来拥有一种语言学习的能力，叫做“语言习得机制”。即儿童天生拥有语法关系及语法范畴的知识，而不是说孩子天生就会说话。）
3. F （乔姆斯基的古典理论有三个特点：(1)重视语言的生成能力，而非规定性；(2)转换规则的介绍；(3)语法描述，不研究意义，而非不研究语言形式。）
4. T （乔姆斯基用“生成语法”这一概念来指“一套用来给句子进行结构描写，定义明确严格的规则系统”。）
5. F （美国结构主义是共时语言学的一个分支，独立地诞生于二十世纪初的美国．它并不是历时语言学的分支。）
6. F （概念功能和人际功能完全相同的两个句子可以有不同的语篇功能。）

IV. Explain the following terms.

1. Ferdinand de Saussure is a Swiss linguist who is often described as "father of modern linguistics". The great work, *Course in General Linguistics*, which was based on his lecture notes, marked the beginning of modern linguistics. Saussure's idea on the arbitrary nature of sign, on the relational nature of linguistic units, on the distinction of langue and parole and of synchronic and diachronic linguistics, etc. pushed linguistics into a brand new stage.
2. Textual function: The textual function is one of the three meta-functions language is composed of. It refers to the fact that language has mechanisms to make any stretch of spoken or written discourse into a coherent and unified text and make a living message different from a random list of sentences.
3. The London School generally refers to the kind of linguistic scholarship in England. The man who turned linguistics proper into a recognized distinct academic subject in Britain was J. R. Firth.
4. Surface structure: It is a term used in generative grammar to refer to the final stage in the syntactic representation of a sentence, which provides the input to the phonological component of the grammar, and which thus most closely corresponds to the structure we articulate and hear. For instance, "John is easy to please." and "John is eager to please." are two sentences with the same surface structure.
5. Transformational-generative grammar is proposed by Noam Chomsky. He postulated a syntactic base of language (called deep structure), which consists of a series of phrase-structure rewrite rules, i. e., a series of (possibly universal) rules that generates the underlying phrase-structure of a sentence. The end result of a transformational-generative grammar is a surface structure that is identical to an actual sentence of a language, after the mediating of a series of rules (called transformations) that act upon the deep structures.
6. Language Acquisition Device: LAD refers to an innate faculty of language in general with which children are born. It is posited by Chomsky, who argues that LAD probably consists of three elements: a hypothesis-maker, linguistic universal, and an evaluation procedure.
7. The "Innateness Hypothesis" of child language acquisition was proposed by Noam Chomsky, who states that language are somewhat innate and that children are born with what he calls a language acquisition device, which is a unique kind of knowledge that fits them for language learning.

V. Short answer questions

1. Saussure occupies such an important place in the history of linguistics that he is often described as "father of modern linguistics":

(1) The book *Course in General Linguistics* (1916), which is the most important source of Saussure's ideas, marked the beginning of modern linguistics.

(2) Saussure was the first to notice the complexities of language. He believed that language is a system of signs, called conventions. He held that the sign is the union of the signifier and the signified.

(3) By providing answers to questions concerning many aspects of language, Saussure made clear the object of study for linguistics as a science. His ideas on the arbitrary nature of sign, on the relational nature of linguistic units, on the distinction of langue and parole and of synchronic

and diachronic linguistics, etc. pushed linguistics into a brand new stage.

2. The three important points developed in Prague School are: (a) It was stressed that the synchronic study of language is fully justified as it can draw on complete and controllable material for investigation but no rigid theoretical barrier is erected to separate diachronic study. (b) There was an emphasis on the systemic character of language. (c) Language was looked on as functional in another sense, that is, as a tool performing a number essential functions or tasks for the community using it.

3. Three points of the Prague School theory are of special importance.

   First, it was stressed that the synchronic study of language is fully justified as it can draw on complete and controllable material for investigation.

   Second, there was an emphasis on the systemic character of language.

   Third, language was looked on as functional in another sense. Based on these ideas, the Prague School practiced a special style of synchronic linguistics, and made great contribution to phonology and the distinction between phonetics and phonology. Its most important contribution is that it sees language in terms of function.

4. Systemic functional grammar, developed by M. A. K. Halliday, is a socially oriented functional linguistic approach and one of the most influential linguistic theories in the twentieth century. Systemic functional grammar is based on two facts:

   Language users are actually making choices in a set of systems and trying to realize different semantic functions in social interaction.

   Language is inseparable from social activities of man. Thus, it takes actual uses of language as the object of study. One point to notice is that it takes clause as the basic unit. It consist of two inseparable parts: systemic grammar and functional grammar.

5. Behaviourism is a principle of scientific method, based on the belief that human beings cannot know anything they have not experienced. Behaviourism in linguistics holds that children learn language through a chain of "stimulus-response reinforcement", and the adult's use of language is also a process of "stimulus-response".

6. For Bloomfield, linguistics is a branch of the positivistic brand of psychology known as "behaviourism". When the behaviourist methodology entered linguistics via Bloomfield's writings, the popular practice in linguistic studies was to accept what a native speaker says in his language and to discard what he says about it. This is because of the belief that a linguistic description was reliable when based on observation of unstudied utterances by speakers; it was unreliable if the analyst had resorted to asking speakers questions such as "Can you say ... in your language?"

Ⅵ. Essay questions

1. Saussure was the first to notice the complexities of language. He believed that language is a system of signs. To communicate ideas, signs must be part of a system of signs, called conventions. He held that the sign is the union of a form (signifier) and an idea (signified), and it is the central fact of language.

   By providing answers to questions concerning many aspects of language, Saussure made clear the object of study for linguistics as a science. Saussure exerted two kinds of influence on modern linguistics. First, he provided a general orientation, a sense of the task of linguistics which has seldom been questioned. Second, he influenced modern linguistics. Many of the developments of modern linguistics can be described as his concepts, i. e. his ideas on the arbitrary nature of sign, on the relational nature of linguistic units, on the distinction of langue and parole and of synchronic and diachronic linguistics, etc. Saussure's fundamental perception is of revolutionary significance, and it is he that pushed linguistics into a brand new stage and all linguistics in the twentieth century is Saussurean linguistics. That's why Saussure is considered being the father of modern linguistics.

2. Halliday's Systemic Grammar is different from other linguistic theories in the following aspects.

   First, it attaches great importance to the sociological aspects of language.

   Secondly, it views language as a form of doing rather than a form of knowing. It distinguishes linguistic behavior potential from actual linguistic behavior.

   Thirdly, it gives a relatively high priority to description of the characteristics of particular languages and particular varieties of languages.

   Fourthly, it explains a number of aspects of language in terms of clines (i. e. ungrammatical → more unusual → less unusual → less usual → grammatical).

   Fifthly, it seeks verification of its hypotheses by means of observation from texts and by means of statistical techniques.

   Lastly, it has as its central category the category of the system.

3. According to Halliday, structure is the outward form of the system, which lies behind the former. Structure, therefore, is less abstract, and closer to the "surface". By studying the constituency structure of grammar, it is assumed that the semantic system above it could become plausible. In the constituency structure, elements are recognized with reference to their functions in relation to the whole. Therefore, in "The huge tiger climbed a tree", only elements like "the huge tiger" not "the" or "the huge" could be recognized, since it is the whole sequence that plays a role in the clause, and in this sentence, the role is Subject. This is the way of bracketing used in Systemic-Functional Grammar.

   This step is followed by labeling, which is to reveal the specific function of that element in relation to the whole. For example, by labeling "the huge tiger" a functional label: "Subject", we get to know the interpersonal function that element plays. It is through these two steps the structures are related to the functions performed by language.

4. According to Chomsky, observational adequacy requires a grammar to be able to produce correct explanations for raw linguistic data; that is, it should be able to capture speakers' intuitions about grammaticality.

   On the second level, that is, on the level of descriptive adequacy, a grammar should not only produce correct explanations for raw linguistic data, but also produce correct explanations for the linguistic competence of the speaker and hearer; that is, it should reflect speakers' competence.

   On the third, and the highest, level, i. e. explanatory adequacy, a grammar that is sufficiently described should reveal linguistic competence and then relate it with universal grammars in order to be related to the initial state of the human mind for the purpose of revealing human cognitive systems; that is, it should account for the learnability of language.

In Chomsky's point of view, it is far from adequate for a grammar to merely distinguish those strings of words which are sentences of the language from those which are not sentences of the language in question. Neither is it for a grammar to assign structures to sentences that match native speaker's intuition about structure and meaning. However, this is where the Structuralistic approach stops. Therefore, Chomsky argues for a generative grammar since it is able to explain how the facts are the way they are and how they arise in the mind of the speaker and hears. And it is after successful descriptions of many languages and subsequent generalizations of universal features of human language that it is possible to explore the initial state of the human mind that contains universal grammars.

5. (1) In the framework of Transformational-Generative linguistics, language is not learnt by innate. While acquiring his mother tongue, he compares his innate language system with that of his native language and modifies his grammar. Therefore, language learning is an activity of building and testing hypothesis.

Although the influence of such a formal and abstract grammar remains limited in the field of language education, there are still various attempts to apply TG grammar to language teaching. In designing teaching materials, for example, sentence patterns with the same deep structure can be closely related, such as the active and the passive. Transformational rules may assist the teacher in the teaching of complex sentence construction. In the teaching of literature, TG grammar provides a new instrument for stylistic analysis.

(2) The Functional linguistics sees language learning from a semantic-sociolinguistic perspective. In particular, Systemic-Functional linguistics, which was proposed by Halliday, sees the formal system of language as a realization of functions of language in use.

Its scope is broader than that of formal linguistic theories. In the field of language teaching, it leads to the development of notion/function-based syllabuses, which have attracted increasing attention.

6. American structuralism is a branch of synchronic linguistics that developed in a very different style from that of Europe. While linguistics in Europe started more than two thousand years ago, linguistics in America started at the end of the nineteenth century. While traditional grammar plays a dominating role in Europe, it has little influence in America. While many European languages have their own historical traditions and cultures, English is the dominating language in America, where there is no such a tradition as in Europe. In addition, the pioneer scholars in America were faced with the urgent task of recording the rapidly perishing native American Indian languages because there was no written record of them. However, these languages were characterised by features of vast diversity and differences which are rarely found in other parts of the world. To record and describe these exotic languages, it is probably better not to have any presuppositions about the nature of language in general. This explains why there was not much development in linguistic theory during this period but a lot of discussion on descriptive procedures.

Structuralism is based on the assumption that grammatical categories should be defined not in terms of meaning but in terms of distribution, and that the structure of each language should be described without reference to the alleged universality of such categories as tense, mood and parts of speech, Firstly, structural grammar describes everything that is found in a language instead of laying down rules. However, its aim is confined to the description of languages, without explaining why language operates the way it does. Secondly, structural grammar is empirical, aiming at objectivity in the sense that all definitions and statements should be verifiable or refutable. However, it has produced almost no complete grammars comparable to any comprehensive traditional grammars. Thirdly, structural grammar examines all languages, recognising and doing justice to the uniqueness of each language. But it does not give an adequate treatment of meaning. Lastly, structural grammar describes even the smallest contrasts that underlie any construction or use of a language, not only those discoverable in some particular use.

7. Stemming from Firth's theories in the London School, Halliday's Systemic-Functional (SF) Grammar is a socially oriented functional linguistic approach and one of the most influential linguistic theories in the 20th century, exerting a strong impact on various disciplines related to language, such as language teaching, sociolinguistics, discourse analysis, stylistics, and machine translation.

   It actually has two components: Systemic Grammar and Functional Grammar. They are two inseparable parts for an integral framework in Halliday's linguistic inquiry. Systemic Grammar aims to explain the internal relations in language as a system network, or meaning potential. And this network consists of subsystems from which language users make choices. Functional Grammar aims to reveal that language is a means of social interaction, based on the assumption that language system and the forms that make it up are inescapably determined by the users or functions which they serve.

8. Chomsky's TG grammar has the following features.

   First, Chomsky defines language as a set of rules or principles.

   Secondly, Chomsky believes that the aim of linguistics is to produce a generative grammar which captures the tacit knowledge of the native speaker of his language. This concerns the question of learning theory and the question of linguistic universals.

   Thirdly, Chomsky and his followers are interested in any data that can reveal the native speaker's tacit knowledge. They seldom use what native speakers say; they rely on their own intuition.

   Fourthly, Chomsky's methodology is hypothesis-deductive, which operates at two levels: (1) The linguist formulates a hypothesis about language structure—a general linguistic theory; this is tested by grammars for particular languages. (2) Each such grammar is a hypothesis on the general linguistic theory.

   Finally, Chomsky follows rationalism in philosophy and mentalism in psychology.